Legal Language

Peter M. Tiersma

Legal Language

The University of Chicago Press * Chicago and London

The University of Chicago Press, Chicago 60637
The University of Chicago Press, Ltd., London
© 1999 by The University of Chicago
All rights reserved. Published 1999
Paperback edition 2000
14 13 12 11 10 09 08   3 4 5

ISBN-13: 978-0-226-80302-9 (cloth)
ISBN-10: 0-226-80302-3 (cloth)
ISBN-13: 978-0-226-80303-6 (paper)
ISBN-10: 0-226-80303-1 (paper)

Library of Congress Cataloging-in-Publication Data

Tiersma, Peter Meijes.
    Legal language / Peter M. Tiersma.
        p.   cm.
    Includes bibliographical references and index.
    ISBN: 0-226-80302-3 (alk. paper)
    1. Law— Language.   2. Law—Interpretation and construction.
I. Title.
K213.T54   1999
340′.1′4—dc21   98-19367
                                                       CIP

CONTENTS

Appendices

ACKNOWLEDGMENTS

In writing this book, I have benefited from comments made by J. H. Baker, QC, Bruce Heitman, Douglas Kibbee, Joseph Kimble, Laurie Levenson, Sam Pillsbury, Lawrence Solan, and Richard Wydick. Obviously, errors and omissions are my own responsibility. I am very grateful to Loyola Law School in Los Angeles for awarding me the Joseph Scott Fellowship, which supported my writing financially. Dale Kim, a former Loyola student, provided excellent research assistance. The students in my language and law seminar at Loyola Law School forced me to clarify my ideas and contributed several examples that I have used in this book. Thanks also to my wife, Matthea Cremers, for reading and helping edit the final manuscript, as well as lending moral support throughout the process of writing and publishing.

All of us working in the field of legal language owe a tremendous debt to Professor David Mellinkoff's classic book on the subject, *The Language of the Law*. Mellinkoff challenged lawyers to use more ordinary English and to abandon antiquated habits that had been passed down unthinkingly from generation to generation. His book was an important impetus to the Plain English Movement. I found it particularly useful in writing part 1, as well as chapter 4 in part 2. Especially those interested in the history of legal English will find Mellinkoff's book to be fascinating reading.

The language of lawyers is an extremely broad and interesting topic. Because of my background, I have emphasized the linguistic characteristics of legal language. Other disciplines, such as literary studies, rhetoric, and semiotics, offer their own insights. The fact that I have not discussed the contributions of those disciplines is not a value judgment, but results from a realistic assessment of my own expertise. Furthermore, I have dealt relatively briefly with some important linguistic topics that are quite relevant to the law. One is meaning and interpretation; the other is speech act theory. Much could be written about both subjects, and I originally planned to discuss them in much greater detail. My failure to do so results simply from a desire to keep this book within manageable proportions.

INTRODUCTION

Our law is a law of words. Although there are several major sources of law in the Anglo-American tradition, all consist of words. Morality or custom may be embedded in human behavior, but law—virtually by definition—comes into being through language. Thus, the legal profession focuses intensely on the words that constitute the law, whether in the form of statutes, regulations, or judicial opinions.

Words are also a lawyer's most essential tools. Attorneys use language to discuss what the law means, to advise clients, to argue before a court or jury, and to question witnesses. The legal rights and obligations of their clients are created, modified, and terminated by the language contained in contracts, deeds, and wills. Few professions are as dependent upon language. The average lawyer's daily routine consists almost entirely of reading, speaking, and writing.

During the past three decades or so, many linguists and social scientists have turned their attention to legal language. For such researchers, the complex language of lawyers is a fascinating topic of study. The results of their work have led to a better understanding of how legal language operates.

Yet there has been remarkably little interaction between language experts and lawyers; neither discipline seems to know very much about the work of the other. This book aims to help fill that gap in knowledge by drawing on both legal and linguistic sources for inspiration. Lawyers, as well as law students hoping to enter the profession, can learn a great deal from language experts about how to make their language more efficient and comprehensible. And linguists can learn that the seeming peculiarities of legal language sometimes serve very legitimate purposes.

At the same time, this book hopes to address the needs of a third group: the public at large. Legal language is not merely the most important tool of the average lawyer, or just an interesting research area for linguists. The law and its language affect the daily lives of virtually everyone in our society. Every time we take a ticket to park in a public garage or to ride the subway, we enter into a transaction that is governed by legal language. Typically, the language is printed in tiny letters on the back of the ticket. Other transactions are less common but far more important: obtaining a credit card from a bank, consenting to a medical procedure, preparing a will, or buying and financing a house. Here, the legal language that governs the transaction may be in a much longer document with a larger typeface, but all too often it is virtually incomprehensible to those most affected by it.

There is no doubt that legal language is decidedly peculiar and often hard to understand, especially from the perspective of the lay public. This book will explain some of the ways in which the language of the legal profession is distinct from ordinary speech. Furthermore, how did it come to be so different? And perhaps most importantly, is the language of lawyers essential to the functioning of the legal system, or can we reform it to better serve both lawyers themselves and the public in general?

Part 1 begins by discussing the history of legal English. It is a fascinating topic not only in its own right, but also because it sheds light on why the profession remains so linguistically conservative even today. The story opens in England, where the language of the law was molded by Celtic-speaking Britons, Anglo-Saxon mercenaries, Scandinavian raiders, Latin-speaking clerics, Norman invaders, and lawyers themselves. Eventually, England established the common law and its language in the far-flung parts of the British Empire. Even today, it remains the legal language of numerous nations around the world. In almost all of these places, it has retained many Anglo-Saxon, Latin, and Norman French relics. At the same time, it has inevitably adapted to local circumstances. Indeed, this theme runs throughout the book: in some ways legal English is extremely stodgy and conservative, while on other occasions it can be highly innovative and creative.

Anyone who has ever seen a legal document realizes that it differs dramatically from everyday speech. In fact, some people have argued that lawyers actually speak a separate language. Consequently, the theme of part 2 is whether and to what extent legal English differs from ordinary language. It is true that at one time, English lawyers did literally have their own language: Law French. At the same time, there is no doubt that today's lawyers use a type of English. Still, in some ways lawyers do still speak a foreign tongue, or at least, a type of language that is quite unfamiliar to the general public. Law students refer to it as "talking like a lawyer." They work hard to acquire this lingo in law school.

We will see that talking like a lawyer requires using long, complex, and redundant sentences, conjoined phrases, impersonal constructions, and arcane words or phrases like *the document aforesaid, witnesseth,* or *to wit.* It can also involve using minor—but potentially quite interesting—deviations in spelling, pronunciation, and punctuation. Lawyers seem to insist on writing *judgment* in place of the more logical *judgement,* for example. They pronounce *defendants* as though they were defending ants. They also have unusual ways of pronouncing Latin and French. Most of these features can be explained as historical relics, but they also serve to create and solidify group cohesion within the profession. In other words, when lawyers use these linguistic features, they subtly communicate to each other that they are members of the same club or fraternity. No wonder that law students strive so hard to imitate the professors and lawyers who teach them!

Other aspects of legal language are aimed at promoting clear and precise communication. We will see that certain characteristics of the language of lawyers, especially the legal vocabulary, do indeed tend to enhance precision. Though not as exact as many lawyers claim, technical terminology promotes communication within the profession by allowing lawyers to express in a word or short phrase what would otherwise require a much longer explanation. But this precision comes at a cost. Most importantly, unusual vocabulary may alienate those who are not part of the profession and may be difficult for them to understand.

Despite claims about the precision of legal English, we will see that sometimes lawyers prefer not to be precise at all, or opt for deliberate obscurity. Like politicians who refuse to accept responsibility when they admit only that *mistakes were made,* lawyers may use devices like passives and nominalizations to downplay their client's culpability. Thus, they might write that *the victim was injured* instead of *my client injured the victim.*

On other occasions, lawyers find themselves in a linguistic dilemma: should they strive to be as precise as possible, or is it better to be more general or even vague? Strategic concerns may dictate one choice over another. As we will see, general or vague language—most notoriously the word *reasonable*—leaves room to maneuver and is adaptable to unforeseen future circumstances. Elsewhere, lawyers prefer to be as exact as possible and try to cover every possibility by making long lists of words, examples, or illustrations.

Because legal English differs from ordinary language, it is also interpreted differently. For example, we will explore how legal definitions are different from ordinary ones. Normally, a definition is simply an aid in understanding how a word might be used in a particular context. Because an ordinary definition is based on usage, it cannot dictate how we ought to interpret something. Yet we will see that this is exactly what a legal definition does. If a legislature defines *person* to include a corporation or association, that is what it means for purposes of the statute in question. What any dictionary might have to say about *person* becomes irrelevant.

Although there is a tendency to treat legal English as a monolithic system, it actually exhibits great variation, depending on the place where it is used, whether it is written or spoken, the level of formality, the genre in which it appears, and other factors. Despite notions that it is hopelessly antiquated, the language of the law can sometimes be quite informal and versatile. During plea bargaining, for instance, lawyers can make very effective use of legal terms like *mal mish* (malicious mischief). Even on a more formal level, the law easily coins innovative terms like *palimony* or *hedonic damages* when the need for a new word arises.

The versatility of legal language is quite evident in court, as we will see in part 3. The courtroom drama is best understood in terms of a story or narrative. The story that unfolds during a trial is similar to an ordinary narrative. A plaintiff who files a lawsuit comes into court telling a tale of some misfortune or problem caused by the defendant. She recites the story in a very formalized manner as a pleading. Yet unlike the ordinary narrative, which is asserted as truth and almost always ends with a resolution of the problem, the story in the pleading is told tentatively; it consists of allegations that must still be proven. And when it is first told to the court, the story in a pleading has no resolution. The purpose of the trial is to decide the truth and then finish the tale by resolving the underlying problem.

The plaintiff proves her story mainly by language in the form of testimony. But the plaintiff and other witnesses normally cannot tell their story in narrative format. Rather, lawyers tend to elicit testimony through a very controlling or coercive questioning format. Typically, lawyers use questions that a witness can only answer with *yes* or *no,* or which allow at most a short response. In fact, during cross-examination lawyers can use a type of question that does not really request information at all, but is more an accusation: *You're lying, aren't you.*

As we explore later in more detail, questioning of witnesses does not just neutrally provide information. The linguistic form of questions can influence the answer, and the structure of both questions and answers can affect judgments of credibility and persuasiveness. For example, jurors tend to assume that witnesses who speak a dialect or nonstandard English are less competent and truthful than those who speak a more "educated" form of the language.

Lawyers not only ask questions during trial, of course. They also use persuasive language to convince the jury to accept their narrative or version of events as being the truth. We will see through an analysis of closing arguments, in particular those in the celebrated murder trial of O. J. Simpson, that lawyers can make very effective use of persuasive language. For example, trial lawyers often use informal and even intimate speech to bond with the jury. A lawyer in the South of the United States might speak with a heavy Southern drawl to convince a local jury to award punitive damages against a large corporation based in New York City. Other lawyers even use rhyme or other poetic devices to impress their theme in the minds of the jurors: *If it doesn't fit, you must acquit.* Trial language also offers convincing proof that when they are properly motivated, lawyers are fully capable of using ordinary English to explain complex topics to a lay audience. They are well aware that legalese does not go over well with a jury.

Unfortunately, once lawyers leave the courthouse and return to the law office, they tend to quickly revert to ponderous, arcane, and obscure legal language. From the point of view of the public, virtually every feature of legal language in some way impedes clear communication. Part 4 thus concludes the book by discussing efforts to reform legal language. It first examines what it is that makes legal English hard for laymen to understand. Especially when consumers are involved, obscure legal language has been the focus of much criticism from the Plain English Movement during the past two or three decades. We will review some of the ways in which people around the world are attempting to deal with the problem, ranging from moral pressure to explicit laws that require that consumer documents be written in plain English.

Finally, we will discuss efforts to make the instructions that judges give to juries at the end of a trial more comprehensible. In death penalty cases, this is truly a matter of life or death. Unfortunately, research indicates that jurors do not understand such instructions very well, a finding that undermines confidence in the very institution of the jury. If we want juries to decide who should live and who should die, they should at the very least be able to understand and follow the guidelines that the judge gives them.

Ultimately, despite gradual and ongoing improvement in legal language, the proverbial man on the street, or even the average juror, will never understand all the intricacies of the law. Lawyers and their distinctive style of speaking and writing will never disappear. But someone bound by a statute should have at least a good general idea of what it prohibits. If judges expect the public to respect their judicial opinions, they should write them so that the public understands the important principles contained in them. Jurors should not be asked to decide critical legal issues without clear instructions. And average consumers should be able to comprehend the legal documents that govern their lives and fortunes. In short, legal language can and should be much less arcane and ponderous, and be much more understandable, than it now is.

Obviously, much remains to be done. I hope that this book will prove intrinsically interesting to lawyers and anyone else who has a curiosity about the law. But most of all, I hope that it will motivate the profession to communicate as clearly, concisely, and comprehensibly as possible.

PART ONE

Origins

The history of legal English begins in ancient Britain and develops as successive waves of invaders—Anglo-Saxons, Scandinavians, Norman French—left their marks not only on the English language in general, but on legal English in particular. The conversion to Christianity, the development of a centralized system of justice, the rise of a legal profession, and the spread of writing and printing were also enormously influential. Eventually, as the invaded became the invaders, the English propagated their legal system and its peculiar language across the globe.

It is impossible to fully appreciate the nature of legal language without knowing something about its history. All the odd characteristics of the speech and writing of lawyers have some historical basis. Knowing the reasons for these features may help us determine their usefulness today. If they no longer serve any communicative function, it may be time to relegate them to the history books.

Often it seems that there is nothing truly new under the sun. In varying degrees, legal language has always differed from ordinary speech. When the differences became large enough, there were generally protests and attempts to improve the situation. Yet after each reform, the gap between legal and ordinary language again gradually widened, leading to yet another round of protests and reform. Perhaps we should learn something from the past, rather than endlessly repeating it.

CHAPTER ONE

Celts, Anglo-Saxons, and Danes

The Celts

Before the time of Christ, the inhabitants of England were Celtic. The Celts inhabited not just much of Britain and Ireland, but large parts of central and western Europe as well.[1] Their language is a branch of Indo-European, so Celtic is ultimately related to English. Nonetheless, English does not derive from Celtic, nor have the Celtic languages left many traces in English. Most of the Celtic remnants in England are place-names, including *Cornwall, Avon, Dover,* and *London.*[2]

Like their language, the law of the British Celts has had little lasting impact on our legal system. We can, however, make some inferences about the legal language of the Britons, based on surviving manuscripts of Celtic law from Wales and Ireland. Like other Celts, the Britons seem to have expressed much of their law in legal sayings or maxims, which were in semi-poetic or rhetorical language, often held together by alliteration. It may well have been that poets were guardians of this oral tradition and that they would "sing out" these legal aphorisms when the need arose. Poets may also have acted as judges. Interestingly, the use of poetic and archaic language to describe the law seems to have been problematic even among the Celts: an Irish legend describes how a king removed the poets from their function as judges because of the obscurity of their language![3]

At the height of their empire, the Romans conquered much of the Celtic territory, including England. Despite the Roman occupation, the Briton masses never switched to Latin.[4] Likewise, Roman law from this period had little lasting impact on the ordinary Briton. Although Roman law operated on Roman citizens in Britain, whatever effect it had on the Celts largely disappeared—along with the Roman legions—in the fifth century.[5]

The Anglo-Saxons

After the Romans had departed, the Britons lost their protection against raids by the Picts and Scots. Long pacified by the Romans, the Britons seem to have lacked the resources and skills to defend themselves. They ultimately appealed for help from some warlike Germanic tribes living on the continent. Beginning sometime around A.D. 450, boatloads of Angles, Jutes, Saxons, and Frisians arrived to do battle with the enemies of the Britons. In fending off the Picts and Scots, however, the Britons exposed themselves to a different threat. The Germanic warriors liked what they saw and decided to stay. Before long, they were joined by others of their tribes and took control of almost all of present-day England. Eventually their domination was so complete that their territory became known as *Angle-land,* ultimately producing the name *England.* Some of the Celtic-speaking Britons who survived the fighting were probably assimilated into the Germanic tribes and adopted their language. Some found refuge in the remote outer reaches of the island: Cornwall and Wales, which remained Celtic-speaking into modern times. In fact, Welsh is still spoken today, and Cornish died out relatively recently. Other Britons fled to the continent, to the Celtic enclave of Brittany in France.[6]

The Germanic invaders spoke closely related languages that came to form what we call **Anglo-Saxon** or **Old English.** After losing their wanderlust, they settled down. Over time, the tribal structure of the Anglo-Saxons was replaced by several kingdoms, including Kent, Essex, Sussex, Wessex, East Anglia, Mercia, and Northumbria. These developing political institutions no doubt increased the desirability of written laws; as early as around 600, King Aethelbert of Kent produced written laws in Old English.[7] Eventually, the several kingdoms were consolidated into a single kingdom of England.[8]

It appears that the Anglo-Saxons had no distinct legal profession.[9] Yet they did develop a type of legal language, remnants of which have survived until today. Examples include the words *bequeath, goods, guilt, land, manslaughter, murder, right, sheriff, steal, swear, theft, thief,* and *ward.*[10]

One of the more significant Anglo-Saxon legal terms to have survived is the word *witness,* which comes from the word for "know" (*witan*). The term *witness* originally meant "knowledge" or "evidence" (as in the Biblical commandment against bearing *false witness*). Currently, *wit* refers to humor more than to knowledge, but its older sense is preserved in expressions like *use your wits* or *have your wits about you*, as well as an archaic phrase still beloved by lawyers: *to wit.*

Anglo-Saxons sometimes used sealed letters to confirm a grant of land or other legal transaction.[11] This document was known as a *gewrit* or *writ;* the word is obviously related to *write.* The later Norman kings retained and expanded the use of writs, which they addressed to the sheriff of a particular county as a means of exercising royal control over the country-side. While differing in function today, writs remain a familiar feature of legal practice.

The Anglo-Saxons had wills. In fact, the term *will* itself harks back to those times. Today, *will* is a modal (auxiliary) verb that refers to the future: *I will give my land to my sister* is a statement of what I plan to do at some later time. In Old English, however, *will* expressed desire. In fact, this meaning is preserved in phrases such as *if there's a will, there's a way* and *if you will.* Wills, therefore, were originally statements of what one *desired* to happen when one died, as indicated by a common expression in Anglo-Saxon wills: *ic wille* ("I desire").[12] There were no guarantees that the next generation would honor those wishes. For this reason, Anglo-Saxons felt it prudent to end the will with a curse on anyone who meddled with its terms.

The Anglo-Saxon word *moot* originally meant "meeting." (*Moot* is related to *meet* through the Old English process of **umlaut,** just as *food* is related to *feed* and *blood* to *bleed.*)[13] A *moot* was an open-air meeting of the population to discuss local affairs and, often, to resolve disputes.[14] In a rough sense, these were the earliest courts. A meeting of wise or knowledgeable men, combining the terms *wit* and *moot,* was the *witenage-mot.* This was a council that advised the king on administrative and judicial affairs.

The word *moot* eventually began to refer to meetings to engage in pleading exercises and to argue hypothetical cases used in the English Inns of Court to train future barristers.[15] That, of course, is the inspiration for the *moot courts* that are so common in American law schools. To say that a case or point is *moot* originally meant that it was unresolved or subject to debate, and by extension, mainly of academic interest.

An Anglo-Saxon legal term that is still extant, but without its original legal meaning, is *doom. Doom* is related to the verb *deem* in the same way that *moot* is connected to *meet.* To *deem* was to render judgment, not too far removed from its present sense of "consider, think." An old word for "judge" is *deemster* or *deemer.* A *doom* was a judgment. Aside from its legal use, the word could refer to God's final judgment (a sense preserved in the phrase to *meet your doom*). Apparently, people in the Middle Ages were not too optimistic about their prospects in the life hereafter. *Doom* soon became not just a neutral description of the last judgment on *doomsday,* but anticipated the worst.

Oath is yet another Anglo-Saxon word that is still with us, although its function has changed over time. To swear an oath today is to promise to tell the truth; lying under oath is punishable as perjury. In Old English times, however, the oath was taken by one of the parties, who swore that his case was true. Often he would have with him a number of neighbors, called "oath helpers," who backed up his word. The case was decided by successfully taking the oath; presumably, God rendered judgment by not striking the oath-taker dead.[16]

A physically more demanding means of deciding a dispute was by various forms of *ordeal.* Like *doom,* this word meant "judgment," and once again, it was God who judged. The process was, however, quite an ordeal, to use the term with its modern meaning. Its operation is illustrated by the medieval story of Tristan and Isolde.[17] Tristan was a knight in the service of King Mark of Cornwall. Under the influence of a love potion, Tristan falls madly in love with Isolde, the king's wife. Before long, the king accuses Isolde of infidelity; she must undergo trial by ordeal.

Isolde approaches the place of the trial by boat. As the lovers have agreed, Tristan, dressed as a pilgrim and recognized only by Isolde, awaits the boat on the shore. At Isolde's request, he carries her to the beach. In accordance with their plan, he stumbles and they fall down together, ending up in each others' arms on the ground.

Despite this mishap, the trial proceeds. Upon answering the question regarding her marital fidelity, Isolde must grasp the hot iron—if her hands are later unscathed, she will be deemed to have told the truth.[18] When the moment of truth arrives, Isolde declares that she has never been in any man's arms other than the king's and, of course, those of the pilgrim who just carried her across the water. She seizes the smoldering iron and God renders judgment (*ordeal*) through her unblemished hands: she has spoken truthfully.

Besides illustrating the nature of the ordeal, this story suggests that words had an almost talismanic power in early medieval society. Isolde's answer to the question regarding her infidelity was blatantly misleading, and the deception was carefully premeditated. Yet no matter how deceitful they might have been, the only thing that seems to have mattered—even to God—was that the words were truthful on a strictly literal level.

The power of words at this time is also reflected in the widespread use of exact verbal formulas in legal transactions and proceedings. For instance, a plaintiff might begin a suit against someone who owed him money by saying (translated into modern English):

> In the name of the living God, as I money demand, so have I lack of that which N. promised me, when I mine to him sold.[19]

The defendant would deny the charge with the following oath:

> In the name of the living God, I owe not to N. sceatt or shilling, or penny, or penny's worth; but I have discharged to him all that I owed him, so far as our verbal contracts were at first.[20]

Failing to repeat the formula word for word, or even stammering, could be fatal to one's case.[21]

Exact repetition of formulaic phrases evokes an age when people believed in magic and divine intervention. No doubt that was part of the reason for these rituals. Yet there may be a psychological basis for them as well. Someone who believes that God might strike him dead for lying, or that he might be condemned to hell, will become very nervous if he is swearing falsely, and might very well forget a few words or stammer. This principle also applies to trial by ordeal. Someone who believes that God will let his hands burn or wounds fester if he speaks falsely may decide to confess before undergoing the procedure. These "primitive" processes are not so different from modern lie detector tests, which largely measure how nervous a person is, rather than detecting lying per se.

Another Anglo-Saxon characteristic that has left traces in legal English is **alliteration.** It was widely used in poetry, as illustrated by the following passage from *Beowulf,* the famous Anglo-Saxon epic written in the seventh or eighth century:

> Hafa nū ond geheald hūsa sēlest,
> gemyne mǣrþo, mægenellen cȳð,
> waca wið wrāþum.

> "Have now and hold house most noble,
> keep mind on valour, strong courage show,
> watch against foe."[22]

As opposed to rhyme, where the ends of words are phonetically the same, alliteration requires that words *begin* with the same sound. Anglo-Saxon poetry strove to have two or three words in each line alliterate. Thus, in the third line, all three words begin with the sound *w*. Similarly, in the first line, *hafa, geheald* (ignore the prefix *ge-*), and *hūsa* all begin with the letter *h*.

Alliteration was common in the laws of all the Germanic tribes, as pointed out by the philologist Jacob Grimm (who is better known for his fairy tales).[23] It is not only poetic but has the utilitarian function of making phrases easier to remember—an important feature in a largely preliterate society. In fact, the phrase *to have and to hold,* which occurs in the first line of the Beowulf example, has survived into modern English.

Like other Germanic tribes, Anglo-Saxons made extensive use of alliteration in their legal language, no doubt in part because legal acts were performed orally in front of witnesses and required remembering exact verbal formulas. Recall that a defendant denied that he owed *sceatt or shilling* (two types of coins). Similarly, a grant of land to Bury St. Edmunds contained the following words:

> also so it stonden
> mid mete and mid manne
> and mid Sake and Sokne
> also ic it aihte

> "as they stand
> with their produce and their men
> and with rights of jurisdiction
> as I owned them."[24]

The alliterative phrases *mid mete and mid manne* and *sake and sokne* are pervasive in Anglo-Saxon land grants, which were made orally and could thus benefit from such mnemonic devices. The full text of the land grant is reproduced as appendix A.

A related phrase, also divided into lines to show its poetic nature, is the following:

> sker & sacleas
> sake & sokne
> tol & team

> "free and quit,
> [with rights of] jurisdiction
> toll and vouching to warranty."[25]

Although most Anglo-Saxon alliterative phrases have disappeared from our language, the process itself has not died out completely. An Old English poet could almost have coined the phrase *rest, residue and remainder,* a ponderous but poetic expression that is still encountered in many wills, as is *hold harmless* in contracts. Of more recent vintage are some favorites of American judges when writing opinions: *assuming arguendo* and *provide in pertinent part* (as in: *Assuming arguendo that it applies, the Act provides in pertinent part . . .*). Other alliterative phrases—some legal, others not—include the following:

> aid and abet
> any and all
> bed and breakfast
> clear and convincing
> fame and fortune
> house and home
> might and main
> mind and memory
> new and novel
> part and parcel
> rack and ruin
> rest and relaxation
> rhyme or reason
> safe and sound

In fact, we will see in a later chapter on language in the courtroom that lawyers use alliteration as a mnemonic device even today during closing argument to the jury.

Alliteration survived mainly in **conjoined phrases** (sometimes also called **binomial expressions** or **repetitive word pairs**). For our purposes, a conjoined phrase is one where two parallel elements are connected by a conjunction such as *and* or *or.* Most examples consist of two or perhaps three adjectives, nouns, or verbs.

Even without alliteration, parallelism was an important stylistic feature of Anglo-Saxon legal documents.[26] A witness sometimes had to swear that an event was something that *I with my eyes saw and with my ears heard.*[27] Obviously, the conjoined parallel structures give the oath a rhetorical force it would have lacked if the witness simply swore to speak truthfully. In fact, even today witnesses swear to tell *the truth, the whole truth, and nothing but the truth.*

Written laws became structurally more complex during the later Anglo-Saxon period. The early laws, like those of other Germanic tribes, were mostly straightforward *if-then* statements: *Gif thuman ofaslaeh, XX scill'* "if somebody cuts off someone else's thumb, then he shall pay 20 shillings compensation."[28] As Risto Hiltunen has noted, there appears to be a "continuous development towards more and more complex sentences from Ethelbert through the laws of Ine and Alfred to Cnut."[29] Compare one of the later laws of Canute the Dane (King of England from 1016–1035; also known as Cnut or Knut):

> And, if a priest produces false evidence or swears a false oath or enters into co-operation with thieves, then he will be excluded from the community of the holy orders and (he shall) lose both their companionship and friendship, as well as all respect, except if he shows deep repentance (for what he did) towards God and men in the way (his) bishop instructs him, and if the people of the town find him such that he will from now on ever abstain from suchlike (crimes).[30]

This law not only has the standard conditional clause at the beginning of the law (*if a priest produces . . .*), but has two parallel conditional clauses (*or swears. . .* and *or enters . . .*). Moreover, two clauses at the end contain exceptions (*if he shows . . .* and *if the people . . .*), each of which has yet another embedding within it. No doubt the increasing complexity of Anglo-Saxon political institutions at this time is mirrored by a growing complexity in the structure of their laws.

Christianity and Latin

A significant event for the language and law of England was the landing of Christian missionaries in 597. Christianity had originally come to England during Roman times, but it was only now that it gained a permanent foothold. By the year 601, the church had established itself in Canterbury and consecrated its first archbishop. Not long afterward, Christianity had spread throughout England.[31]

Through the Roman church, the Latin language once again had a major presence in England. Its influence extended to legal matters, particularly by means of the canon law, through which the church regulated religious matters such as marriage and the family.[32] Latin was also the language of learning and literature in the Middle Ages. Consequently, many laws and other legal documents were written in Latin. In fact, the spread of Christianity in England promoted not merely writing in Latin, but literacy in general. The first written laws in the Anglo-Saxon language—those of Aethelbert of Kent, around A.D. 600—directly followed the arrival of Christian missionaries to his kingdom.[33]

Use of Latin as a legal language introduced terms like *client, conviction, admit, mediate,* and *legitimate* into the English lexicon. Another Latin word to influence the law was *clerk*, which meant "priest" (compare the modern word *cleric*).[34] People with religious training were among the few who could write in those days. With one or two exceptions, none of the kings of Anglo-Saxon England were literate.[35] Eventually, clerics became roughly synonymous with scribes, with the result that a *clerk* today is someone who writes and keeps records, including the official documents of a court.

The Scandinavians

During the eighth century, Vikings from Scandinavia began raiding the English coast. Over the next few hundred years, they sacked churches and monasteries. Like the Angles and Saxons before them, some of the Northmen decided to settle down and occupied substantial portions of land. In the ninth and tenth centuries, Scandinavian law—known as the **Danelaw**—governed parts of eastern England. Scandinavian influence probably reached its height when Canute the Dane became king of England in the eleventh century.

The languages of the Anglo-Saxons and Scandinavians were fairly close at that time; there must have been at least some degree of mutual comprehensibility. At any rate, the Scandinavians had a lasting impact on the English language. Such basic words as *they, their, skin, sky,* and *take* are of Scandinavian origin.

In the legal arena, the Anglo-Saxons borrowed from the Scandinavians the most important legal word in the English language: the word *law* itself. One of the Anglo-Saxon terms for law, *riht*, has survived into modern English as *right*. But the word *law* derives from the Norse word for "lay" and means "that which is laid down." Etymologically speaking, therefore, the phrase *to lay down the law* is a repetitive redundancy.

And, of course, from *law* we get *lawyer*. Someone who does *work* is a *work-er;* someone who does law is a "*law-er*." Because people found "*lawer*" hard to pronounce (they had the same problem with someone who *saws*, a "*saw-er*"), they inserted a *y*, creating *lawyer* (and *sawyer*).

Other legal words of Norse origin include *gift, loan, sale,* and *trust*.[36] In fact, English adopted quite a few Scandinavian legal terms, such as *hamsocn* "house-breaking or the fine for that offense" and *stefnan* "summon," but most disappeared after the Norman Conquest.[37]

CHAPTER TWO

The Norman Conquest and
the Rise of French

A different group of Scandinavians had a far more profound and lasting impact on the legal language of England. These were the **Normans,** whose name comes from *northman.* The Normans were originally Vikings who conquered the region of Normandy, which is now part of France, during the ninth and tenth centuries, at around the same time their fellow Scandinavians were harassing the English. In the course of a few generations, the Viking invaders of Normandy became French both culturally and linguistically; the Northmen had become Normans.[1]

William the Conqueror Invades England

William, Duke of Normandy, claimed the English throne and invaded England in 1066. He defeated the English king Harold at the Battle of Hastings and was crowned king of England. Before long, the English-speaking ruling class was largely supplanted by one that spoke Norman French. As a consequence, virtually all significant words relating to the English government, aside from *king* and *queen,* were and still are French: *authority, chancellor, council, country, crown, exchequer, minister, nation, people, power, state, govern, government, realm, reign,* and *sovereign.*[2] Perhaps not surprisingly, the Conquest has often been viewed as a linguistic cataclysm in which William the Norman deposed the English language, installing in its place a "barbarous" French dialect that would function for centuries thereafter as an "evident and shameful badge . . . of tyranny and foreign servitude."[3]

In actuality, the transition from English to French in public life generally and in legal language specifically evolved more gradually. Part of the reason was that William encouraged some use of English in order to reinforce his claim that he was not just a foreign interloper, but the legitimate heir to the throne. In the words of Mellinkoff, use of English "emphasized the continuity of kingship, law, and property rights."[4]

Eventually, however, as more and more Normans took on positions of prominence, Norman French became the language of power. For some time after the Conquest, English was primarily the lower-class language of a subjugated people. As stated much later by Sir Walter Scott in his novel *Ivanhoe:* after the Norman Conquest, "French was the language of honour, of chivalry, and even of justice, while the far more manly and expressive Anglo-Saxon was abandoned to the use of rustics and hinds, who knew no other."[5] Scott surely exaggerated the point, but it is true that the literary use of English was limited largely to religious compositions intended for the edification of "lewde" (uncultivated) people.[6]

The inferior status of English during this time became the stuff of legend. It has been suggested that the people most likely to see meat on the table were the aristocracy, who spoke French. As a result, it is said, English words for meat as food derive from French: *mutton, veal, beef,* and *pork.* In contrast, it was the English-speaking peasants who tended the animals while on the hoof. Hence, the words for farm animals are Anglo-Saxon: *lamb, calf, cow* and *pig.* Scholars now believe that this dichotomy is exaggerated. Still, the overall conclusion that French was the language of the aristocracy, while English remained the language of the masses, is generally accurate.[7]

Despite its prominence as the spoken language of the aristocracy, not a single document in French has come down to us from the reign of William the Conqueror. William's writs and charters were in Latin or English.[8] Anglo-French (the type of French spoken by the Normans living in England) was apparently not used in an official legal document until around a century and a half after the Norman Conquest.[9] This does not mean that English thrived, however. On the contrary, by the reign of Henry I (1100–1135) the occasional use of English in legal documents ceased, to be replaced by Latin exclusively.[10]

The main impact of the Norman Conquest on *written* legal language was thus to replace English with Latin.[11] Before the Conquest, both English and Latin were used to write legal documents. After the Normans arrived, the use of English rapidly declined. The Normans were accustomed to writing in Latin.[12] Consequently, while the Norman Conquest did depose English as a written legal language, it did not immediately enthrone French.

The first statute in French dates from 1275, over two hundred years after the Conquest. The time from 1275 to around 1310 is a transitional period, in which statutes were apparently written indiscriminately in

either French or Latin. Beginning in 1310, the normal language for statutes was French. Although there are occasional statutes in Latin through
1460, most seem to have been in that language for a reason. The great
majority of the Latin statutes after 1310 were directed to or concerned
the church, which still used Latin regularly, or were in the form of writs
addressed to the sheriffs; the traditional language for writs was also Latin.
This state of affairs continued until the end of the 1480s, when the language of statutes suddenly shifted to English.[13]

Incidentally, even while statutes were being drafted in French, there
are indications of oral usage of English in Parliament as early as 1362
and increasingly thereafter.[14] It seems likely that statutes continued to be
recorded in French for several decades after the members of Parliament
began conducting their affairs in English.

Written commentary on the law followed a similar course. The treatise
De Legibus et Consuetudinibus Angliae, attributed to Glanvill and written
around 1187, was entirely in Latin. Bracton's treatise (early to mid-
1200s) was also in Latin, but from time to time he would translate a term
or expression into English (not French!). Six times he used the English
term "ebb and flood," for example. Most of these translations into
English were legal terms, which suggests that even at this late date, educated readers were familiar with English legal terminology, perhaps
more so than French.[15]

Other evidence of continuing Anglo-Saxon influence on the law
comes from English glosses of Latin terms during this period. For example, Latin terms in a royal charter to the monks of Colchester were
sometimes accompanied by English equivalents.[16] Yet by the end of the
thirteenth century, there was already a need for legal commentary
in French.[17] In the centuries thereafter, a substantial legal literature
emerged in French.[18]

With regard to the spoken language of the law, the course of the transition to French is less certain. William, who strove to project himself as
legitimate heir to the throne, was proclaimed king in both French and
English. Mellinkoff suggests that in the immediate post-Conquest period, much litigation continued to be conducted in English in the local
courts.[19] In fact, J. H. Baker notes that there is no evidence that French
was used in the law courts until the middle of the thirteenth century,
roughly two hundred years after the Conquest.[20] Woodbine concludes
that it is difficult if not impossible to say when French became regularly
used in English courts, but the general use of French in oral pleading
may not have happened until long after the Conquest, perhaps as late

as the time of Edward I (1272–1307).[21] Most likely, we will never know exactly. It seems certain that proceedings in the Curia Regis, a royal council with certain judicial functions, were in French immediately after the Conquest. On the other hand, local courts may well have conducted much of their business in English, particularly because litigants in those courts would have spoken little, if any, French.[22]

We do know that by the end of the thirteenth century, the expanding royal courts were conducting their oral proceedings at least partly in French. Beginning in the 1280s and continuing through 1535, anonymous writers created reports of oral proceedings in court, which were compiled in the **year books.** (A case from the year books is contained in appendix B.) All of these year books, made for the edification of law students and lawyers, were in Anglo-French.[23] Further support that French was gaining prominence in the courts during this time comes from a Latin tract from around 1275; it suggests that pleadings in royal courts were in French. Another tract from around 1285 explicitly states that this is so.[24]

Unfortunately, how much French was actually being spoken in the courts at any period of time is extremely difficult to say. Although the year books probably reflect actual French speech in the courts when they began, they continued in French long after the predominant language of the courtroom must have become English. In other words, speech in one language could be, and often was, written down in another.[25]

In any event, the evidence suggests that French was not enthroned as the main language of English law directly as a result of the Norman invasion. It is only in the latter half of the thirteenth century—two hundred years after the Conquest—that statutes arising in Parliament and oral pleadings in the royal courts are definitely in French, although it quickly becomes the norm. For the next century or two, French maintained its status as England's premier legal language, at least with respect to written documents.

What is odd about this linguistic development is not just that it happened so late, but that the use of French in the English legal system grew at the very time that its survival as a living language was in serious question. During the thirteenth century, most of the gentry were not native French speakers, although the royal court and magnates retained the language.[26] Baker observes that outside the legal sphere, Anglo-French was in steady decline after 1300.[27] As early as 1295, Edward I attempted to garner support for a war against Philip IV of France, declaring in a summons to the leaders of the church that the French king proposed to wipe the English language from the face of the earth. This suggests that some, perhaps most, of England's bishops and abbots—who after the Conquest were all French speakers—had shifted their loyalties to English.[28]

Over the course of the fourteenth century, French declined among the nobility as well. Robert of Gloucester, at around 1300, could still conclude that "people of rank" spoke French.[29] In actuality, most likely these "people of rank" were bilingual in English by this time. And the number of French speakers was small: perhaps one in a hundred.[30] Furthermore, various outbreaks of the Plague killed over a third of the English population during the mid– to late fourteenth century; an epidemic in 1361 was especially devastating to the upper classes, and thus to the French language.[31] By 1400, if not before, even the upper echelons of the nobility must have been mostly native English speakers.

The final holdouts were members of the royal household. It was only in 1417, while fighting the French, that King Henry V finally broke all linguistic ties with his Norman ancestry. He decided to have many of his official documents, including his own will, written in English.[32] His successor, Henry VI, ascended to the throne in 1422, using his mother tongue—English—to make his formal challenge for the crown.[33]

By 1300, therefore, Anglo-French was in serious decline among the general population, and by 1400 it was close to a dead language even in the royal household. Why is it, then, that in precisely this century the use of French as the language of the law was in ascendancy? Recall that statutes shifted decisively to French in 1310 and continued in this language through the 1480s.

In an odd sense, the adoption of French as a legal language might be viewed as a progressive measure, designed to make the law more accessible to those subject to it. When statutes began to appear in French around 1275, it was still spoken by much of the nobility. Thus, French was quite possibly the native language of most members of Parliament at this time. And those who sought the king's justice in the royal courts, as well as its advocates and judges, would have been mainly aristocrats who were native speakers of French or spoke it quite well.[34] Those who made and used the law thus had access to it in a language that they understood, as opposed to a dead language—Latin—used mainly by academics and clerics. Adoption of Anglo-French did nothing to make the law more accessible to the English-speaking masses, of course, but this was hardly a democratic era, and in any event ordinary folks were probably more affected by local custom than by royal statutes.

It is also significant that there was a fair amount of interaction across the English Channel during this period. For example, the reservoir of French speakers increased when Henry III (1216–1272) married Eleanor of Provence. The result was another French invasion of the island as Eleanor brought along her relatives and courtiers from France. These French immigrants landed important positions in the royal administration, creating hostilities between the king and the English barons, who resented their presence.[35] The fighting ended with a victory by the king and his French allies. No doubt such continuing contacts with the Continent reinvigorated the French language in England and contributed to its adoption as the primary language of the law.

Moreover, French was becoming a language of culture throughout much of Europe. According to M. T. Clanchy, "[i]t was not primarily the Norman Conquest but the advance of French as an international literary and cultural language, particularly in the thirteenth century, which caused its increasing use as a written language for English records."[36]

The cause of French was further advanced by the creation of a centralized system of royal justice. As Douglas Kibbee has observed, "[t]he centralization of judicial authority also points to a centralization of judicial language."[37] Although the king and his council (the Curia Regis) had always had certain judicial functions, the king gradually "delegated" his judicial powers to professional judges in specific courts (such as King's Bench and the Court of Common Pleas), and at the same time opened the royal courts to a larger number of litigants.[38] The king's courts would naturally be conducted in the king's language: French. Thus, the growing jurisdiction of the royal courts of justice concurrently promoted the expansion of French as a legal language. Furthermore, this change to French seems to have filtered down to other courts as well. According to Pollock and Maitland, by the end of the thirteenth century cases were sometimes pleaded in French even in local courts.[39]

Finally, the triumph of French as the distinctive language of the law was doubtless aided by the development of a professional class of lawyers, the first signs of which appear around 1200.[40] This development was stimulated in the mid–thirteenth century, when the church banned its priests from serving as legal representatives in lay courts.[41] Not long after, by the time of Edward I (1272–1307), there is indisputable evidence of a group of technically trained lawyers who appeared regularly as pleaders in the royal (common law) courts; these men used French in pleading.[42] Once lawyers constituted a profession, it made some sense for them to develop their own professional language. And because lawyers were trained not at the university (where the language of instruction was Latin), but by other lawyers at the Inns of Court, the mechanism was in place for French to be passed down from one generation of lawyers to the next, even after it died out among the rest of the population.

The Continuing Use of Latin

Despite the emergence of French, Latin remained an important legal language in England, especially in written form. Court records, writs, and some other legal documents were in Latin as late as the eighteenth century.[43]

To the modern mind, writing in Latin—the language of the clergy and the educated elite—rather than in the language of the people, might seem like just another way of oppressing the masses. After all, Anglo-Saxon had been a written language before the Norman Conquest. Yet a problem with using English was that it had many dialects, often very different from each other. Latin, in contrast, was a standardized language, with a set grammar and spelling. A sheriff in some parts of England might have had trouble following the king's spoken English, but Latin writs were understood throughout the country (and indeed, all of Europe). The advantage of Latin was therefore that it could operate as a lingua franca in a country where dialect differences could be substantial.

As might be expected, the Latin used by the legal profession was soon adapted to the needs of the English law. Eventually, it developed into something called **Law Latin.** As time went on, Law Latin frequently employed English when quoting an utterance that was originally in English, or when the Latin word did not come to mind, or did not exist. In court records regarding defamation cases, for instance, the allegedly slanderous statement was generally interposed in the original English:

> Et tunc et ibidem inter cetera verba et plures communicationes Thomas Morpath dixit Thome Mowberlay thow art an heretyke.

> "And then and there among other words and several communications Thomas Morpath said, 'Thomas Mowberlay thou art a heretic.' "[44]

The occupations of the parties might also be listed in English: *barber, husbondman, inholder,* or *yoman,* for instance, are interspersed in the Latin records.[45] Some English words were Latinized, as in *murdrum* "murder."[46] Clerks might also provide an English gloss for readers who did not know the Latin term: *sorceri vocati wytches* "sorcerers, called witches."[47] Law

Latin also borrowed words from French, generally with Latinized forms: *barganizando* "bargaining,"[48] *attornatus* "attorney" and *juratores* "jurors,"[49] and *seisitus* "seised."[50]

The fact that writs were drafted in Latin for so long explains why even today, many of them have Latin names. Writs are letters issued in the name of the sovereign, typically addressed to a sheriff and ordering him to undertake some action.[51] The Latin name for the writ often came from the first word or two, or from another critical phrase in the text. Thus, there were several types of *praecipe* writs. After the greeting from the king to the sheriff (*Rex vicecomitati X salutem* "the king to the sheriff of X, greetings") one such writ continued with the Latin words *praecipimus tibi* "we command you." The writ called *mandamus* "we command" has a similar meaning. A writ of *habeas corpus* "you should seize the body" directs law enforcement officers or prison officials to have the body of a prisoner brought before the court. Other Latin writ names that have survived, at least in the United States, are *certiorari, quo warranto, subpoena,* and *supersedeas.*

Latin was also extensively employed for legal canons or maxims, which are sayings about the law. Some maxims concern the law in general, whereas others deal with the interpretation of legal language in particular. Even today they tend to be phrased in Latin, as in *ubi jus, ibi remedium* ("where there is a right, there is a remedy") and *expressio unius (est) exclusio alterius* ("the expression of one thing implies the exclusion of the other"). Others include *de minimis non curat lex, ejusdem generis, in pari materia* and *noscitur a sociis.* One Latin maxim is still widely known among the public: *caveat emptor.*

The use of Latin and tireless repetition by judges have endowed these legal maxims with a sense of timelessness and dignity, often undeserved by the content. Nonetheless, they reflect an oral folk tradition in which legal rules are expressed as sayings, typically with a certain rhythm or rhyme as an aid to remembrance. It was an ancient practice among Germanic peoples, for example, to express legal principles in rhymed and alliterative sayings.[52] This tradition continued in England. One such rhyme is the following:

> Wo so boleth myn kyn
> ewerc is the calf myn

> "No matter who bulls my kine
> the calf is mine."[53]

In this light, note the rhyme and roughly dactylic meter (stressed-unstressed-unstressed) in

> expressio unius
> exclusio alterius.

Amazingly, these poetic features are still occasionally found in legal language. Brenda Danet has identified features such as alliteration, assonance, rhythm, and rhyme in a contemporary bank promissory note.[54] For a popular rhymed saying about the law, consider:

> Finders keepers
> Losers weepers.

In fact, we will see later that trial lawyers are not above using rhyme to impress an argument on the minds of jurors.

Latin has also persisted in expressions relating to the names of cases and parties. Examples are *versus, ex rel., et al., pro se, in personam, in rem, in propria persona, in forma pauperis, in re, ex parte,* and *pro hac vice.* In England, the term for the crown in criminal case names is *Rex* or *Regina.* These procedural phrases probably reflect the fact that records of legal proceedings were kept in Latin for many centuries.

A substantive area of the law with a relatively high level of Latin vocabulary is defamation. This may be because the law of libel and slander developed in the ecclesiastical courts, which used Latin in their proceedings.[55] Thus, the following words are either Latin, or are Anglicized forms derived from Latin: *colloquium, defamation, innuendo, libel, mitior sensus,* and *per quod.* It appears that when the common law judges took jurisdiction over defamation from the ecclesiastical courts, they borrowed much of the terminology as well. We should not make too much of this point, however. Virtually every sphere of the law mixes words of Anglo-Saxon, French, and Latin origin; identifying a specific legal area with a particular language is not a hard science.

Other Latin words or phrases still in common usage include *actus reus, amicus curiae, corpus delicti, ex post facto,* and *malum in se.* Words describing mental states are typically in Latin: *mens rea, scienter, animus revocandi,* and *animus testandi* are examples.[56] And there are, of course, a large number of English words, like *demonstrative, testament,* and *testify,* that derive from Latin but have been Anglicized.

Law French

Once Anglo-French died out as a living tongue, the French used by lawyers and judges became a language exclusive to the legal profession, known as **Law French.** Modern complaints about the difficulty of understanding legal language pale in comparison to the language barrier that existed then between the legal profession and the population. Law French was a distinct language that had to be learned by aspiring lawyers; it was incomprehensible not only to their English clients, but probably to speakers of ordinary French as well.[57]

Unhappiness about this state of affairs led to what might be considered the first plain English law. In 1362 the Statute of Pleading was enacted, condemning French as "much unknown in the said Realm" and noting that parties in a lawsuit "have no Knowledge nor Understanding of that which is said for them or against them by their Serjeants and other Pleaders." In order that "every Man of the said Realm may the better govern himself without offending of the Law," the statute required that all pleas be "pleaded, shewed, defended, answered, debated, and judged in the English Tongue." Records could still be kept in Latin. Ironically, the statute itself was in French and seems to have had limited effect.[58]

The preservation of Law French for hundreds of years after French died out as an ordinary language in England underscores the inertia and linguistic conservatism of the legal profession. Indeed, it foreshadows the resistance that the profession has shown—even today—to reforming its language.

There may also be a more sinister motive for the retention of French. Remember that the emergence of a profession of lawyers may have assisted in the original adoption of French as language of the law. The profession's subsequent desire to monopolize the provision of legal services no doubt encouraged it to retain French long after it had become obsolete in ordinary life. As Mellinkoff has suggested: "What better way of preserving a professional monopoly than by locking up your trade secrets in the safe of an unknown tongue?"[59]

Of course, lawyers had other explanations. Perhaps the most interesting justification for keeping the law in an "unknown tongue" was given by Sir Edward Coke: to protect the public. Coke suggested that legal materials were not published in English "lest the unlearned by bare reading without right understanding might suck out errors, and trusting in their conceit, might endamage themselves, and sometimes fall into destruction."[60] Much the same argument was made for keeping the Bible and other religious texts in Latin. If ordinary people could read the Scriptures, they might reach their own conclusions and question the official teachings of the Church; translating the Bible into the vernacular was therefore heresy.[61] Perhaps not incidentally, keeping spiritual as well as temporal laws in a foreign language preserved the status of priests and lawyers as interpreters and intermediaries.

Most of the defenders of Law French offered somewhat more palatable arguments, similar to those that lawyers make today in defense of modern legal language. The formalized phrases of Law French were regarded as a convenient shorthand for summarizing legal arguments on paper. Law French also contained many terms for which there were no English equivalents. Over six hundred years after the Norman Conquest, Roger North could still claim that "the law is scarcely expressible properly in English."[62]

Additionally, Law French was considered much more precise than English. Using the example of *an heir in tail rebutted from his formedon by a lineal warranty with descended assets,* Maitland contended that "[p]recise ideas are here expressed in precise terms. . . . [T]he chemist could hardly wish for terms that are more exact or less liable to have their edges worn away by the vulgar."[63] Not only did Law French allow for precise terms of art, but its terminology was considered more resistant to change and therefore relatively immune to the "corruption" and changes in usage that affected all spoken language.[64]

Of course, whatever validity these arguments might have had, they justified at most the retention of French technical terms, not wholesale preservation of a dead language. No one has seriously contended that all French articles, prepositions, and verbs were more precise than their English equivalents. Basic words like *the, with,* and *is* are just as clear in English as in French, for the most part. As we do today, lawyers could have continued to employ Law French technical terms, with all their vaunted precision and resistance to change, but embedded those terms into ordinary English sentences. The fact that they chose instead to preserve—as best they could—an entire foreign language lends credence to the conspiratorial view.

Law French gradually underwent drastic simplification. When it was still a natural language, it would have had its own pronunciation. There would have been sounds that did not exist in English, just as in modern French and most other languages. Over time, however, its distinct phonetic and phonological features seem to have been lost; lawyers pronounced it as though it were English.[65] Incidentally, a noteworthy aspect of the pronunciation of Law French, which it shares with other Romance languages, was its aversion to having *st, sp,* or *sk* (written as *sq*) at the beginning of a word (as in *state, stop* or *squire*). To break up these clusters, an *e* was added to the beginning of the word, creating *estate, estop,* and *esquire,* which makes these words easier to articulate. Frequently, both the form with initial *e,* as well as that without it, survived into modern English, albeit with differences in meaning. Thus, *espouse* is related to *spouse, establish* to *stable,* and *escheat* to *cheat.*

As in standard French, an *s* was commonly dropped before consonants (compare French *forêt* with English *forest*). Thus, the Law French term *puisne* (from *puis* "after" and *ne* "born"), meaning "younger" or "junior," was pronounced without the *s.* In modern English legal usage it is pronounced *pyoonee* and refers to a junior or associate judge. The word eventually entered ordinary speech as *puny,* with a derogatory connotation that no doubt offends most *puisne* judges, whose status is far from puny.

French adjectives normally follow the noun that they modify. Several such combinations are still common in legal English:

accounts payable / receivable
attorney general
condition precedent / subsequent
court martial
fee simple absolute
fee tail
letters patent
letters testamentary
malice aforethought
notary public
solicitor general

There were exceptions to this rule. As in modern French, the words for "large" (*grand*) and "small" (*petit* or *petty*) preceded the noun that they modified, as reflected in *grand larceny* and *petty theft.*

The infinitive form of the Anglo-French verb, which took the suffix *-er,* could be used as a noun, called a **gerund.** Many of these gerunds have entered legal English as ordinary nouns, including *demurrer, interpleader, joinder, merger, ouster, remainder, reverter,* and *waiver.* On the other hand, when Law French terms were adopted into English as verbs, they dropped the infinitive ending: *demur, interplead, join,* and so forth.[66] Another way to create nouns from Anglo-French verbs was to add the suffix *-al.* Many legal words still reveal this process: *acquittal, denial, proposal, rebuttal, trial,* and *estoppel* or *estoppal.*

Verbs in Law French often formed the past participle by adding *-e* or *-ee*. Thus, the infinitive *lesser* "let, lease" had the past participle *lessee* "leased." These past participles later came to be used as nouns to indicate the person who was the recipient or object of the action ("the person leased to").[67] In contrast, the suffix *-or* indicated the actor, or person engaging in the action. These processes created numerous sets of legal terms indicating the actor and object of an action, respectively: *lessor/lessee, vendor/vendee, mortgagor/mortgagee,* and so forth.

By far the most lasting impact of French is the tremendous amount of technical vocabulary that derives from it, including many of the most basic words in our legal system: *agreement, arrest, arson, assault, crime, damage, easement, felony, heir, larceny, marriage, misdemeanor, money, profit, property, slander, tort,* and *trespass,* to name a few.[68] The French influence on legal vocabulary is pervasive. As Pollock and Maitland pointed out, an American or English lawyer who wished to write about the law using only original English words would be "doomed to silence."[69]

Certain areas of the law seem to have an especially heavy concentration of words from French. For instance, the English law of real property was greatly influenced by feudalism, mostly imported to England by the Normans.[70] Consequently, real property terminology is overwhelmingly French: *cestui que use, chattel, conveyance, curtesy, dower, easement, estate, fee simple, fee tail, lease, license, profit a prendre, property, remainder, rent, seisin, tenant, tenure, trespass.*

Recall that there are some uncertainties about the extent to which French was actually used as a spoken language in English courts following the Conquest. Nonetheless, it is remarkable that the vast majority of words referring to courts, their officers, and procedures, come from Law French. They include *action, appeal, attorney, bailiff, bar, claim, complaint, counsel, court, defendant, demurrer, evidence, indictment, judge, judgment, jury, justice, parol, party, plaintiff, plea, plead, process, sentence, sue, suit, summon, verdict,* and *voir dire.* This overwhelmingly Romance vocabulary suggests that court proceedings were largely in French for a substantial period of time, and certainly during the formative years of the English judicial system.

As we saw earlier, Anglo-Saxon had many phrases that joined two words with closely related meaning. These conjoined phrases were often alliterative as well. *To have and to hold* is a remnant of this practice. Mellinkoff has pointed out that this doubling continued in Law French, but with some variations.[71] For one thing, alliteration was far less characteristic of French. More importantly, the doubling often involved the pairing

of a native English word with the equivalent French word. Because many
people at the time would have been only partially bilingual, this practice
ensured that they would always understand at least one of the terms.
Some examples follow, with the English member of the pair in italics:

> devise and *bequeath*
> *breaking* and entering
> *acknowledge* and confess
> *goods* and chattels
> *had* and received
> *will* and testament
> *fit* and proper
> *free* and clear

The use of conjoined phrases later became more a matter of style or
fashion.[72] The linguist Otto Jespersen cites several examples from Chaucer, who must have assumed that his readers were familiar with both the
French and the English:

> poynaunt and *sharp*
> At sessiouns ther was he *lord* and sire
> *olde* and auncyent doctours
> *fowle* and dishonestly
> I toke a *glasse* or a mirrour[73]

Conjoined expressions remain fashionable in the profession, even
though there is no longer a need to translate French into English, or
vice versa.

Eventually, Law French descended ever further along the path to becoming merely technical vocabulary of the legal profession. Baker estimates that by the sixteenth century, "the active vocabulary of law French
had diminished to less than a thousand words, and legal writers un-
ashamedly inserted English words when their knowledge of French
failed them."[74] An illustration of the curious mingling of the two languages is an argument by Coke in a 1585 defamation case about an allegation of *faulsifyinge de recorde,* in which the word *falsifying,* though of
Latin origin, clearly shows English morphology with its *-ing* suffix. Coke
argued that the defamation consisted of *parolx in heate et anger sicome home
que est angrie ove son councellour dit que il est ambideuxter.*[75] *In heate* is an
English phrase, while *anger* and *angrie* are also English (though they ultimately derive from Norse).

One case report has become a notorious portrayal of this mixture of
French and English:

> Richardson Chief Justice de Common Banc al assises de Salis-
> bury in Summer 1631 fuit assault per prisoner la condemne pur
> felony, que puis son condemnation ject un brickbat a le dit jus-
> tice, que narrowly mist, et pur ceo immediately fuit indictment
> drawn per Noy envers le prisoner et son dexter manus ampute
> et fix al gibbet, sur que luy mesme immediatement hange in
> presence de Court.[76]

Not only does this passage mix French and English words with abandon
(English words include *summer, narrowly mist, drawn,* and *hange,* as well
as the *-ly* suffix on *immediately*), but it throws in some Latin (*dexter manus*)
for good measure.

Another report of the same incident by Mr. Justice Hutton adds some
flavor and again reveals how English was interspersed through the text.
Hutton wrote that "per le negligence del gaoler" the prisoner was not
"manacled come est use." The prisoner

> sudenment throwe ove grand violence un great stone al heade
> del dit Seignior Rychardson quel per le mercy del Dieu did
> come close to his hatt et missed him . . . et le stone hitt the
> wanescott behind them and gave a great rebound, quel si ceo
> stone had hitt le dit Seignior Rychardson il voet have killed him.

While the penalty of amputation seems extreme by modern standards,
Mr. Justice Hutton provided a rationale that no doubt resonates well
even today: this was "un bon example de justice in cest insolent age."[77]

To be fair, the brickbat example has been called "the worst specimen
of Law French yet discovered."[78] The reason is surely the subject matter.
When the topic was something beyond the predictable phrases that pop-
ulated the law reports of the time, their French escaped them; lawyers
had no alternative but to resort to their native English. By the seventeenth century, therefore, Law French was barely more than a large number of technical terms glued together with a few oft-repeated function
words.

Trilingualism and Code-Switching

During much of its history, the English legal profession was trilingual,
using English, French, and Latin in differing situations, and with varying success. Lawyers engaged in what linguists have come to call **code-
switching.**[79] People who speak more than one language often switch from
one code to another, depending on the topic, context, or participants.
This is exactly what lawyers of this period had to do. Many written plead-

ings and legal records were in Latin. Speech directed at nonlawyers—such as discussions with clients or questioning of witnesses in court—would necessarily have been in English. And interchanges with other barristers or judges in court—especially oral pleading—would have been in French, at least for part of this period. Lawyers would therefore have needed at least a working knowledge of all three languages.

The extent to which these languages were intertwined is well illustrated by a report of *Hawes v. Davye,* a case dating from the middle of the sixteenth century in the Court of Common Pleas. Case reports were still typically in Law French during this period, and thus it begins in that language. But it quickly switches to English because that is the original language of the bond at issue, while throwing in the Latin phrases *verbatim, in haec verba,* and *scilicet:*

> En dett sur obligation le defendant ad oyer del obligation enter verbatim, et del condition in hec verba, scilicet If the obligour doe pay. . . .

> "In debt on a bond, the defendant had oyer of the bond entered verbatim, and of the condition *in haec verba:* 'if the obligor do pay. . . .' "

The plea of the defendant is then presented in Latin, because that is the language of the record:

> Defendens dicit quod actio non. . . .

> "The defendant says that the plaintiff ought not to have the action. . . ."

The report then concludes in Law French:

> Et lopinion del court fuit pur le plaintife. . . .

> "And the opinion of the court was for the plaintiff. . . ."[80]

Law has always been a profession of words, but in some respects that may have been even more true in medieval England than it is today.

CHAPTER THREE

The Resurgence of English

The Demise of Latin and Law French

The legal profession's use of three different languages makes the Middle Ages an interesting period linguistically, but it did not always promote the fair and efficient administration of justice. We have already seen that as early as 1362, Parliament tried to legislate the greater use of English in pleading, to little avail. Complaints about the situation continued to mount. In 1549, Thomas Cranmer, the first Protestant archbishop of Canterbury, recounted that "I have heard suitors murmur at the bar because their attornies pleaded their cause in the French tongue which they understood not."[1] Later, John Warr asked why the law was still kept in an unknown tongue. Before the Conquest, he noted, the law was in English, and a man could be his own advocate. But the "hiddenness" of the law—caused in large part by use of a foreign language—forced people of the time to "have recourse to the shrine of the lawyer."[2]

Parliament finally took action during the Commonwealth, when the Puritans assumed power and beheaded the king. The Puritans seem to have had a zest not just for plain living, but for plain language as well. They toyed with the idea of abolishing the common law, including its courts and practitioners, and replacing it with a pocket-sized code in ordinary English.[3] More realistically, in 1650 Parliament passed a law that required all case reports and books of law to be "in the English Tongue onely." It directed that earlier reports of judicial decisions and other law books be translated into English.[4] But in 1660, after the monarchy had been restored, the "pretended act" requiring English was repealed and the old state of affairs returned: many of the case reports were again in Law French, and court records in Latin.[5]

During the rest of the seventeenth century, Latin and Law French continued their slow decline. Recall that statutes had been in English since the end of the 1400s. Even the courts, long bastions of French and Latin, had largely switched to English. For instance, the bills and answers in the Star Chamber, a court established in 1487 and known for its harsh sentences, were in the vernacular.[6] Similarly, the court that developed in the Chancery kept pleadings regarding its equitable jurisdiction in English, starting around the mid–fifteenth century, and its proceedings may have been in English even earlier.[7] By 1704, law reports of all the courts were in English.[8] Consequently, when Parliament permanently ended the use of Latin and French in legal proceedings in 1731, it was delivering mainly a *coup de grâce*. Unfortunately, it turned out to be difficult to translate many Law French and Latin terms into English. Two years later, another statute provided that the traditional names of writs and technical words could continue to be in the original language.[9]

The Increasing Importance of Writing and Printing

Throughout the history of English law, legal language has been spoken. Originally, of course, legal language was exclusively oral. One of the most profound developments over the centuries has been the increasing significance of writing, in addition to—or in place of—spoken legal language. The impact of writing was compounded by the invention of printing, which was introduced to England in the 1470s.[10]

On one level, there should be very little difference between spoken and written legal language. Linguists have emphasized that human language is based on speech, while writing is clearly derivative.[11] In this sense, writing is nothing more than a way of representing and preserving speech, much like a tape recorder.

This was the state of affairs in Anglo-Saxon England. Legal language was almost entirely oral; any writing was simply a record or evidence of the spoken event. For example, from the fifth century to the Norman Conquest, transfers of land and wills were customarily made orally, usually with witnesses present, and often accompanied by a symbolic handing over of a clod of dirt. Eventually, the clergy began to make written records of property transfers as aids to remembering.[12] As Brenda Danet and Bryna Bogoch point out, these documents were simply "after-the-fact records of the binding event that already had taken place."[13] In other words, the written documents were *evidentiary* of the oral ceremony, rather than *operative* or *dispositive* legal documents in the modern sense.[14]

Commencing in the late Anglo-Saxon period, there are indications of a new trend in which legal documents were no longer just evidence of grants or wills. While the process took centuries to complete, ultimately the writing and signing of the document itself became the legally operative or dispositive act.[15] For instance, transfers of real property by will had to be in writing under the Statute of Wills of 1540. After the Statute of Frauds in 1677, such transfers also had to be signed by the testator in the presence of witnesses.[16]

As a consequence, the emphasis shifted from what was *said* to what was *written*. Stated somewhat differently, written legal language originally had the function of merely recording an oral event. The focus remained on the oral ceremony. Later, the focus became the written document itself. In fact, with the development of the **parol evidence rule,** which largely prohibited introduction of evidence of oral discussions regarding the content of the document, this evolution was complete. What mattered now was solely what was written on paper. Anything the parties *said* regarding the transaction became legally irrelevant, subject to some limited exceptions.

A similar evolution took place with reports of judicial proceedings. The year books were compiled by "reporters" in the literal sense of the word: they simply reported speech in the courtroom, including questions of judges and argument of counsel. (See appendix B for an example.) An innovation that began in the middle of the fifteenth century indicates that lawyers were beginning to treat descriptions of court proceedings not just as interesting or educational reports of what happened in court, but as actual sources of law. Notably, lawyers began making and printing **abridgments.** Much like today's digests, the abridgments consisted of alphabetical headings, like *abatement,* followed by synopses of cases dealing with that topic.[17] This made it much more convenient for lawyers to find and cite cases dealing with a particular legal proposition. Gradually, reports of court proceedings revealed a growing emphasis on what the judge said, and less on the arguments of the lawyers. In a sense, this is the beginning of the notion of **precedent.**

The final step of this process began in the United States at the end of the eighteenth century, when judges systematically began to issue written opinions.[18] Even though books containing such opinions are still called *reports* in the United States, they are no longer the result of a "reporter" going to court and "reporting" the proceedings. Rather, they consist almost entirely of opinions written by the judges themselves and are normally published verbatim. The end result is that today, what an American appellate judge *says* is virtually irrelevant. All that matters, for legal purposes, is what judges *write* in their opinions. And because they come straight from the horse's mouth, so to speak, lawyers focus intensely on the exact words of the opinion.

Legislation, the other major source of law, seems to have undergone much the same development. Anglo-Saxon compilations of laws mainly recorded rules or customs that existed independently in the community. Legislation enacted by a parliament was rare until the end of the thirteenth century. Even then, such legislation was not, according to J. H. Baker, authoritative text in the modern sense.[19] In other words, the written legislation was viewed primarily as a report of an oral proceeding. This conclusion is bolstered by the fact that at least in some cases, the drafting of the text was done by clerks and judges *after* Parliament had given its assent. Furthermore, the written versions of the texts were often inconsistent with one another and were quite freely interpreted.[20]

Toward the end of the fifteenth century, parliamentary legislation underwent a significant change and became "the deliberate adoption of specific proposals embodied in specific texts."[21] Along with this new concept, according to Baker, came "a new reverence for the written text."[22] In our terms, the written document was no longer simply evidence of the law, but constituted the law itself.

A related event with a major impact on the law was the invention of printing. Beginning in the 1600s, the publication of law books grew rapidly. By 1800, the printed literature on English law included over fifteen hundred distinct titles.[23] Printing not only led to a vastly larger legal literature, but it also made those writings—including statutes and reports of cases—widely available.

Taken together, these trends infused tremendous power into written words, imbuing them with great authority. An important characteristic of legal documents that function as reports of oral proceedings is that they are generally written by an observer rather than the participants. Clerics wrote down Anglo-Saxon wills, law students may have written many of the reports in the year books, and clerks recorded early acts of Parliament. The result was that the written words were not especially authoritative. On a more practical level, the transcription of the event might be incomplete or wrong.

Later, the written text came to *constitute* the will of the testator, the contract between the parties, the opinion of the judge, or the act of Parliament. The author of the text, in theory if not always in practice, was now the testator, judge, or legislator himself. The result was that the legal profession could now fixate on the exact wording of a text in ways that it would not have before.

In many respects this development is reminiscent of the Anglo-Saxon emphasis on exact repetition of oaths and other legal formulas. Yet the main issue for the Anglo-Saxons seems to have been whether the oral ritual was correctly performed; the meaning of the ritual itself was predetermined. In contrast, the development of written legal text shifted the emphasis to what was on paper or parchment. Even with writing, of course, ritualistic language remained important. But as legal transactions and statutes became more complex, the meaning of documents drew more attention. And increasingly over time, that meaning could be derived only from the writing itself.

Sometimes the fixation on written text was so extreme that rules— such as the **plain meaning rule** and the parol evidence rule—prohibited consideration of oral statements by the author in determining its meaning. Thus words—the *exact* words—of legal authorities have come to matter very much to the profession. Recasting an authoritative text in your own words is dangerous, perhaps even subversive. Once established, legal phrases in authoritative texts take on a life of their own; you meddle with them at your risk.

Printing contributed to this trend by helping to standardize legal language. Before printing, there were often divergent records of cases or statutes in manuscript form, none exactly like the other. It is almost impossible to overly concentrate on the exact wording of a statute when there are competing versions of the same text. Printing eliminated the need for handwritten copies, with all their limitations and inconsistencies. It allowed the development of a single version (or at most, a few versions) available to the profession at large. The final step to standardization of statutory text occurred when Parliament itself caused an authoritative version to be published. Squabbling over the placement of a comma now became a realistic possibility.

Furthermore, once a law is fixed in written form, and especially if it is published, it is endowed with a *permanence* that it would not have—or would have to a far lesser extent—if it were oral. A law that is decreed by the king from the throne will be in language that members of his court will understand, at least if the king hopes to be obeyed. If the law is still heeded a few decades or centuries later (which is itself unlikely with an oral decree), people will probably express it differently; language naturally evolves over time and no one will recall the exact words of a spoken edict. With authoritative written texts, on the other hand, the law is ossified. The words will remain the same, even if the spoken language, and indeed the surrounding circumstances, have changed. And lawyers will continue to refer to the exact language of the statute, even if the public no longer understands it. Once this happens, reliance on a professional class trained in the ancient language of the texts is inescapable.

Writing and printing also made possible the doctrine of precedent, which has had a very conservatizing effect on the law. A strict notion of precedent would be very difficult to maintain without written opinions. Most judges and lawyers could not remember and follow a decision that was made fifty or a hundred years before. Even if they had heard of the decision, they would be able to conveniently "forget" it if it was not worth following. With authoritative written opinions, however, judges have felt themselves bound by decisions made generations or even centuries ago. In citing those opinions, lawyers and judges often repeat—and thus keep on life support—ancient verbiage that should long since have died out.

None of this should be taken as an indictment of writing. There is much to be said for a written law; indeed, modern society could not exist without complex written codes. And written law provides important safeguards against arbitrary exercises of power by the government. At the same time, it is evident that writing has encouraged the conservative linguistic practices of the legal profession and its fixation on words.

Further Developments in England

Even today, the language of pleading has a tendency to be relatively formal and ritualistic. The term *pleading* generally refers to a document that sets forth the claims or defenses in a case, and thus defines the parameters of a lawsuit. For various reasons, the rules regarding the language of pleadings became highly technical around the sixteenth and seventeenth centuries.[24] In the words of Justice Hale, pleading "began to degenerate from its primitive Simplicity . . . and to become a Piece of Nicety and Curiosity." In part, this became possible because pleadings were now drawn up in writing, leading to careful scrutiny by opposing counsel, ever vigilant for a "slip to fasten upon." The result, according to Hale, was that "Causes are not determined according to their Merits, but do often miscarry for considerable Omissions in Pleading."[25]

An example is a case that was reversed because a writ to the sheriff misspelled the Latin word *praecipimus* ("we command") as *praecipipimus*.[26] In another case from 1625, the plaintiff alleged that the defendant had slandered him by saying *Thou art as arrant a thief as any is in England; for thou hast broken up J.S. chest, and taken away forty pounds.* The plea was held bad because the plaintiff failed to allege (or prove) that there were any thieves in England; if there were none, the statement was obviously not defamatory! Furthermore, the plea used the word *taken,* which did not necessarily allege that the plaintiff had unlawfully stolen the money.[27] On the other hand, judges were not entirely unreasonable. Another plaintiff claimed to have been slandered when the defendant said: *As sure as God governs the world, and King James this kingdom, so sure hath J.S. committed treason.* Here, the court drew the line; the plaintiff did not need to plead (and later prove) that God indeed governs the world, or King James the kingdom.[28]

Such requirements for verbal precision were an important reason for the development of form books, which contained illustrations of effective pleas.[29] Obviously, extreme pickiness by judges in how pleadings are phrased would lead lawyers to copy, as far as possible, timeworn examples that had passed muster in the past. This tendency would contribute to making legal language quite conservative. In fact, pleading form books continue to be widely used today, at least in the United States. Although rules of pleading have been greatly liberalized, so that minor slips are no longer fatal to a case, lawyers would still rather be safe than sorry. Why experiment with stating a complaint in your own words when you can consult a book with forms that have received a judicial seal of approval? No matter that the language in the form books might be decades or even hundreds of years old!

During roughly this same time, legal language became ever more verbose. One of the main causes was that clerks were paid by the page for the documents they wrote. Moreover, they often adopted very large handwriting and wide margins, making documents many times longer than they needed to be.[30] An oft-repeated story concerns a man who made the mistake of submitting an overly lengthy document to a court towards the end of the sixteenth century. The exasperated judge ordered that a hole be cut through the pleading, that the man's head be inserted through the hole, and that he be paraded through Westminster Hall, where the royal courts were held.[31] Many judges today, frustrated by the verbosity of lawyers, might wish they still had the power to impose such creative sanctions.

It is hardly surprising that the legal profession found itself in low repute. Hale wrote in the seventeenth century: "Their multitude is so great, that they are not able to live one by another; and upon this account they stir up suits, and shark upon the few clients they have, and are apt to use tricks and knavery to gain themselves credit with those that employ them."[32] Consider also how Jonathan Swift described English lawyers and their language to the Houyhnhnms in *Gulliver's Travels,* written in the early part of the eighteenth century: "there was a Society of Men among us, bred up from their Youth in the Art of proving by Words multiplied for the Purpose, that *White* is *Black* and *Black* is *White,* according as they are paid. To this Society all the rest of the People are Slaves."[33] Swift elaborated that if a person became involved in a lawsuit, it was "against all Rules of *Law* that any Man should be allowed to speak for himself." Instead, he would be forced to hire a lawyer, a member of a society that "hath a peculiar Cant and Jargon of their own, that no other Mortal can Understand, and wherein all their Laws are written. . . ."[34] Obtuse, archaic, and verbose legal language, employed most vigorously for those best able to pay, is surely even today a major reason for antipathy toward the legal profession.

English statutes, as well as other legal writing, remained relatively obscure and anachronistic, despite the many criticisms, and even though they had now been in the English tongue for centuries. In 1827 the *Edinburgh Review* wrote, "The language and composition of our legal Instruments, including our Acts of Parliament, are a disgrace to the intelligence and information of the Country."[35] Another British commentator, one year later, noted that for the lay public, trying to understand a statute was like trying to interpret a runic inscription or hieroglyphics.[36]

Oddly enough, therefore, the switch to English was not a panacea. The language that lawyers spoke and wrote remained obscure to outsiders. Whereas previously some people believed that lawyers stuck to French as a way to retain their monopoly, later critics suggested that lawyers were now using their peculiar variety of English for precisely the same purpose.

No less a figure than Jeremy Bentham seems to have been a proponent of this conspiracy theory, referring to "lawyer's cant" as "an instrument, an iron crow or a pick-lock key, for collecting plunder."[37] Even in modern times, critics suggest that legal prose retains its "arcane, ponderous and technical qualities" to help lawyers justify their fees. "It is in the lawyer's self-interest to keep legal prose unreadable. If money, power, and prestige are all protected by keeping the layperson confused and awestruck, why should any lawyer opt for clear, concise, communicative prose?"[38] Another critic is even more blunt: "The easiest way to create a monopoly is to invent a language and procedure which will be unintelligible to the layman. . . . In many ways, it is . . . the art of the ancient and noble profession of the law."[39]

That lawyers actually created legal English as a means of keeping the public in the dark and protecting their monopoly on legal services seems greatly exaggerated. As we have seen, there are many other reasons why legal language developed as it did. Nonetheless, it seems that after every attempt to force the profession to communicate more clearly, lawyers quietly reverted to their old ways.

Legal English throughout the World

English settlers and colonial officials transported their memories of the English law and its language to the British colonies throughout the world, including those in North America. When the Pilgrims arrived in the New World, they drafted a type of constitution for their colony, known as the *Mayflower Compact,* in 1620. After stating the aims of the colony, the Compact continued that its signers

> Do by these presents, solemnly and mutually, in the presence of God and one another, covenant and combine ourselves together into a civil Body Politick, for our better Ordering and Preservation, and Furtherance of the ends aforesaid: And by Virtue hereof to enact, constitute, and frame such just and equal Laws, Ordinances, Acts, Constitutions and Offices, from time to time, as shall be thought most meet and convenient for the general Good of the Colony; unto which we promise all due Submission and Obedience.[40]

Clearly, the Pilgrims brought with them from the Old World not only their earthly possessions but also their conceptions of how a proper legal document should sound.

At the same time, many of the American colonists resisted wholesale importation of the English legal system. Often they were suspicious of lawyers and dreamed of creating law books that any person could read and understand without needing to consult a member of the legal profession.[41] For a while, Massachusetts forbad lawyers from serving in its legislature and required that parties in court represent themselves rather than engage an attorney.[42] With few lawyers, at least in the beginning, legal proceedings would necessarily have been informal, and the law was based to varying extents on custom, notions of fairness, and—in some colonies—religious precepts. Strict adherence to English common law and statutes would have been difficult, even if the colonists had felt so inclined.[43]

Nonetheless, as the colonies developed they needed a more formal legal system, and the only familiar model was the English one. Even in the earliest period, the common law—to the extent that the colonists remembered it—must have had a fair amount of influence, and many British statutes did apply.[44] Of course, the interpretation of those statutes and the proper application of the common law would require recourse to reports of English judicial decisions. As a result, the libraries of American lawyers before the Revolution were filled almost entirely with English law books, something that changed only gradually after independence.[45] All of this virtually guaranteed that English legal language would transplant itself to the New World, despite occasional yearnings for a lawyerless paradise.

The influence of English legal language continued unabated after independence. Despite their revolutionary zeal, early American lawmakers did not exactly cast off the yoke of English legal language and style when they drafted their first constitution. Here is part of Article IV of the Articles of Confederation, relating to privileges and immunities:

> The better to secure and perpetuate mutual friendship and intercourse among the people of the different States in this Union, the free inhabitants of each of these States, paupers, vagabonds and fugitives from justice excepted, shall be entitled to all privileges and immunities of free citizens in the several States; and the people of each State shall have free ingress and regress to and from any other State, and shall enjoy therein all the privileges of trade and commerce, subject to the same duties, impositions and restrictions as the inhabitants thereof respectively, provided that such restrictions shall not extend so far as to prevent the removal of property imported into any State, to any other State of which the Owner is an inhabitant; provided also that no imposition, duties or restriction shall be laid by any State, on the property of the United States, or either of them.[46]

Like English legal writing of this period, early American documents are replete with long conjoined phrases, archaic vocabulary, exceptions within exceptions, and convoluted syntax.

The emergence of a legal profession no doubt reinforced American ties to English law. Almost half the signers of the Declaration of Independence and a majority of delegates at the Constitutional Convention were trained in the law.[47] In the 1780s, the first American law school, the Litchfield School, was founded in Connecticut. Its course of study was modeled on Blackstone's *Commentaries,* so that English law, as well as its language, had a substantial impact on the lawyers who were trained there. University lectures in law followed in the decades thereafter.[48] At least in the beginning, American legal education relied heavily on English materials.

In establishing a legal system of their own, the independent Americans continued to use statutes, precedents, and forms—and consequently, legal language—from their former colonial masters. Most of the new states provided for the continued validity of English common law and at least some British statutes after independence.[49] Although most states later repealed or modified the statutes, virtually all retained the common law.[50] Because there were few published American judicial opinions during the colonial period and the early republic, the courts and legal profession were forced to rely on English case reports, which were cited extensively in the early years.[51] In fact, as much as fifty years after independence, over half the citations in reported New Jersey chancery cases were still to English precedents.[52] The continuing use of English statutes, cases, and other legal literature resulted in a lasting British influence on the American legal system and its language.

Perhaps it need not have been so. Many of the states that had adopted English statutes early in their existence later systematically reviewed these laws, revising and readopting some of them, while repealing others that were inappropriate or repugnant to their democratic ideals. Thomas Jefferson was a member of such a committee in Virginia. Jefferson later wrote that his committee seriously considered abolishing the entire existing system of laws, to be replaced by a "new Institute" like that of Justinian or Bracton. Such an initiative might have created a truly revolutionary—and truly American—legal system. In the process, it might also have cast off the ponderous legal language inherited from the English.[53]

But the Virginia committee decided that such an undertaking would be too ambitious. Ironically, the possibility of ridding the law of its antiquated vocabulary was viewed not as a golden opportunity, but as a critical drawback. The committee feared that creating a new system of laws from scratch would lead to the meaning of many of the novel words and phrases becoming

> a subject of question & chicanery until settled by repeated adjudications; that this would involve us for ages in litigation, and render property uncertain until, like the statutes of old, every word had been tried, and settled by numerous decisions, and by new volumes of reports & commentaries. . . .[54]

Jefferson thus concluded that it would be best

> not to vary the diction of the antient statutes by modernizing it, nor to give rise to new questions by new expressions. The text

of these statutes had been so fully explained and defined by
numerous adjudications, as scarcely ever now to produce a question for our courts.[55]

But while wishing to preserve most technical vocabulary, Jefferson did
feel that it would be beneficial to improve upon the *style* of statutes,

> which from their verbosity, their endless tautologies, their invo-
> lutions of case within case, and parenthesis within parenthesis,
> and their multiplied efforts at certainty by *saids* and *aforesaids,*
> by *ors* and by *ands,* to make them more plain, do really render
> them more perplexed and incomprehensible, not only to com-
> mon readers, but to lawyers themselves.[56]

Perhaps Jefferson's aversion to the worst aspects of legal style help
explain the remarkable elegance and relative simplicity of the Declaration of Independence and the Constitution, both of which he helped
draft. In fact, the Framers of the Constitution seem to have agreed that
it should be in the "plain common language of mankind," rather than
in the "scientific language of law."[57]

Overall, however, despite the prestige and influence of Jefferson and
like-minded men, American legal language came to resemble the statutes of King George III much more than the Declaration of Independence or Constitution. Whatever reforms may have flowed from the
American Revolution, improving legal language was not among them.

The Americans could have looked to traditions other than the English
in establishing a truly American legal system, but seldom did so. While
Native American law is still important within many of the tribes themselves, it has had little influence on American law in general and even
less on legal language. The same is true of the law—and legal language—of other European settlers. For example, while Dutch law and
legal terminology briefly survived the English takeover of New York, the
English common law and its language eventually supplanted it.[58] French
and Spanish law did have a more lasting, but nonetheless fairly limited,
impact in certain regions of the present United States.[59] In California,
for example, the notion of *pueblo* lands is still sometimes legally significant.[60] And, of course, the French language is still quite influential in
Louisiana, with its civil law tradition.

The colonies in other parts of the world remained under British rule
for much longer. Because of the extent of the former British empire,
some type of legal English is used in a vast number of countries throughout the world, including many African nations, Australia, Canada, India,

Malaysia, New Zealand, and Singapore, to name just a sampling. Despite the diversity of cultures in these far-flung parts of the globe, their legal language retains many Anglo-Saxon, French, and Latin grammatical features and technical terms that can only be fully appreciated in light of the history of the English legal system. Remarkably, a Malaysian judge with the Chinese name Lim Beng Choon can discuss the defendant's contention that the plaintiff has no *locus standi* to sue in a dispute regarding *the said land,* located in Kuala Lumpur and duly registered in the *Pendaftar Tanah Wilayah Persekutuan.*[61]

At the same time, each one of these systems will continue to develop independently, and the legal language in each country will reflect those developments. Just as their language long ago ceased to be the sole property of the Anglo-Saxon people, legal English is being adapted to the laws and customs of the areas of the world in which it is now used.

Yet much as the English eventually ousted Law French, residents of former British colonies in which the majority of the population does not speak English may eventually enact their own Statute of Pleading. It is likely that most of these nations will replace English legal language with a more local tongue, as many have already done, at least partially. Even after these countries adopt a local language, however, legal English will continue to exert a powerful influence, in the same way that Latin and Law French continue to have an impact on the language of English-speaking lawyers.

Conclusion

There is no single, easy answer to the question of how legal language came to be what it is. Much of the explanation lies in a series of historical developments, each of which left its mark on the language of the law. At the same time, the profession's resistance to change played a heavy role as well. The Norman Conquest may have brought French to England, and the Crown's desire to establish royal justice may have introduced it to the courts, but it was the conservatism of the profession that kept French alive for such a long time after it should by all rights have become obsolete. The fact that speaking an obscure language made it virtually impossible for litigants to represent themselves was, no doubt, an added benefit and one more reason to preserve the status quo. As we will see in the rest of this book, this resistance to change has ebbed somewhat recently, but in many ways is still very much with us.

PART TWO

The Nature of Legal Language

We have seen that the legal profession long had its own distinct language, Law French. Of course, during the past centuries, virtually all legal affairs in common law countries have been carried out in English. Yet the type of English used by lawyers can be quite different from ordinary speech and writing. Could it be that lawyers, while ostensibly switching to English, have managed to preserve an exclusive language of their own? Or is the language of the law simply another variety of English, a technical jargon like the language of dentists or carpenters?

Although some have suggested that legal English is a separate language, it seems best to regard it as a variety of English. For the most part, legal language follows the rules that govern English in general. At the same time, it diverges in many ways from ordinary speech, far more than the technical languages of most other professions. In this part we therefore consider what makes legal language distinct: how the language of the law differs from normal speech and writing.

CHAPTER FOUR

Talking Like a Lawyer

Language is much more than merely a means of communication. It is also a way of signaling, consciously or unconsciously, that we come from a particular area, or belong to a certain social group. In the United States we can hear from a person's speech whether he is from the South, from New York, or from Boston. Regional differences are even more marked in England, where the way that people speak may relate not just to geography, but to their social status. The result is that some accents are very prestigious, while others are associated with membership in more ordinary socioeconomic circles. In fact, certain accents or dialects can be heavily stigmatized.

At the same time, people can use the way that they speak in a more positive way: to mark themselves as members of a group. Like others in society, lawyers use language to set themselves apart from the mass of the population and to create group cohesion. In the words of the iconoclast Jeremy Bentham, legal language serves lawyers as a "bond of union: it serves them, at every word, to remind them of that common interest, by which they are made friends to one another, enemies to the rest of mankind."[1] Whether lawyers' language makes them "enemies" of mankind is debatable, but it clearly helps set them apart.

Pronunciation and Spelling as Markers of Group Cohesion

Some of the clearest examples of "talking like a lawyer" are also, in a sense, the most trivial: minor quirks in pronunciation, spelling, and punctuation. The legal profession, especially in England, has its own idiosyncratic way of pronouncing a few words. In a book for English law students, Glanville Williams noted that lawyers pronounce the noun form of *record* like the verb, with the stress on the second syllable. The term for an insured person, *assured,* is three syllables, the last rhyming with *red.* And *cognisance* and *cognisable* are pronounced without the *g.*[2] These all appear to be traditional pronunciations of the profession. The fact that they have been preserved over the centuries is nonetheless telling.

A more modern innovation is the growing popularity, at least among lawyers in the United States, of pronouncing the word *defendant* with a full vowel in the final syllable, in such a way that the plural *defendants* rhymes with *defend ants* (as though the attorney were defending insects). Normally, *defendant* should rhyme with *appellant, attendant,* or *descendant.* Before long, lawyers will be pronouncing *respondent* to rhyme with *dent, sentence* to rhyme with *tense,* and *justice* to rhyme with *ice!*

This aberrant pronunciation may well have originated with pedantic law professors who grew weary of students misspelling *defendant* as *defendent,* which is a logical enough way to write it. Perhaps these professors began to articulate the word with added (but unnatural) emphasis on the *a* in the final syllable, stressing the final vowel and coloring it to rhyme with *ant.* Students, ever eager to begin "talking like a lawyer," quickly mimicked their instructors.[3] Whatever its origins, this unusual articulation is now perceived as a badge of membership in the legal fraternity. In fact, reporters and commentators on television have begun to imitate it, even if they have no formal legal training.

For the most part, the spelling of legal terms is the same as ordinary English. An interesting deviation is *judgment.* In nonlegal writing, *judgement* and *judgment* both occur. The Oxford English Dictionary lists both alternatives, although *judgement* comes first and is presumably preferred. As a logical matter, *judgement* makes more sense: just add the suffix *-ment* to the word *judge.* Nonetheless, in legal circles one always encounters *judgment,* the less logical alternative; *judgement* is a virtual pariah. I was specifically told during law school that lawyers spell the word without an *e.* The same principle applies to *abridg(e)ment* and *acknowledg(e)ment,* where the form without *e* is likewise favored in legal usage, although less consistently than *judgment.* The reason, I believe, is not merely tradition; like the aberrant pronunciation of *defendant,* spellings such as *judgment* have come to be perceived as signaling membership in the profession.

It was once thought that legal language—especially statutes—were unpunctuated as a matter of principle. Mellinkoff has exposed this as a "canard."[4] Certainly today, all varieties of legal language use ample punctuation. Nonetheless, as with pronunciation and spelling, the legal profession has at least one minor eccentricity. The normal rule with a series of three or more items is to place a comma before the conjunction.[5] (This is also known as the *serial comma.*) Yet legal writers prefer to omit the comma, in my experience. The phrase *rest, residue and remainder,* ubiquitous in wills, most often has no comma before the *and*. Law firm names also exhibit this tendency: *Smith, Shabazz, Cohen & Sanchez*. Notably, this is merely a trend; it is far less universal than the spelling *judgment*. Yet once again it reveals lawyers' penchant for setting themselves apart. As Lawrence Friedman has suggested, a "common vocabulary and style enable lawyers to recognize one another as lawyers and to distinguish themselves collectively from laymen."[6]

Despite a desire to separate themselves from the ordinary public, as well as their linguistic conservatism, lawyers are not immune to trendiness and a desire to conform. One of the best illustrations is the pronunciation of Law French and Latin words. Traditionally, in the words of Glanville Williams, "Latin words and phrases are generally pronounced in the same old barbaric way as they were in the Middle Ages, that is to say, as if they were English." Following this Anglo-Latin tradition, the phrase *res judicata* is pronounced "rees ju-di-KATE-uh" and *rea* in *mens rea* is "REE-uh."[7] Most law dictionaries still favor the traditional Anglo-Latin articulation. Thus, *nisi* roughly rhymes with *eyesight*, not *easy*. The word *res* is "rees" in several surveyed dictionaries. The pronunciation of *amicus* is listed as "uh-MIKE-us." While the Anglo-Latin practice may seem "barbaric" to some, it reflects the fact that many legal words were adopted into English centuries ago and have therefore participated in the same phonetic changes that have affected the rest of the language.

Law French words are likewise traditionally pronounced as though they were English. Consider the simple word *oyez*, the Law French equivalent of *hear ye*, which is chanted three times to announce the opening of some courts of law. If we were to follow the historical pronunciation, trying to imitate the Norman invaders, we would probably have to say "o-YETS." Of course, we do not pronounce English words the way they were in 1066, nor is there any good reason to pronounce Anglo-French in that manner. We should look to the usage of older practitioners for guidance, rather than speculating on how the Normans might have pronounced French. In the case of *oyez*, this word is traditionally called out as "o-YES" or "o-YEZ," with the accent on the second syllable.[8] Only with this pronunciation can we understand the pun made by an English writer in 1842: "when the Crier cried 'O yes!' the people cried, 'O No!'."[9]

It seems logical, therefore, that where words of foreign origin have become part of legal English, they should be pronounced in the traditional style of the English bar. Furthermore, we would expect law students struggling to learn how to "talk like lawyers" to imitate older practitioners. Yet the emerging trend with both Law French and Latin is to ignore the customary legal practice and to use the pronunciations that are taught in schools.

In the case of Latin words, the trend is to use the **Classical** Latin pronunciation, which is often taught in high school or university Latin courses and attempts to reconstruct how the ancient Romans might have spoken. Thus, *res judicata* is commonly pronounced "race ju-di-KAH-tuh." Incidentally, this is also roughly the **Italianate** pronunciation, which derives from later Latin and is used by the Roman Catholic church, including canon law.[10] One problem for those wishing to go back to the "original" articulation of Latin terms is how consistently to do so. Most American lawyers who strive for the Classical Latin pronunciation of *res judicata* get the vowels approximately right, but use English consonants, pronouncing the first syllable in *judicata* as "Jew." In both Classical and Italianate Latin, it is pronounced "you." The same is true for *vivos* in the phrase *inter vivos*, where many lawyers say "veevos." The classical articulation would be "weewos," which is virtually never heard and sounds decidedly odd.

Just as many lawyers strive for the Classical pronunciation of Latin, Law French is increasingly pronounced as modern French. Thus, *oyez* is sometimes heard as something like "o-YEH," with the accent on the second syllable. This is how the word might be pronounced in the Gallic heartland today, and it is decidedly ahistorical. *Oyez* is not modern standard French but derives from the dialect spoken by the Normans. Pronouncing Law French as if it were present-day Parisian French has little merit, as a matter of logic: it is the wrong dialect and the wrong historical period. As Williams observed, "it is a solecism to utter [Law French terms] as if they were modern French."[11]

As a consequence of these recent trends, uncertainty and inconsistency prevail. Many older lawyers adhere to the traditional legal pronunciation. But younger lawyers are increasingly pronouncing Law Latin in the style of Julius Caesar, and Law French in the style of Brigitte Bardot.

In a delightful parody of these conflicting pronunciations, the British writer A. P. Herbert portrayed the case of *Rex v. Venables and Others*.[12] Mr. Ambrose Wick, an advocate appearing before the court for the first time, applied for a writ of *certiorari,* which he pronounced in the Classical fashion as "kairtiorahree." He spoke of an order "pro hahk weekay" (*pro hac vice*) and the "day yooray" (*de jure*) tenant.

The judge was not amused. Finally, the lawyer admitted that he was using the "new" Latin that he had been taught in school. His Lordship retorted:

His Majesty's judges will not permit the speaking of the Latin tongue after that fashion in the King's Courts. . . . [I]t is not for the King's judges to remodel their diction according to the whims of pedagogues or the habits of the Junior Bar. The bitter conclusion is, Mr. Wick, that you must go away and learn to pronounce the Latin tongue correctly, according to the immemorial practice of your profession.[13]

Unfortunately, there is no longer a generally accepted usage today, even among the "senior" bar and the judiciary. Many legal terms are commonly pronounced in two or three different ways. One and the same attorney may alternate almost randomly from one style to another. Virtually all lawyers pronounce *prima facie* with English vowels, but those same lawyers may give many other Latin words, like *res judicata*, classical Latin vowels (and modern English consonants!). At least for the foreseeable future, these variants will simply have to coexist peacefully.

A possible explanation for this inconsistency is that the pronunciation of foreign terms presents lawyers with a difficult dilemma: they must choose between "talking like a lawyer," which requires using pronunciations that sound odd and uneducated to the modern ear, or imitating the more prestigious accents of classical Latin and modern Parisian French, which are taught by the schools as the correct standard. Usually, talking like a lawyer is automatically the prestigious choice, making the decision an easy one. Here, however, lawyers are torn between the traditions of their own profession and what is regarded as prestigious by the rest of society. The result is that inconsistency reigns.

Lengthy and Complex Sentences

Some of the other characteristics of "talking like a lawyer"—or writing like one—can best be described as matters of **style.** Style relates to the fact that given any proposition that you wish to communicate, there are typically many alternative ways in which you can express the proposition in words. When we say that a person or group has a particular style, we generally mean that they tend to prefer one method of expression over the other possibilities.

Of course, some styles communicate more clearly than others. Lawyers often adopt a style that does not communicate all that well, at least to the general public. Sometimes there may be legitimate reasons for such a choice. In other cases, the stylistic choice is merely a matter of habit, because this is how lawyers traditionally speak or write.

One prominent feature of legal style is very long sentences. Bentham noted that lawyers favored "longwindedness" and suggested that "[t]he shorter the sentence the better."[14] His advice has been followed mainly in the breach. In an analysis of the British Courts Act of 1971, Marita Gustafsson found that the shortest sentence had 10 words and the longest had 179. Sentences in the Act had a mean length of 48 words. This contrasts to scientific prose, which according to one study had a mean sentence length of 27.6 words, and dramatic texts, which in one corpus contained an average of only 7 words per sentence.[15] Even lengthier sentences were found by Risto Hiltunen in his analysis of the first two parts of the British Road Traffic Act of 1972. Hiltunen calculated a mean sentence length of 79.25 words; the shortest sentence had 7 words and the longest had 740.[16] Similarly, in one set of jury instructions, the average sentence was 102 words long.[17]

Long sentences are not confined to statutes and jury instructions. An American patent application must be a single sentence: an extra period might be cause for rejection.[18] Nor is the "single sentence" phenomenon restricted to English. For example, all decisions of a French court, the Cour de Cassation, consist of one single, highly structured sentence.[19] Naturally, such sentences tend to be long and complex. Commenting on the tendency to draft English statutes as one long sentence, Bentham observed: "With as much reason, and with similar utility, might the whole of Coke-Littleton [a legal treatise] have been squeezed into one sentence, or the whole of a Serjeant's-Inn dinner have been mashed up together into one dish."[20]

A motivation for lengthy sentences is the desire to place all information on a particular topic into one self-contained unit.[21] Presumably, this tendency reduces the ambiguity that might result if conditions on a rule or provision are placed in separate sentences. Legal drafters seem to fear that if they place a condition on a rule in a separate sentence directly following the statement of the rule, some lawyer will later be free to argue that the condition does not apply.

The result is not just very long sentences, but complex ones, with many conjoined and embedded clauses. Gustafsson found that sentences in the British Courts Act had an average of 2.86 finite clauses per sentence, and there were relatively few simple sentences. One sentence had nine dependent clauses. In Hiltunen's corpus, sentences had an average of 6.74 clauses (the number is higher than Gustafsson's in part because Hiltunen's figure includes both finite and nonfinite clauses). Not only does legal English have more embedding, but the embedding is significantly deeper than occurs in most journalistic, literary, or scientific texts.[22]

An illustration of the length and complexity of legal drafting is the following penal statute from California:

> Every person who insures or receives any consideration for insuring for or against the drawing of any ticket in any lottery whatever, whether drawn or to be drawn within this State or not, or who receives any valuable consideration upon any agreement to repay any sum, or deliver the same, or any other property, if any lottery ticket or number of any ticket in any lottery shall prove fortunate or unfortunate, or shall be drawn or not be drawn, at any particular time or in any particular order, or who promises or agrees to pay any sum of money, or to deliver any goods, things in action, or property, or to forbear to do anything for the benefit of any person, with or without consideration, upon any event or contingency dependent on the drawing of any ticket in any lottery, or who publishes any notice or proposal of any of the purposes aforesaid, is guilty of a misdemeanor.[23]

There is obviously a great deal of legalese in this statute, which partially explains why it is so hard to process. More important, however, is that a huge amount of information has been compressed into a single sentence, which accounts for its length and grammatical complexity. Furthermore, that single sentence contains several conditions and exceptions, and exceptions within exceptions, which are expressed by conjoined or embedded clauses. Observe also that all these conditions and exceptions precede the main verb (*is*); the main verb does not occur until the last few words of the sentence. Typical for legal syntax, there is a tremendous quantity of information inserted between the subject (*every person*) and the verb phrase (*is guilty*).

The statute would be far more comprehensible if it were broken down into parts. As long as all these parts are expressly linked to one another, or simply follow one another under a single heading, there is no realistic danger that any provisions or exceptions will be missed by the reader. It should be evident, in other words, that the parts form a single text.

For example, the statute could begin by stating the overall prohibition in general terms (I leave the wording of the statute essentially unchanged, so that we can concentrate on the structure):

> 1. Every person who insures a ticket in any lottery whatever is guilty of a misdemeanor.

Of course, to *insure* a lottery ticket can involve a number of different activities. This can be handled by making a list of specific activities that are prohibited:

> 2. Insuring a ticket in a lottery includes any of the following acts:
> A. Insuring or receiving any consideration for insuring for or against the drawing of any ticket in any lottery whatever, whether drawn or to be drawn within this State or not;
> B. Receiving any valuable consideration upon any agreement to repay any sum, or deliver the same, or any other property, if any lottery ticket or number of any ticket in any lottery shall prove fortunate or unfortunate, or shall be drawn or not be drawn, at any particular time or in any particular order. . . .

and so forth.

Note that there are four major activities that are prohibited by this statute, including one in A and one in B. In the original statute, these are indicated by repetition of the word *who* before each of the major activities. Obviously, breaking the statute down into numbered subsections makes it far easier to process than looking for more subtle cues like the repetition of the word *who*. Even then, each of these major prohibited activities could be further broken down. As I understand provision 2(B) above, it could be rephrased as follows:

> B. Receiving money or property under a lottery insurance agreement. For purposes of this statute, a lottery insurance agreement refers to an agreement to provide the other party with money or property on any of the following conditions:
> i. that any lottery ticket or number of any ticket win or lose;
> ii. that any lottery ticket or number of any ticket be drawn or not;
> iii. that any lottery ticket or number of any ticket be drawn at any particular time; or
> iv. that any lottery ticket or number of any ticket be drawn at any particular order.

Whatever historical reasons there may be for drafting legal rules in single sentences, there is little justification for it today. A long sentence is normally much harder to follow than one that is broken down into pieces. Interestingly, this is a lesson that many drafters of statutes seem to be learning. The statute under discussion was enacted in 1872. While statutes are still quite long and complex, drafters are increasing the use of headings, division into subsections, and similar devices to help the reader parse the language.

Wordiness and Redundancy

Unfortunately, while the length of individual sentences may be declining somewhat, legal documents overall are becoming ever longer. Much of this results from the growing complexity of the world around us. Yet the legal penchant for wordiness and redundancy is surely also part of the problem.

Lawyers continue to reach for familiar words or phrases out of habit, without pondering whether the words contribute anything to the meaning that they hope to convey. Much of this is what those in the legal profession call **boilerplate**: a standard provision that is routinely added to a particular type of document. It seems likely that the growth in word processors and document assembly software, which enable lawyers to churn out extremely lengthy documents in a matter of minutes, will only make things worse. Part of the problem is that lawyers virtually never *delete* a clause from their standard will or contract forms, even if it serves no evident function; who knows when it might turn out to valuable? Generally, they only *add* material to cover additional possible (but usually quite unlikely) contingencies. The result is ever more words.

An example of a boilerplate provision that is often useless is a **no contest clause,** added unthinkingly to almost all wills. These provide that if anyone challenges the will (in what is called a **will contest**), that person forfeits any legacy that he or she might stand to receive. Suppose that parents disinherit a child. Upon the death of her parents, the daughter might challenge the will on the ground that her parents lacked mental capacity. If she loses the suit, the no contest clause will prevent her from obtaining anything under the will. But the will left her nothing in the first place! Hence the clause has absolutely no effect. Such clauses only work if the drafter is clever enough to "throw a bone" to a possible challenger, thus giving her something to lose if she engages in a contest. All too often, however, lawyers slavishly insert the clause without thinking the matter through.[24]

Another contributor to wordiness is the inclination to use prepositional and other phrases in place of simple adverbs or prepositions. Various commentators have observed that lawyers prefer adverbial phrases (like *at slow speed*) over simple adverbs (like *slowly*). The same is true of prepositions and conjunctions. Some lawyers seem incapable of using short and simple words such as *if*, *before*, and *after*, preferring instead to say or write *in the event that*, *prior to*, or *subsequent to*. Other common examples of such complex phrases include *during the time that* instead of simply *during*, *until such time as* in place of *until*, and *in order to* for *to*.

Of course, eliminating redundancy and wordiness requires some thought, and tradition often gets in the way. Consider the familiar title of almost every will: *Last Will and Testament of Jane Smith*. *Will and testament* is redundant; either term alone would be adequate. And if you think about it, the adjective *last* is unnecessary verbiage. All that need be written is *Will of Jane Smith*. Of course, if Jane executed three wills, only the most recent one will be probated, so it is important to find the *last* one. But labeling it the *last* will and testament provides no evidence whatsoever in this respect. In fact, all three of the wills (including her *first* will) are almost certainly entitled the *last* one!

Just as useless—and equally ubiquitous—is the alliterative recitation in most wills that the testator is of *sound mind and memory*. Of course, the testator must be mentally competent. But adding to a will that you are of sound mind and memory proves absolutely nothing. It does make sense for the *witnesses* to swear that you seem to be competent, so it is worth adding to the attestation clause, which is what the witnesses sign. But the more that someone insists that she is perfectly sane, the less onlookers are likely to believe it.

Ironically, there is another sense in which legal language is not verbose at all, but rather too compact or dense. The illustration above of the statute against insuring a lottery ticket shows how much information can be compressed into a single sentence. Decompressing it into manageable parts and making it more comprehensible could very well make it longer. While that might have been problematic in an age of expensive parchment, it is far less an issue today, when new methods of information storage are extremely cheap. As Reed Dickerson, an expert on statutory drafting, has written: "Tight compression of language does not insure clarity and simplicity. . . . Sometimes the longer statement is the simpler."[25]

The problems of overly compact statutes are illustrated by a law that intends to make it (1) illegal to sell a prohibited substance (defined elsewhere) to a minor child, but only (2) if the seller knows that the child is a minor. Typically, statutory drafters compress these two thoughts into one shorter phrase, making it illegal for any person to *knowingly sell a prohibited substance to a minor*. But the scope of the adverb *knowingly* is virtually always ambiguous in such sentences and has spawned endless litigation. Does the seller merely have to know that the substance is illegal, or also that the sale was made to a minor?[26] Clarifying a sentence of this type will produce a longer statute, not a shorter one. The point is not that the legal profession should consistently use more words, or fewer. Rather, it should re-examine its linguistic habits so that it uses words as effectively and unambiguously as possible.

Legal language is not inherently verbose or compact; the incentives under which lawyers operate make all the difference. Lawyers who draft private documents, like contacts, deeds, and wills, are normally paid by the hour and may feel a need to impress their clients—or justify their fees—with the length and complexity of their prose. They are thus naturally inclined towards liberal use of redundancy and a verbose style, just as clerks in the Middle Ages reacted to the incentives of being paid by the word. In contrast, judges who must read aloud jury instructions, or who have to wade through a protracted "brief," have exactly the opposite incentive. Unnecessarily long documents waste their valuable time. They therefore have little patience with wordiness, and want the instructions or brief to be as compact and to-the-point as possible. Lawyers are well aware of these differences and vary their style accordingly. Given that lawyers can, with the proper incentives, get to the point quickly and succinctly, it is hardly a radical proposal to suggest that they do so more consistently.

Conjoined Phrases and Lists of Words

Another typical feature of legal style—which can be a further contributor to wordiness—is joining together words or phrases with the conjunctions *and* and *or*. As described previously, these conjoined phrases have a long history, going back at least as far as early Germanic times. Sometimes conjoined phrases and lists have a legitimate function. Elsewhere they are a creature of habit, used in contexts where a single word or phrase would do just as well.

Conjoining words and phrases is common enough in ordinary language. Yet it seems endemic in legal writing. One study found that **binomial expressions** (a technical linguistic term for two parallel words joined by a conjunction, like *any and all*) were used five times as often in legal writing as in other prose styles. And legal writers tend to use the same limited set of such expressions repeatedly; in other prose styles there is more variation.[27]

The possibilities of creating tremendously long phrases and sentences by use of conjunctions like *and* and *or* are virtually limitless. In theory, a speaker could create an infinitely long sentence by continually tacking on further information, rather than ending the sentence with a period. Linguists refer to this property of language as **recursion:** "given any grammatical sentence of the language, it is always possible to form a sentence that is longer."[28] All you need is an *and*.

Lawyers have taken up this challenge with a vengeance. It is hardly a recent development. For example, in a defamation case in an English ecclesiastical court in 1424, the complaining party *presents, gives and exhibits the subscribed petitions and articles . . . in the defamation cause . . . initiated and pending in the court of York* and intended to prove that he *was and is a trustworthy man, of good fame, honest conversation and of unblemished reputation and so was openly, publicly, commonly and notoriously held, named and reputed for such.*[29] In fewer words, he had a good reputation. Some three hundred years later, this trend had only accelerated. The 1731 statute requiring the use of English in court could have stated that it applied to *all oral and written legal proceedings.* Instead, the statute explicitly pertained to:

> all Writs, Process and Returns thereof, and Proceedings thereon, and all Pleadings, Rules, Orders, Indictments, Informations, Inquisitions, Presentments, Verdicts, Prohibitions, Certificates, and all Patents, Charters, Pardons, Commissions, Records, Judgments, Statutes, Recognizances, Bonds, Rolls, Entries, Fines and Recoveries, and all Proceedings relating thereto. . . .[30]

By 1835, the Englishman Arthur Symonds severely criticized the verbosity of lawyers and Parliamentary draftsmen. He lampooned their affection for long word lists by suggesting that in legal English, the phrase *I give you that orange* would be rendered as follows:

> I give you all and singular, my estate and interest, right, title, claim and advantage of and in that orange, with all its rind, skin, juice, pulp and pips, and all right and advantage therein, with full power to bite, cut, suck, and otherwise eat the same, or give the same away as fully and effectually as I the said A.B. am now entitled to bite, cut, suck, or otherwise eat the same orange, or give the same away, with or without its rind, skin, juice, pulp, and pips, anything hereinbefore, or hereinafter, or in any other deed, or deeds, instrument or instruments of what nature or kind soever, to the contrary in any wise, notwithstanding.[31]

Anyone who pages through some current statutes or other legal documents will soon discover that this tendency is as vital now as it was in the past.

Lawyers conjoin not only nouns, but other linguistic categories as well. Consider the strings of verbs in the following language from a standard publishing contract:

> While this agreement is in effect, the Author shall not, without the prior written consent of the Publisher, *write, edit, print, or publish,* or cause to be *written, edited, printed or published,* any other edition of the Work, whether *revised, supplemented, corrected, enlarged, abridged, or otherwise.* . . .[32]

Apparently, the lawyer's most important drafting tool is an extensive thesaurus. Observe also that often legal drafters wish to prohibit not only the doing of *X,* but also *causing* or *inducing* anyone else to do *X.* Thus, in the above example, the string of forbidden acts must be listed twice: the author may not *write,* etc., nor *cause to be written,* etc.

This prolixity may seem silly; why not just say that the author may not produce any other version of the work, in whatever form? If the parties could assume that they both would act in totally good faith, such language might indeed suffice. Unfortunately, lawyers must take the position that the other side will not always act with the best of intentions, and that the author might try to circumvent the agreement by producing a modified version of the work, which might then be sold to a competing publisher for an additional fee. Or the author might have a friend or relative sell an abridged form of the work to someone else. Lawyers want to anticipate and deal with every possible future contingency, a trait that encourages long lists of semantically related words as the lawyers conceive of ever more (and more remote) possibilities.

Even prepositions, seldom paired in ordinary language, are routinely strung together in legal documents. A publisher promises in a contract to publish a work *in accordance with and subject to* the agreement.[33] A standard textile sales contract provides that the credit limit of the Buyer

> may be fixed or varied from time to time *at and in accordance with* the sole discretion and opinion of the Seller, or its factor. . . .[34]

All too often, this doubling of prepositions serves little purpose; *under the agreement* or *at the sole discretion of the Seller* seems quite sufficient.

A different reason for conjoined phrases and word lists is that they have a certain rhetorical value. They may give an air of elegance or significance to what we say, as Charles Dickens, in *David Copperfield,* recognized:

> In the taking of legal oaths, for example, deponents seem to enjoy themselves mightily when they come to several good words in succession, for the expression of one idea; as, that they utterly detest, abominate, and abjure, and so forth. . . . [W]e are fond of having a large superfluous establishment of words to wait upon us on great occasions; we think it looks important, and sounds well.[35]

Whatever the aesthetic reasons for using "several good words in succession, for the expression of one idea," a serious drawback is that it may lead to ambiguity. It is a general principle of legal interpretation that each word must be given effect and that no word is to be considered "surplusage."[36] This sounds quite reasonable, but consider language from countless wills that contain phrases similar to the following: *I give, devise and bequeath the rest, residue and remainder of my estate to Samantha.* Because the drafter has inserted all three terms, one would logically assume that *rest, residue,* and *remainder* are distinct terms of art, carefully selected to convey subtle shades of meaning and to cover every contingency. One would thus expect that another will might give the *rest* and the *residue* to Samantha, while giving the *remainder* to Jonathan. In actuality, although attempts are sometimes made to distinguish them, there is absolutely no relevant difference among these terms. *Rest, residue and remainder* is not a finely-tuned legal phrase consisting of three carefully-defined technical terms. At best it has become a redundant idiom. The same is true of *give, devise and bequeath.* Despite occasional attempts to differentiate them, they are now used completely interchangeably. Thus, *I give the rest of my estate to Samantha* is perfectly adequate.[37]

Judges are well aware of the redundancies of legal style. Instead of giving meaning to each word in accordance to the surplusage rule, many judges are cognizant of the "habits of conveyancers and the mode in which legal instruments are drawn," and therefore are "never very much embarrassed by the suggestion that when a man used ten words where two would do, I am bound to affix a separate meaning to every word of the ten."[38] Such judges apparently assume that many of these words convey no additional meaning and effectively ignore them.

So, which is it? Should we assume that each word in a list must add something to the meaning (under the surplusage rule), or should we be free to ignore most items in a list because long strings of words are simply a meaningless "habit of conveyancers"?

Of course, *give, devise and bequeath* and *rest, residue and remainder* have, like *null and void, cease and desist,* or *any and all,* become established idioms; lawyers realize that they convey only a single meaning. In contrast, conjoined phrases that are not idioms will often be ambiguous.[39] Stringing together long lists of words that serve no purpose is therefore not just bad style, but could introduce the sort of ambiguity that lawyers generally work so hard to avoid.

Unusual Sentence Structure

A further characteristic of "writing like a lawyer" is use of sentence structures that are theoretically possible in ordinary English, but tend to be quite unusual. An illustration in a book by linguists Crystal and Davy comes from an insurance contract: *a proposal to effect with the Society an assurance.*[40] When a verb (V) is followed by both a prepositional phrase (PP) and noun phrase (NP), the common word order in modern English is for the noun phrase to come first: V-NP-PP, as in *a proposal to effect an assurance with the Society.* Yet as the above example shows, legal language often uses the order V-PP-NP.

Crystal and Davy further mention that in written legal texts, adverbials often precede a participle: *herein contained* or *hereinbefore reserved.*[41] Although *herein* or *hereinbefore* can hardly be considered "ordinary" adverbials, the normal word order would be for the adverbials to follow the participle: *contained herein* and *reserved hereinbefore.*

Legal writing also reflects a fondness for non-finite clauses that follow the nouns that they modify: *rent hereinbefore reserved and agreed to be paid.*[42] Of course, it would be awkward and probably ungrammatical to write of *the hereinbefore reserved and agreed to be paid rent,* but it is not difficult to make the sentence sound more natural without a loss in meaning. For example, one could speak of *the reserved and agreed-upon rent,* or *the reserved rent that the tenant has agreed to pay.* Very likely, simply writing *the rent* would be sufficiently clear from the context.

Part of the explanation for these usual sentence structures almost certainly goes back to use of Latin for records and legal documents. Because Latin had relatively free word order, sentence elements could be moved around with ease. In contrast, word order in English is relatively fixed. The odd word order of much legal English seems to originate in a slavish, word-by-word translation of Latin phrases.

Another feature of legal style is to place dependent clauses next to the words they modify, even when this results in a position that is avoided in more normal language. For example:

> The defendant or the prosecutor, *if dissatisfied with the place of trial as fixed by the magistrates' court, or by the Crown Court,* may apply. . . .

Or the clause may be placed between the auxiliary and main verb:

> The Lord Chancellor may, *with the concurrence of the Minister for the Civil Service as to numbers and salaries,* appoint. . . .[43]

Ordinarily, people try to avoid separating the subject and verb with too much material. They also try not to insert too much material inside the verb complex. It has been argued that the legal word order allows adverbials and other modifiers to appear "with logical exactitude next to the words they determine."[44] Perhaps this does indeed decrease the possibility of ambiguity, but it simultaneously reduces comprehension.

Negation

It is sometimes claimed that legal language has an unusual amount of negation. While this element of legal style has not, to my knowledge, been statistically substantiated, it is quite possibly accurate, at least in certain types of legal writing. The profession's favoring of the negative may be related to the age-old notion that whatever is not explicitly forbidden is permissible. Consequently, the law is primarily about what people *cannot* do, and is logically phrased mainly in the negative. Consider the Ten Commandments. Although some contain both positive and negative admonitions, at least eight are primarily negative (*thou shalt not . . .*).

Negatives include not just words like *not* or *never,* but any element with negative meaning, like the prefix *mis-* in *misunderstand* or *un-* in *unreal,* and even semantic negatives like the word *deny.* Multiple negation is all too frequent in legal language. An example from a California jury instruction is the phrase "innocent *mis*recollection is *not un*common,"[45] which contains no less than three negative elements in a five-word phrase.

Judges also tend to favor injunctions that are negative in form rather than positive. It is easier to tell people what they cannot do, rather than what they can. In fact, the preference for the negative is reinforced by the rule that a positive (mandatory) injunction is automatically stayed on appeal, while one that is negative (prohibitory) remains in force.[46]

Although commands, orders, and related speech acts are often in the negative, there are many legal genres, such as judicial opinions, briefs, or letters to clients, which do not especially favor the negative. Whether greater use of negation is a general characteristic of legal style therefore remains an open question.

Impersonal Constructions

The law tends to be phrased in a highly impersonal manner. An illustration of this impersonal style is the tendency to steer clear of first and second person pronouns (*I, we,* and *you*). Rather than beginning an argument to judges by saying *May it please you,* a lawyer typically starts with *May it please the court,* addressing the judge or judges in the third person, and using a noun instead of a pronoun.

In spoken language, first and second person pronouns are ubiquitous. If we had to order or command someone to do something, we would use the second person pronoun *you* (*you must register with the police*). Yet legal documents are almost always in the third person: *the sex offender shall register. . . .* The same normally holds for pleadings (*plaintiff alleges* rather than *I allege*) and contracts (*Buyer shall pay Seller,* or *the party of the first part shall pay the party of the second part,* in place of *I shall pay you*). Other examples of impersonal constructions include the common phrase *it shall be unlawful* or the provision that certain sorts of acts are *punishable as a misdemeanor.*

One reason for using the third person in documents like statutes is that they are meant to be of general applicability and address several audiences at once. If a statute were simply directed to those who are to obey, it could realistically be phrased in the second person *you,* just like in the Bible (*Thou shalt . . .*). But statutes must also instruct police officers about what is permissible behavior, and they instruct the courts on how to deal with violations. To use the second person, the statute would not only have to direct sex offenders that *you must register with the police,* but it would separately have to tell police that *you should arrest any sex offenders who do not register,* and it would need a further provision informing the courts that *you should punish any sex offenders who violate this statute.* It is more economical to declare, in the third person, that *sex offenders shall register with the police,* leaving the various affected parties to figure out when this means *you.*

There is a similar reason for using the third person in contracts. Suppose that Smith tells Jones: *I promise to convey my house to you,* and Jones responds, *I promise to pay you $100,000 for the house.* The written contract containing these reciprocal promises cannot use *I* (or *you*) since the *I* could refer to either Smith or Jones and would thus create great ambiguity. To use the first and second persons, there would have to be two documents, one in which *I* (Smith) promise *you* (Jones) that I will convey my house, and a second in which *I* (Jones) promise *you* (Smith) that I will pay you the money. This seems very cumbersome. The better way is to draft a single contract in the third person: *Smith promises X* and *Jones promises Y.*

The third person also promotes an aura of objectivity, greatly desired by lawmakers. Judges are reluctant to say that *I find* something to be the case; such a finding seems too personal and vulnerable. An alternative is the **editorial we,** which is often used in formal or scientific writing by a single individual.[47] This (*we find*) seems more impressive and objective, but it resembles the plural of majesty and may appear pompous. Thus, many judges prefer the third person: *this court finds.* It appears as an objective and powerful finding, made not by one frail human being, but endorsed by a venerable and powerful institution. As Peter Goodrich has noted, use of the third person suggests that judges are not mere mortals, but the embodiment of law and justice.[48] This usage thus helps legitimate the judicial system by making it appear to be above the fray of human emotions and biases.

Lawyers, always eager to show respect to judges, also use impersonal language when addressing them: *Has the court made a ruling yet?* or *May I approach the bench?* Along the same lines, lawyers normally address the judge as *your honor* (U.S.) or *your lordship* (England), rather than *you: I shall now call my last witness, if it please your lordship.*

But legal language is not always impersonal. It is normal practice to use the first person in wills: *I appoint John Stienstra to be my executor.* Here there is no possible ambiguity regarding the identity of the *I;* unlike a contract, most wills have a single "speaker." In addition, multi-judge courts seem less reluctant to refer to themselves in the first person plural (*we hold that . . .*), perhaps because several judges are inherently more authoritative than just one.

An interesting custom is when judges use *we* to refer not merely to themselves, but to the entire institution throughout time. Without flinching, the United States Supreme Court was able to refer in 1996 to *our earliest opinion* on a subject; the opinion dated from 1827![49] While

Supreme Court justices are famous for their professional longevity, it seems safe to say that none were on the bench in the early nineteenth century. Here, the first person may help stress the continuity of the law, which legitimates the legal system in another way.

Conclusion

The examples in this chapter are just some of the ways that law students learn—often subconsciously—to talk and write like lawyers. Many of these lawyerly quirks or aspects of legal style serve little or no function besides marking that an utterance or writing is in some sense legal, or at least associated with the profession. That would be harmless enough. If lawyers want to pronounce *defendant* in their own idiosyncratic way, or spell *judgment* without an *e,* no one will be the worse off.

But other stylistic features are less innocuous. For one thing, emphasis on group cohesion necessarily excludes those who do not belong and who have not learned to "talk like lawyers." When dealing with the public, that is obviously the wrong message to send. Furthermore, long and complex sentences with unusual word order and other odd features make legal language convoluted, cumbersome, and hard to comprehend. Unless they have a legitimate function that cannot be otherwise conveyed, these stylistic features of legal language have little to commend them.

CHAPTER FIVE

The Quest for Precision

Much of the linguistic behavior of the legal profession is geared towards speaking and writing as clearly and precisely as possible. Indeed, the legendary precision of Law French, unadulterated by ordinary usage, was one of the main justifications for keeping it alive long after the royal household itself had switched to English. Even today, the need for precision is offered as a justification for the many peculiarities of legal language. In this chapter we examine some of the ways in which legal language is indeed precise, as well as characteristics that undermine precision. Another very important method for increasing precision—the use of technical vocabulary—is the subject of a later chapter.

Avoiding Pronouns: "Player Promises That Player Will Play . . ."

One of the most salient ways in which lawyers try to enhance precision is by avoiding pronouns. Lawyers prefer to repeat nouns, hoping to avoid ambiguity, rather than using the pronouns that are common in ordinary speech. Combined with the impersonal style mentioned in chapter 4, this means that in legal language pronouns are a rare species.

To understand how pronouns normally work, consider the sentence below:

John kissed John's girlfriend

If John is kissing his own girlfriend, this sentence sounds rather odd. Roughly speaking, when we refer to a person or thing more than once in the same discourse, we use the name or a full noun only the first time, to identify the referent. The next time we wish to refer to that same person or thing, we typically use an appropriate pronoun. If John is kissing his own girlfriend, we would therefore say:

John kissed *his* girlfriend

One of the problems with pronouns is that the antecedent (the noun that the pronoun refers back to) is often uncertain. In the above, the most likely interpretation is that John was kissing his own girlfriend, so *his* refers to *John*. But if the speaker had been talking about James, there is another possible antecedent, and *his* could refer to either James or John. Pronouns become especially ambiguous when there are two possible antecedents in the same sentence:

> John told James to kiss *his* girlfriend

Without further information, it is impossible to tell whether John or James is the antecedent for *his*, and thus we do not know whose girlfriend John wants kissed.

Because pronouns can have ambiguous reference, the legal profession tends to shy away from them. At least in written legal language, lawyers are inclined to repeat a name or full noun over and over. In fact, manuals on legal drafting caution that pronouns can create ambiguity and recommend repeating a noun instead.[1] Consequently, lawyers use pronouns only where the antecedent is very evident, and even then may decide to use the name or a noun instead.

Avoiding pronouns makes sense in documents such as contracts, where it is essential to carefully distinguish the rights and obligations of two or more parties. In a standard football player contract, for example, there are two parties (the *Player* and the *Club*), and an interested third party, the National Football League (the *League*). The player's duties under the contract are triggered by acts of the club and the league, and it is therefore important to keep these parties distinct, as is done in this excerpt:

> Player will report promptly for and participate fully in Club's official pre-season training camp, all Club meetings and practice sessions, and all pre-season, regular-season and post-season football games scheduled for or by Club. If invited, Player will practice for and play in any all-star football game sponsored by the League. Player will not participate in any football game not sponsored by the League unless the game is first approved by the League.[2]

Obviously, whether the club or the league sponsors or schedules an event may matter; using nouns instead of pronouns makes this clear. Thus, the player must attend club meetings, but not league meetings. Use of *it* or *its* would create ambiguity, because there are two possible antecedents for that pronoun: the club and the league.

Yet there are numerous occasions where the contract could easily employ pronouns with no real loss of precision. The continual repetition of *Player,* for instance, is unnecessary. There is only one human male that this contract could possibly refer to, so there is absolutely no danger in using *he* or *his* more often. Yet as Crystal and Davy have observed,

> it is not simply that referential pronouns are avoided only when their use could raise genuine confusion; they seem to be eschewed as a species. And in environments in which even the most bizarre misreading would be unlikely to find an undesirable meaning, the lexical item is solemnly repeated . . . .[3]

It should be pointed out that there is an additional benefit to repetition of nouns, at least when dealing with standardized forms. Substituting a pronoun for the various repetitions of *Player* in a preprinted form would probably lead to using *he* as the traditional generic pronoun. On the other hand, *Player* is gender-neutral. Though probably unintended, this is one more reason that the legal profession will probably continue its habit of repeating nouns.[4]

All in all, the reluctance of lawyers to use pronouns does indeed make their language more precise. Unfortunately, as we will see below, there are other characteristics of legal English that undermine or even contradict this goal.

Undermining Precision: "The Masculine Shall Include the Feminine"

Another characteristic of legal language does little to enhance precision, and could even sow confusion. This is the penchant for declaring that one morphological category will include another. For instance, statutes commonly declare that the masculine gender will include the feminine and the neuter.[5] Thus, the pronoun *he* includes *she* and *it,* and *man* presumably includes *woman.* Oddly, although the masculine can include the feminine, the opposite is not normally true. Thus, a pension plan providing a benefit to *widows* has been held inapplicable to widowers.[6]

Women have argued that using the masculine to refer to people in general perpetuates sexism, and the better practice these days is to avoid such constructions. Most legal journals endeavor to do so, although the profession as a whole seems slow to follow suit. Nonetheless, California now encourages its judges to "use gender neutral language in all local rules, forms, and court documents. . . ."[7] Further, one court has held that jury instructions containing exclusively the male pronoun may have confused the jury in the homicide prosecution of a woman. It explained that "the persistent use of the masculine gender leaves the jury with the impression the objective standard to be applied is that applicable to an altercation between two men."[8] Here, obviously, the male does not include the female.

Along those same lines, legal documents and statutes often declare that the present tense shall include the future, and sometimes the past, and that the singular shall include the plural, and vice versa.[9] Applying all these redefinitions together leads to the rather absurd result that *one man is* could be legally equivalent to *two men were* or *two women will be.* Of course, these redefinitions are supposed to be used only when appropriate in context. If the context requires it, however, there should be no need for a separate rule.

These odd redefinitions seem to have arisen for quite a legitimate reason: to counter the trend of needlessly repeating nouns and verbs.[10] In the past, statutes often applied to *any person or persons,* for instance. Such repetitions could become quite tedious, as this deed from 1674 illustrates:

> I, Simon Leach . . . *have* granted, surrendered, remised, released, and for ever quit claimed, and confirmed, and by these presents *do* grant, surrender, remise, release, and for ever quit claim, and confirm. . . .[11]

To the extent that these redefinitions help lawyers overcome their penchant for needless repetition, they are certainly welcome. Yet if a law prohibits *any person* from doing something, surely it applies just as well when two people do the forbidden act! A contrary interpretation is absurd. Nor is there any good reason to fiddle with the normal meaning of verb tenses. If I legally grant something by a deed, it is unnecessary to say that I also *have granted* it in the past. If I really *granted* it in the past, I do not need to do so again by saying *I do grant.* Finally, if every reference to a male can include a female, it becomes very problematic to refer unambiguously to men only, as one might wish to do in a military conscription act, or an act requiring medical examinations for prostate cancer. At best, these redefinitions seem useless, and at worst they can lead to unintended mischief. Precision is hardly promoted by such a device.

Strategic Imprecision: Obscuring the Actor through Passives and Nominalizations

Despite claims about the precision of legal language, some of its attributes are deliberately *imprecise.* For example, passives and nominalizations often obscure the identity of the actor; whether done intentionally or not, it can only reduce precision.

The basic sentence in English consists of a noun and then a verb, optionally followed by another noun: *The man injured the girl.* We know that *the man* is the subject of the sentence—and the actor—because it precedes an active verb. And we know that *the girl* is the person or object that was injured, because this noun phrase follows the verb. All we have to do is reverse the nouns (*The girl injured the man*) to change the girl into the subject and the man to the object.

Because this such a basic structure, we tend to anticipate that whenever a noun occurs at the beginning of the sentence, it will be the grammatical subject, as well as the actor (the person doing the action described by the verb). With such basic sentences, it is difficult to obscure the actor. The sentence must have a subject, and the subject is normally the actor. And what the actor did—injure the girl—is also straightforwardly stated by a simple verb.

Yet it should come as no surprise that frequently lawyers wish to obscure or at least downplay the fact that their client was the actor who engaged in some kind of wrongful conduct. Their aim is obfuscation, not precision. Two major linguistic devices that can function to obscure the actor—intentionally or not—are passive verbs and nominalizations.

Legal language is often excoriated for overreliance on passive constructions.[12] A passive sentence is, in a way, the opposite of an active sentence, in which the grammatical subject is also the actor. In contrast, the grammatical subject of a passive sentence is the *object* of the action, rather than being the actor.

Active sentences like *The man injured the girl* can be converted to passives in a few easy steps:

1. Move the object (*the girl*) to the beginning of the sentence;
2. Move the original subject of the sentence to the end, behind the verb, into a prepositional phrase that begins with *by;* and
3. Change the active verb (*injured*) into the appropriate passive form (*was injured*).

Performing these actions will produce the passive sentence *The girl was injured by the man.*

Unlike the active sentence, the subject of the passive sentence (*the girl*) is not the actor (after all, it is the man who did the injuring). Passives thus deviate from the basic sentence pattern of English, because we normally expect the grammatical subject to be the actor as well.

More noteworthy for our purposes is what happens to the original subject: in a passive sentence, the actor (*the man*) is found in what is sometimes called the "*by* phrase" (*by the man*). Critically, such a *by* phrase may be left out. It is possible to say just that *the girl was injured*, omitting any reference to the responsible party. Consider also the mantra of many politicians when something goes wrong: *mistakes were made.*

No doubt the possibility of leaving out the actor explains much of the profession's affection for the passive construction. Even the United States Supreme Court has noticed this feature:

> When Congress writes a statute in the passive voice, it often fails to indicate who must take a required action. This silence can make the meaning of a statute somewhat difficult to ascertain.[13]

Of course, passives can occur for more legitimate reasons as well. The function of de-emphasizing the actor may explain why passives are common in statutes and court orders.[14] Legislators and judges want their commands to appear maximally objective, to give them the greatest possible rhetorical force. For legislators to state *we shall punish those who skateboard on sidewalks* seems too personal, perhaps even vindictive. A passive sounds more authoritative: *Those who skateboard on sidewalks shall be punished.* The same holds true for court orders. To appear as authoritative as possible (and to avoid the first person), judges typically start an order not with *I order . . .* but with *it is ordered, adjudged and decreed. . . .* Indeed, in a recent series of orders by the United States Supreme Court, virtually every verb was in the passive voice:

> The petitions for writ of certiorari *are granted . . .*
> The cases *are consolidated . . .*
> . . . one hour *is allotted* for oral argument.
> The briefs of petitioners *are to be filed . . .*
> The application for stay of execution . . . *is denied.*
> The application for stay . . . *is granted* and *it is ordered . . .*

Virtually the only active constructions among dozens of passives were statements that a particular rule of court did not apply, which is an impersonal, objective formulation even in the active voice, and that a certain justice *took no part in the consideration or decision of this application,* which is unavoidably a bit personal, while still being as impersonal as possible in that it fails to state why.[15]

Passives seem less common in contracts, where the drafters are very concerned with specifying as precisely as possible who can or should do what, and hence need to emphasize the actor. For example, in a standard publishing agreement, virtually all of the verbs, which mostly deal with rights and duties of the parties, are in the active voice:

> The Author *shall prepare* and *deliver* . . .
> The Publisher *shall publish* . . .
> The Author *grants and assigns* . . .
> The Publisher *shall pay* . . .[16]

On the other hand, when the contract deals with the choice of law to govern the contract, it does so in the passive: *This Agreement shall be interpreted and governed by the laws of the State of New York* . . . Because of uncertainty at the time of making the contract as to who will be doing the interpreting (i.e., the actor is uncertain), use of a passive makes sense here.

Another syntactic device, like passive constructions, also can have the effect of de-emphasizing or obscuring the identity of the actor. This is the phenomenon of **nominalization.** At least historically, a nominalization is a noun derived from another word class, usually a verb. For example, the nominalized form of the verb *injure* is *injury.* Compare also these verbs and corresponding nominalizations:

Verb	**Nominalization**
construct	construction
demonstrate	demonstration
insure	insurance
judge	judgment
see	sight

As noted in the previous chapter, many nominalizations were created in Law French by the addition of *-al* to the verb (as in *try/trial* or *propose/proposal*) or by the suffixation of *-er* (as in *demur/demurrer* or *waive/waiver*). Nouns can also be created from verbs by adding the suffix *-ing* to the verb, thus forming a **gerund:** *Injuring the girl was unforgivable,* or *kayaking is fun.*

Like passive constructions, nominalized verbs allow the speaker to omit reference to the actor. Rather than having to admit that *the defendant injured the girl at 5:30 P.M.,* the defendant's attorney can write that *the girl's injury happened at 5:30 P.M.* In fact, the lawyer can depersonalize the incident even more by leaving out mention of the girl entirely: *the injury happened at 5:30 P.M.* These are, of course, further illustrations of strategic imprecision.

A more legitimate reason for nominalizations is that by allowing the actor to be omitted, they enable legal drafters to cover the possibility of *anyone* doing a specified act. This permits laws to be stated as broadly as possible. A California law defines a number of acts as trespass, all of them expressed in the form of nominalized verbs (gerunds). Below are just a few examples from the statute:

> *Cutting down, destroying or injuring* any kind of wood . . .
> *Carrying away* any kind of wood or timber . . .
> *Digging, taking, or carrying away* . . . any soil . . .
> *Building* fires upon any lands owned by another . . .

And so the list goes on, each applying to anyone who does one of the enumerated acts.[17]

Consider further this sentence from the standard publishing agreement (part of which was quoted previously):

> If there is an *infringement* of any rights granted to the Publisher
> . . . the Publisher shall have the right, in its sole discretion, to
> select counsel to bring an action to enforce those rights . . .[18]

The use of the nominalization *infringement* seems calculated to cast as wide a net as possible; it names no actor and thus covers anyone who might happen to infringe. Obviously, this usage is not very precise at all, for the simple reason that the drafter is unable to specifically list every person, or even class of people, who might infringe the rights of the publisher in the future.

One might suggest replacing this nominalization with a verb: *if any person infringes any rights* . . . Instead of *any person,* one might write *whoever infringes* . . . , or use the archaic *whosoever.* Yet here the cautious drafter might become concerned by the possibility of infringement by something like a corporation, which may or may not legally be subsumed under the terms *any person* or *whoever.*[19] The drafter wants to include every possible infringer, which is achieved by the nominalization.

Elsewhere, the legal profession's use of nominalizations is just a bad habit. A California jury instruction provides a prime example:

> *Failure* of *recollection* is common. . . .[20]

In other words: *people commonly fail to recollect things.* More plainly yet, we could simply say that *people often forget things.*

Like so many features of legal language, the profession uses passives and nominalizations strategically. When there is a need to be precise, lawyers avoid them. On the other hand, when lawyers want to downplay or obscure the identity of the actor, or have a provision apply as broadly as possible, these linguistic devices can be very handy.

Flexible, General, or Vague Language

As we have seen above, lawyers often strive to be as precise as possible. At the same time, legal language is described as full of words and expressions with general, vague, or flexible meanings.[21] Lawyers sometimes deliberately employ terminology exactly because of its pliability. As Reed Dickerson has noted, vagueness in legal language is often "a positive benefit."[22]

Perhaps the best known illustration of flexibility is the word *reasonable* in expressions like *reasonable care, beyond a reasonable doubt* and the legendary *reasonable man*. Obviously, such flexible terms may be quite useful. What is "reasonable" in any particular situation may not be capable of precise articulation in advance. What would a "reasonable" person do when confronted with someone having a heart attack? A reasonable person who knows cardiopulmonary resuscitation might react differently than a reasonable person who does not. Likewise, if a hospital is very far away, it might be reasonable to transport the victim there in an automobile. But if there are paramedics or an ambulance in the area, the only reasonable course of action might be to call them and wait for professional help.

Furthermore, standards of reasonableness may change over time. Formerly it was deemed prudent, when someone is bitten by a venomous snake, to cut a cross on the wound, try to suck out as much of the poison as possible, and apply a tourniquet. Nowadays, this is no longer recommended; experts advise us to transport the victim to medical facilities as soon as possible.[23] Conceivably, therefore, someone who accidentally injured a snakebite victim in the past by applying a tourniquet would have been acting "reasonably" and would have no liability. That same person today might be responsible for any damage because it is no longer reasonable to apply the tourniquet in the first place. As the Supreme Court recently noted in reference to *due process* (another flexible term):

> " 'Due process' . . . is not a technical conception with a fixed content unrelated to time, place and circumstances, but is flexible, calling for such procedural protections as the particular situation demands."[24]

Other notoriously flexible or vague terms are words like *obscene* or *indecent*. Many governments around the world claim the power to ban *obscene* or *indecent* materials. But what exactly is obscene? Justice Stewart of the Supreme Court admitted that he could not define it intelligibly, but claimed that "I know it when I see it."[25] At best, people might agree on a vague (and somewhat circular) definition of these terms, something along the lines of "offensive to one's standards of decency." Yet people differ dramatically on what those standards of decency are and how to apply them to any particular situation.

The problem is that if a term is too flexible, it gives a judge, jury, or government official tremendous latitude in deciding what should be banned as "obscene." On the other hand, if a law avoids the flexible term, and instead tries to be as precise as possible (forbidding the use of certain words or acts, for instance), it may fail to recognize that what is offensive can differ widely across place and time. The Supreme Court at one point dealt with this problem by formulating a test for obscenity: the "average person" had to apply "contemporary community standards" in determining whether "the dominant theme of the material taken as a whole appeals to prurient interest."[26] At least in theory, formulations of this type allow the standard to retain much of its flexibility, while simultaneously giving some minimal guidance to the judge or jury.

Despite its limitations, vague or flexible language therefore has several useful functions. It allows a legislature to use a general term without having to articulate in advance exactly what is included within it, something the legislators might not be able to agree on even if they had the time to try. It permits the law to adapt to differing circumstances and communities within a jurisdiction. And it enables the law to deal with novel situations that are certain to arise in the future, as well as changing norms and standards.

For these reasons, flexible and often quite abstract language is typical of constitutions, which are ideally written to endure through time. As the Supreme Court noted in 1816, "[t]he constitution unavoidably deals in general language."[27] Elsewhere, Justice John Marshall wrote that the Constitution was not a "legal code" that contained "immutable rules" for every possible contingency.[28] Consequently, the Constitution—especially the Bill of Rights—has many quite general or flexible terms, including *due process, freedom of speech, liberty, probable cause, property, unreasonable search,* and *cruel and unusual punishment.* Because these terms are so malleable, their meaning will naturally evolve with our changing society.

Elsewhere, flexibility may be less appropriate. Perhaps the greatest problem arises under the criminal law: those who have to obey a law should know precisely what conduct is prohibited, something that vague or flexible language generally does not convey well. If a statute expressly prohibits uttering the word *breast,* the public knows how to comply. But if the law vaguely bans any *indecent* language, it may be very problematic to decide which words are permissible and which are not, even under a "community standards" test. Likewise, when drafting private documents, such as contracts and wills, lawyers are often leery of vague or flexible language, fearful that in the future it may be interpreted in a way that they do not intend. Consequently, although in some legal contexts flexible language is useful or even necessary, in other circumstances lawyers will strive instead for maximum precision.

The Tension between Flexibility and Precision

The choice between flexibility and precision is seldom an easy one: increasing precision generally reduces flexibility, and vice versa. This tradeoff is perhaps best illustrated by the distinction between general terms versus lists of specific examples. Frequently, legal drafters must choose between using a single flexible and rather general term that encompasses a large number of things or actions, or a more precise word list that attempts to enumerate all the specific things or actions that the writer intends to include. For example, women sometimes obtain what are commonly called **restraining orders** aimed at preventing men from "harassing" them (and occasionally vice versa). Yet in many American jurisdictions, such an order may not be enforceable if it just orders the man not to *harass* the woman. This is a fairly general or even vague term that gives the man limited notice regarding what he can and cannot do. Does telephoning the woman or sending her a birthday card constitute "harassment"? Hanging around the neighborhood of her house? What about going to a party that he knows she is likely to attend? For that reason, these orders almost inevitably resort to lists of specific activities that are prohibited: do not come within 100 feet of her residence or person, do not call her on the telephone, do not send her any mail, and so forth. A word list provides more specific guidance than general or flexible terminology.[29]

Solving vagueness problems by the use of lists is nicely illustrated by the history of a 1985 Connecticut law that made it unlawful to *interfere with* or *harass* a hunter. Clearly, whacking the hunter's aimed rifle with a baseball bat would constitute harassment. But what about shouting *run for your life!* at Bambi when the gunman moves in for the kill, or loudly chanting *hunting is immoral* at the silently stalking hunter? It is less evident that this is harassment. In fact, it might be regarded as free speech protected by the Constitution. The "hunter harassment" law was therefore struck down as overly vague.[30] In other words, its use of the general term *harass* was insufficiently precise.

Undeterred, the Connecticut legislature redoubled its efforts to protect the beleaguered hunter. It amended the statute to include a specific list of prohibited activities, providing that a person violates the statute when he intentionally or knowingly:

> (1) Drives or disturbs wildlife for the purpose of disrupting the lawful taking of wildlife where another person is engaged in the process of lawfully taking wildlife;
> (2) blocks, impedes or otherwise harasses another person who is engaged in the process of lawfully taking wildlife;
> (3) uses natural or artificial visual, aural, olfactory or physical stimuli to affect wildlife behavior in order to hinder or prevent the lawful taking of wildlife;
> (4) erects barriers with the intent to deny ingress or egress to areas where the lawful taking of wildlife may occur;
> (5) interjects himself into the line of fire;
> (6) affects the condition or placement of personal or public property intended for use in the lawful taking of wildlife in order to impair its usefulness or prevent its use; or
> (7) enters or remains upon private lands without the permission of the owner or his agent, with intent to violate this section.[31]

Notably, lists of specific items may not only limit the reach of vague or flexible terms, but may also expand their meaning and make them more comprehensive, with the aim of casting as broad a net as possible. Calling a woman on the telephone is not normally *harassment,* but using a list allows it to be added to the inventory of prohibited activities.

In contrast to the hunter harassment statute, there are times when word lists turn out to be too precise and must be replaced by a broad, flexible term. This is illustrated by the law governing the investments that a trustee can make with the assets of a trust. The older approach was for legislatures to create statutory lists of specific classes of investments that were deemed safe. Such lists might include government bonds of the United States and the individual states, municipal bonds, and first mortgages on real property. The trustee could purchase any investment on the list without fear of liability if the trust later lost money.

The great advantage of statutory lists was their precision: the trustee knew exactly what type of investments he could buy. Yet what was gained in precision was lost in flexibility; trustees could not put trust assets in novel types of investments until the statutory list was amended, even if the investment was safe and would increase the yield to the beneficiaries. Remember that trustees are personally liable for losses from imprudent investments. Consequently, many states have abandoned the statutory list approach and adopted the general and more flexible **prudent investor rule** (originally the "prudent man rule"), which simply requires that the trustee act like a prudent investor. As usual, the flexibility carries a cost. Under the older approach, the trustee was safe as long as he chose investments on the list. With the general standard, the trustee cannot hide behind the safety of the list; he can be held liable for making any investment that the court later deems imprudent. Furthermore, the general approach might well lead to more litigation regarding which investments are prudent and which are not.[32]

Yet the precision of lists also has its costs. Assume that X is a general term and that it consists of the specific items a, b, c, d, and e. Even if the list is exactly equivalent to the general term, use of one or the other may have interpretive consequences. One possible implication of using a list, as Lawrence Solan has pointed out, is that it tends to lead to a narrower interpretation than a more general definition.[33] If the drafter wishes to be comprehensive or expansive, this may not be the best approach.

Use of specific lists has another consequence: courts encountering a list (a, b, c, d, e) will attempt to interpret each member of the list as being part of some general class such as X, even if the general class is not overtly stated. This is embodied in the maxim *noscitur a sociis*.[34] For example, an English act required factory *floors, steps, stairs, passageways and gangways* to be kept free of obstructions. Literally, this would mean that nothing—including machinery—could be placed anywhere on factory *floors*. Nonetheless, the other items on the list all refer to places for people to pass over. The general category is thus a place for passage, and the court restricted the term *floor* to this meaning as well.[35] While the decision makes sense in light of the presumed purpose of the act, such an interpretation might not always be what the drafter intended.

Another consequence of using a word list is that it suggests that any similar item that the drafter could have included, was indeed included. The absence of an item from a list is therefore deemed significant. For instance, suppose that X is the general class of my cousins, consisting of *a, b, c, d,* and *e.* If you ask me which of my cousins were at a particular wedding, my response that *a, b,* and *c* attended would lead to the implication that the other members of the class (*d* and *e*) were not. This rule of interpretation is captured by the maxim *expressio unius est exclusio alterius.*[36]

It seems that the Ninth Amendment to the United States Constitution was intended to prevent *expressio unius* from being applied to the list of rights contained in the earlier amendments: "The enumeration in the Constitution, of certain rights, shall not be construed to deny or disparage others retained by the people." In other words, if *X* is the class of all rights, and the Bill of Rights lists *a, b, c,* and *d,* the expressed list would normally suggest that remaining possible rights were meant to be excluded. The Ninth Amendment declares that this principle should *not* be applied, however, to the Bill of Rights.

The result of principles such as these is that there is a tendency to interpret lists as being comprehensive. Lists are more precise, but less able to deal with unforeseen contingencies or changing circumstances. Flexible terms, on the other hand, may give too much discretion to a decisionmaker or allow someone to "weasel out" of an agreement.

Many legal drafters recognize the inherent tension between generality and specificity. Hoping to attain the best of both worlds, they strive to marry the flexible to the precise. Thus, where *X* is a general or flexible category, and *a, b, c, d, e* . . . are specific members of that category, lawyers will refer to *any X, including a, b, c, d, and e.* Or the general term may come at the end of the list of items: *a, b, c, d, e, or any other X.* Yet the strategy is not always successful. For example, an English statute from the time of Queen Anne referred to *cities, towns corporate, boroughs, and places.* Birmingham was not a "city," "town corporate," or "borough," although it clearly was a "place." Was Birmingham included within the language of the statute? It could be argued that the act referred generally to all "places" and that "cities," "towns corporate," and "boroughs" was a nonexclusive list of examples or illustrations of this general category. But English courts did not interpret it in this sense. They applied a canon of construction known as *ejusdem generis,* which states that where general words follow an enumeration of persons or things, the general words should not be construed to their broadest extent, but should be limited to persons or things of the same kind or class as those specifically mentioned. In this case, the court observed that the list of specific items consisted only of incorporated places, so it interpreted the general word (*place*) as not including unincorporated places like Birmingham.[37] This holds even though Birmingham is undoubtedly a "place." If the drafters had indeed intended the statute to apply to all places, the accompanying word list obviously thwarted their purpose.

More recently, lawyers have tried to avoid such narrowing interpretations by use of the phrase *including but not limited to* (as in *any X, including but not limited to a, b, c, d, and e*). In fact, *including but not limited to* has become enormously popular in the profession.[38] The phrase is meant to emphasize that the specified items on the list are merely examples or illustrations, and should not in any way limit the scope of the general term. Still, including a list must surely have *some* function. Listing examples (*a, b, c . . .*) will almost inevitably color the interpretation of the general category *X;* in fact, some courts have explicitly so held.[39]

The tension between precision and flexibility is an inherent problem for legal language. Making statutes and contracts as specific as possible, so that they anticipate and constrain future actions and events as exactly as they can, will make the law less flexible and often undermine the intent of the legislators who enacted the statute or the parties who entered into the contract. The use of general or flexible terms creates its own difficulties. Because some vagueness and ambiguity is inherent in language, the problem will never be fully solved.

Conclusion

Professor David Mellinkoff has concluded that the claimed precision of legal language is largely a "myth."[40] He has been joined more recently by critical scholars who emphasize the indeterminacy of language. There is no doubt that lawyers tend to exaggerate the precision of legal language. The huge number of lawsuits each year over the meaning of some word or phrase in statutes and other legal documents, virtually all written by lawyers, is reason enough to question the legendary precision of legal language.

What makes precision so difficult to obtain is not merely the indeterminacy of language, however. For the most part, legal language can be made precise enough for ordinary purposes. While one can be amazed by the large number of disputes regarding the meaning of legal language, it is equally possible to wonder at the vastly larger number of legal documents that function more or less as they should. An equally important impediment to precision in legal language is the fact that there may be competing considerations at stake. Often the legal drafter is forced to choose between the flexible and the precise, knowing that each direction has its own attractions and dangers. In other cases, she may deliberately opt to be imprecise for strategic reasons.

Another aspect of legal language that gives it tremendous precision—or, depending on one's point of view, merely presents the illusion of doing so—is technical vocabulary. It is the topic of the next chapter.

CHAPTER SIX

The Legal Lexicon

There is no doubt that the vocabulary of the law is extensive. To some critics most legal terms are worthless jargon whose main purpose is to befuddle the public. More moderate voices might reject the conspiracy theory, but nonetheless suggest the legal vocabulary is full of hoary words and phrases, many survivors from Anglo-Saxon, Latin, and Law French days, that should long ago have been relegated to the history books. Lawyers, of course, tend to defend their technical vocabulary as essential to communication within the profession, even if it may be difficult for the lay public to understand. Reality, as usual, is more complex.

Legal Archaisms

Some features of legal language are definitely archaic. The following are a few of the more common examples. One of the main justifications for continued use of antiquated vocabulary is that it is more precise than the modern equivalent. As we will see, this is virtually never true.

Antiquated Morphology

Many of us are vaguely familiar with archaic pronoun forms like *ye* and *thou,* or anachronistic verb forms such as *giveth* or *takest.* Archaic morphology can give a quaint flavor to a phrase, as in *Ye olde wine shoppe.*

Legal language has retained several morphological forms that have died out in ordinary speech. *Ye,* the old plural of *you,* has survived in the phrase *Hear ye.* One can still encounter the verb form *witnesseth* in contracts of insurance: *This policy witnesseth that. . . .*[1] In fact, *witnesseth* is now often stripped of any context and placed at the beginning of contracts, as a totemic signal that roughly means, "This is a legal contract; the following are its terms." Another archaic morphological form is *sayeth* in the stock phrase *Further affiant sayeth not.* And until Justice Sandra O'Connor joined the United States Supreme Court, its members referred to each other with the antiquated plural *brethren.* Similarly, lawyers have preserved obsolete word order in certain set phrases, as in the example above regarding the affiant, or a common opening in pleadings: *Comes now plaintiff...*

Somehow, these anachronisms lend a dignity or stateliness to the occasion that it would otherwise lack. Consider the modern English equivalents to some of these phrases: *Listen up!* (for *Hear ye*), *The affiant has nothing else to say,* or *Here comes the plaintiff. ...* Perhaps preserving a small number of archaic phrases is not so bad, after all. As long as the significance is clear, beginning a court session with *hear ye* or *oyez* is at worst rather quaint.

Same

A more problematic archaic feature of legal language is the use of *same* as a substitute for a pronoun:

> She made an offer in a letter to buy the machinery, and I accepted *same.*

Writing *the same* in this context is marginally more acceptable, but it also is anachronistic. Observe that in ordinary speech, *same* usually implies *comparison* to a similar object or person; that implication is lacking in the legal sense, which refers to *identity* of reference.[2]

Lawyers tend to believe that archaic language of this sort is quite precise, but that is simply not correct. One might argue that *it* (*I accepted it*) would be ambiguous in the above example, because there are at least two possible antecedents: *it* could refer to either the offer or the letter (or maybe even the machinery). Critically, only accepting the offer would create a contract. But *same* is ambiguous in exactly the same way; *I accepted same* does not clarify whether I accepted the offer or just the letter. In the above sentence, therefore, *it* is just as clear (or unclear) as *same* and has the added benefit that it is acceptable modern English.

Same may, in fact, be more ambiguous than a regular pronoun. For one thing, *same* can be singular or plural, whereas *it* or *them* specifies the number. Furthermore, *same* is ambiguous between its ordinary meaning and the common legal usage: *She sold Bill the machinery and I want the same.* Do I want similar machines (ordinary usage), or am I intent on getting my hands on those that Bill bought (legal usage)? Fortunately, *same* in this sense has been dying a slow death; we should quickly put it out of its misery.

Said and Aforesaid

Another common and ancient legalism is the use of *said* as an article or demonstrative pronoun:

> Lessee promises to pay a deposit. *Said* deposit shall accrue interest at a rate of five percent per annum.

Here, *said* could easily be replaced by *the* or *this*. Used in this way, it is clearly an oddity from the point of view of standard English. *Said* may also be used as an ordinary adjective: *the said deposit* is equally possible, and equally archaic.

A variant of *said* is *aforesaid*. It seems to mean exactly the same as *said*, because anything *said* was necessarily said before or "afore." Thus, *aforesaid* simply takes up more space while contributing nothing to the meaning. Unlike *said*, *aforesaid* occasionally occurs with the French word order, which makes it even worse: *the indebtedness aforesaid*.

Said and *aforesaid* do nothing to eliminate ambiguity when there is more than one possible antecedent:

> Lessee promises to pay a *cleaning deposit* of $200 and a *damage deposit* equivalent to one month's rent. *Said deposit* shall accrue interest at a rate of five percent per annum.

What does *said deposit* refer to? *Said* can indicate any deposit that has already been mentioned, so it could refer to the first mentioned deposit, the second, or perhaps even both. In this context, it is no more and no less ambiguous than writing *this deposit*. If the drafter wishes to refer to the cleaning deposit, she should write that interest will be paid on the cleaning deposit. *Said* just muddles the issue.

The uselessness of *said* and *aforesaid* is further illustrated by a case from Texas, where a man named Mack Brown accused another man, also named Mack Brown, of stealing some of his cattle. The indictment continued by alleging that the cattle were the personal property of the *said Mack Brown,* and that they were stolen with the intent to appropriate them to the benefit of the *said Mack Brown.*[3] If Mack White had stolen cattle from Mack Brown, *said* would be unnecessary: the indictment could simply allege that Mack White stole cattle from Mack Brown. Yet when Mack Brown steals cattle from someone with the same name, use of *said* is not just unnecessary, but positively dangerous. It suggests that *said Mack Brown* refers consistently to one person, whereas in fact it must logically refer on one occasion to one Brown, on another to the other Brown.

Same, said, and *aforesaid* are almost certainly literal translations from Latin or perhaps Law French.[4] The records of medieval and Renaissance English courts, which were in Latin, typically introduced the parties by stating their full name, their occupations, and place of residence, as in this case from the Court of Common Pleas in 1562:

> Thomas Pyckeryng nuper de Isham in comitatu predicto generosus attachiatus fuit ad respondendum Johanni Humfrey generoso . . .

> "Thomas Pyckeryng, late of Isham in the aforesaid county, gentleman, was attached to answer John Humfrey, gentleman . . ."[5]

Once introduced, the parties were generally referred to by their first names only: *idem Johannes* "the same John," *predictus Thomas* "the aforesaid Thomas," *dictus Johannes* "the said John," and so forth. Thus, words like *said, aforesaid,* and *the same* referred back to a person or thing that had been more fully introduced earlier in the text.

While this system possesses a certain elegance, the repetition of *said* and *aforesaid* is unnecessary and can become quite tedious. Furthermore, these Latin terms were no more useful than their English translations in avoiding ambiguity. If there was only one *John* in the case, there would be no need to refer to *the said John*. But if there was more than one person with the same first name, *the said John* was ambiguous; it became necessary to add the last name. Thus, in a suit in 1509 between Thomas Moberlay and Thomas Morpath, it would have been problematic to write that *said Thomas* called *said Thomas* a heretic; which Thomas is the heretic? Last names were essential here, although the clerk still did not drop the *said* (Latin *dictus*), referring to the already introduced Thomas Morpath as *the said Thomas Morpath!*[6] Obviously, *said* was as useless in Latin as it is in English.

These expressions were also used in Law French. Phrases like *le dit justice* "the said justice" or *le dit case* "the said case" are common in legal documents in that language. One can only conclude that *said, same,* and so forth, are not just attributes of legal English. In a very real sense, these features—and others like them—transcend language. They are characteristics of a style that began in medieval England and has spread along with the English legal system itself.

Admittedly, there is one way in which *said* or *aforesaid* is theoretically more precise than *this*. Specifically, *this* can be utilized **anaphorically** (referring to a specific antecedent in previous text or discourse) or **deictically** (referring to something outside the discourse or text).[7] *Said* and *aforesaid* are exclusively anaphoric, in that they can only refer to something that has been mentioned previously. Within a legal text, however, there is virtually no possibility of a demonstrative like *this* being used deictically: *this deposit* or even *the deposit* in a contract or lease can logically only refer to a deposit previously mentioned in the same text, not to some hypothetical other deposit in the outside world. So as a practical matter, it would be pointless to keep *said* on life support, especially when the less cryptic *above* or *above-mentioned* is always available in a pinch.

Such

A related anachronism is the legal use of *such*. Normally, *such* is an adjective meaning "that sort" or "this sort." If you tell me about your terrific new job, and I reply that I would like to get *such employment,* you would not take this as a threat to your livelihood. I do not covet your job, but merely want the same type of work. Now consider how *such* is used in a 1993 opinion by a California appellate court that decided that a trial court's order should be overturned:

> We conclude that the trial court's order constituted an abuse of discretion in the procedural posture of this case which compels us to set aside *such* order.[8]

Here, *such order* means "this (specific) order." *Such* performs exactly the same function as *this,* and appears indistinguishable from *said* or *aforesaid.* Furthermore, use of *such* is potentially confusing because it might be interpreted to mean "this kind of" (especially in the plural).

The legal profession's long retention of *said, aforesaid, same,* and *such* cannot be justified as adding precision or clarity to the text. A drafter who wants to clearly refer to a noun that has been introduced previously can do so in modern English by the use of *the deposit,* or if necessary, *the above-mentioned deposit* or *the above deposit. This* or *that* is a better choice than *said* or *such.* And *it* will usually replace the legal sense of *same.* There is no need for these anachronisms.

To Wit

Few things sound as lawyerly as the phrase *to wit.* Beyond sounding lawyerly, however, it fulfills absolutely no function. This is illustrated by the famous case of *Raffles v. Wichelhaus,* in which each party to a contract seems to have had in mind a different ship named *Peerless.* The plea alleged

> That the said ship mentioned in the said agreement was meant and intended by the defendants to be the ship called the "Peerless," which sailed from Bombay, *to wit,* in October [while the plaintiffs intended to refer to] another and different ship, which was also called the "Peerless," and which sailed from Bombay, *to wit,* in December.[9]

Such usage has led David Mellinkoff to declare the phrase "worthless."[10]

Nonetheless, *to wit* did once arguably have a function. Recall that in the past, English writs and pleadings were very formulaic; the plaintiff essentially took a predetermined verbal formula and filled in some blanks. The repetition of the formula ensured that the plaintiff had a recognized cause of action, while the individualized insertions in the blanks gave the defendant more specific information about the indictment or complaint. Thus, a writ or plea alleging trespass might state (in Latin) that the defendant, *with force and arms, broke the close* of the plaintiff. The phrase *to wit* (Latin *scilicet* or *videlicet*) allowed some details to be added to the writ, as in an example from around 1470:

> the said Richard . . . with force and arms, *to wit,* with swords, bows and arrows, broke the close of the said archbishop. . . .[11]

To wit served as a marker that what followed was not the formulaic language of the writ, but individualized details of this specific complaint.

To wit has virtually died out in ordinary language. Remarkably, however, a computerized search of California cases encountered the phrase well over twelve thousand times, including many quite recent examples.[12] Part of the reason is that *to wit* is still very common in criminal complaints, and for much the same reason that it was historically. Here is an example from a 1996 case charging that the defendant engaged in assault with a deadly weapon:

> On or about July 14, 1990, [the defendant] did willfully and unlawfully commit an assault upon [the victim] with a deadly weapon, *to wit,* HANDS. . . .[13]

Fortunately, the California Supreme Court recently decided that bare hands should not be considered a deadly weapon.[14] Besides this, not much has changed in half a millennium. As was true then, the drafter here was trying to insert the required words about assault with a deadly weapon (thus tracking the language of the statute and identifying the crime), while adding some details to notify the defendant of the factual basis for the charge. While the survival of *to wit* may be understandable, is it really essential? A colon or comma would serve as well.

Subjunctives

There are various kinds of subjunctives, virtually all of which have died out in modern English, especially in spoken language. One type of subjunctive is a construction called the **formulaic subjunctive,** which involves use of a verb in its base form and conveys roughly the same meaning as *let* or *may.* It has quite correctly been characterized as formal and old-fashioned.[15]

In legal usage, the formulaic subjunctive is still very much alive, as in the frequent phrase *know all men by these presents.* It is even more common in the passive. Some examples are *be it known* and *be it remembered.* Another illustration is the British enactment clause, which is found at the beginning of all statutes:

> *Be it enacted* by the Queen's most Excellent Majesty, by and with the advice and consent of the Lords Spiritual and Temporal, and Commons, in this present Parliament assembled, and by the authority of the same. . . .

This clause illustrates not just the subjunctive, but several other common features of legal English: French word order (*Lords Spiritual and Temporal*), formal or pompous language (*Queen's most Excellent Majesty*), conjoined phrases (*by and with, advice and consent*), odd word order (*in Parliament assembled*), and use of *same* as a pronoun. Although a paragon of legalese, it also has a majestic flair that would be hard to achieve with more banal phraseology. Phrases such as this one surely go far in explaining why lawyers are so reluctant to give up their idiosyncratic language.

Here-, There-, and Where-

Legal English has long been characterized by another archaic trait: constructions of the type *hereunder, therein,* and *wherewith.* These words were common in medieval English. Rather than saying *under it* or *under that,* a speaker of Middle English could say *hereunder* or *thereunder.* And instead of using *with what* or *with which* in questions, Middle English speakers would generally say *wherewith.*

Although similar constructions still exist in Germanic languages like

Dutch and German, they have died out in English. At best, speakers of modern English might encounter them in passages from the King James version of the Bible, or in the works of Shakespeare. As a result, people today have trouble understanding these phrases.

Consider what Juliet meant when she stood on the balcony and pined, "O, Romeo, Romeo! *wherefore* art thou Romeo?"[16] The modern reader almost invariably thinks that Juliet cannot find her lover in the garden below, and—peering forlornly into the dark bushes—is calling out to him: *Where are you, Romeo?* In fact, *wherefore* is the interrogative form of *therefore* and means "for what reason" or "why." A translation of the sentence in modern English is "Oh, Romeo! Romeo! Why must you be *Romeo?*[17] The popular misinterpretation obscures the whole point of the scene. Juliet is looking directly at Romeo and is asking *why* his name is Romeo Montague, marking him as a member of an enemy clan and keeping them apart. Only in this context can we properly understand the famous lines that soon follow: "What's in a name? That which we call a rose by any other name would smell as sweet."[18]

Despite the archaic nature of these words—or perhaps because of it—lawyers continue to sprinkle their prose with *hereunders* and *thereins*. Mellinkoff pilloried this habit, arguing that the terms are archaic and often imprecise.[19]

Admittedly, words like *herein* and *therein* may sometimes lead to economy of expression when they replace a longer phrase like *in this document* or *in that clause*. Of course, verbal economy has not always been a significant goal for most legal writers, who are known more for verbosity than conciseness. Moreover, the economy comes at a cost. Consider the following provision from a standard textile sales contract approved by the American Textile Manufacturers Institute in 1986:

> Delivery to a carrier, or in the absence of shipping instructions, the mailing of a covering invoice after completion of the manufacture shall constitute good delivery or tender of delivery, subject to the Seller's right of stoppage in transit, and subject to Seller's security interest *therein* as elsewhere *herein* provided.[20]

Observe that the *there* in *therein* acts like a pronoun, because it refers to a preceding noun phrase ("in that _____"). But what do we place in the blank? To what does *therein* refer? The only realistic candidate is the noun *delivery*, but it seems odd to have a security interest in the act of delivering. Most likely, the security interest is in the merchandise that is being delivered. Although we can figure this out from the context, *therein* is not exactly precise. In fact, if we have to determine the nature of the security from the context, *therein* is entirely superfluous. If we wished to be more precise, we could refer to a *security interest in the delivered merchandise,* which would be just a little longer, more exact, and less anachronistic. *Herein* suffers from the same deficiency: does it mean "in this sentence" or "in this clause" or "in this contract"? The cases are in disarray. As the Supreme Court of California concluded almost a century ago, the meaning of *herein* must be determined by the context; "it may refer to the section, the chapter, or the entire enactment in which it is used."[21]

Again, to write *as provided in this contract,* or *as provided in paragraph 2,* would be less arcane and much more informative. The same is true, as E. A. Driedger pointed out, with the words *hereinbefore* and *hereinafter,* both of which lead to similar difficulties of interpretation.[22]

Why Is Legal Vocabulary So Conservative?

As we have seen, the legal lexicon has many obsolescent or obsolete English words and grammatical constructions, as well as outdated Latin and French terms.[23] It is very evident that these outdated words and constructions do absolutely nothing to enhance communication; in many cases they impede it by introducing ambiguity or lowering comprehension. So why do these anachronisms persist?

One reason for conservative or archaic language is that it is considered more formal than everyday speech. Language continually changes. Most people today combine *data* with a singular verb (*the data is convincing*), use *input* as a verb (*I inputed some data into the computer*), and readily employ new and useful coinages like *prioritize* and *finalize.* Yet many writers avoid these innovations in formal prose until the winds of change prove irresistible. Formal and archaic language are thus closely related. As we discuss in somewhat greater detail below, because legal language often strives toward great formality, it naturally gravitates towards archaic language.

It is worth comparing legal language to another major area in which language is very conservative: religion. The Roman Catholic church clung to Latin as the language of religion for well over a millennium after it died out as a vernacular. In the same way, Jews have maintained Hebrew, and Hindus retain Sanskrit as sacred languages. Some religions have experienced "plain language" movements, just as with the law. The best known is the Protestant Reformation; one of Martin Luther's major reforms was to translate the Bible into German so that ordinary believers could read and understand it. The King James version of the Bible was similarly motivated. Curiously enough, however, the natural tendency towards linguistic conservatism quickly reasserted itself among many Protestants, who cherish the language of the King James Bible as if God spoke Elizabethan English.

Much of this linguistic conservatism derives from an attribute that most major religions share with the law: a veneration of authoritative texts. Many Christians, for example, regard the Bible as divinely inspired, believing that every word was dictated by God Himself. When every syllable in a text is holy, translating it into another language can be problematic, or at a minimum would produce something less reliable or authentic than the original. The same is true for updating the text to more modern language.

Just as the Bible or the Koran is the authoritative source of religion for believers, documents like statutes, constitutions, and judicial opinions are the main sources of law for the legal profession. These sources are obviously not sacred in a religious sense, although many American lawyers show great reverence for the United States Constitution. Yet they are clearly regarded as authoritative. It would be almost unthinkable to establish a commission of scholars to rewrite the Constitution in more modern English, even though certain parts of it have become difficult for citizens to understand. Not surprisingly, therefore, the archaic vocabulary and grammar of authoritative older texts continues to exert great influence on contemporary legal language.

A related reason for not modernizing archaic legal texts is that specific words and phrases may have received authoritative interpretations over the years. Rewriting statutes and constitutions could wreak havoc with decades of court decisions that have clarified what those texts mean and how they are to be applied. This does not mean that legal texts cannot be modernized, but it does inspire caution.

Two further reasons for the conservatism of legal language are safety and convenience. In the legal sphere, the safest course of action is almost always to reuse the same worn phrasing time and again. As we will see later, jury instructions are often very difficult for jurors to comprehend. But judges keep reading the same tired instructions to the jury because it is safe. To paraphrase the instructions in more modern terms might invite a reversal by a higher court because of some perceived change in meaning. Likewise, if lawyers learn that a particular format and phrasing in a complaint has passed judicial scrutiny in the past, they will be extremely reluctant to deviate in the future. If it worked before, it should work again.

Not only is it deemed safer, but it is far more convenient and economical to keep recirculating the same forms. Over the years, law firms build up collections of documents that were drafted in the past and can serve as samples for the future. Moreover, published collections (form books) are available commercially. The result is that stilted language that may have been written decades or centuries ago is continually reincarnated, virtually without change, in modern legal documents.

Archaic language also seems particularly authoritative, perhaps even majestic. Using antiquated terminology bestows a sense of timelessness on the legal system, as something that has lasted through the centuries and is therefore deserving of great respect. Witness the British enactment clause. Somehow language that has withstood the test of time seems more potent and valuable than innovative phrasing. Few people know how much a *score* is these days, but the *four score and seven years* of Abraham Lincoln's Gettysburg Address has a ring to it that *87 years* clearly lacks.

Although lawyers are reluctant to admit it, archaic language also happens to help justify the profession's monopoly, an age-old theme that we encountered in previous chapters. Clients confronted with an impenetrable legal document have no choice but to seek the advice of a lawyer as interpreter, just as medieval clients sought out lawyers to translate Law French. Whether this is as strong a factor as in centuries past is hard to say. The law has become so complex in recent years that it would be foolhardy for most people to represent themselves in a complicated legal matter, even if legal language were as straightforward as could be. Still, many lawyers show little inclination to encourage self-helpers by modernizing legal vocabulary and making the law more accessible to the general public.

Linguistic Creativity

New Wine in New Bottles

Although there is plenty of archaic usage in legal contexts, the point should not be exaggerated. Lawrence Friedman has observed that most legal vocabulary is not especially ancient: "spendthrift trust" is only about one hundred years old, and "zoning" is very recent.[24] In fact, it is easy to add examples of innovative legal terminology to Friedman's list, some of very recent vintage. The development of securities law during the past half-century or so required the creation of a whole new vocabulary, including terms such as *antitrust, blue sky laws, poison pill, predatory pricing,* and *tying arrangement,* to name just a few. Innovations in the law of contracts, torts, and damages has led to the coining of neologisms like *cramdown, hedonic damages, lost volume seller, palimony, sexual harassment, toxic tort,* and *wrongful birth.* Lawyers now *Shepardize* cases and make sure the police have properly *Mirandized* their clients.

Even as lawyers create new vocabulary for novel areas of practice, old terms tend to die out with the obsolescence of the legal concepts to which they refer. Terminology relating to feudal property law has become obsolete along with feudalism itself. Words or phrases like *demesne, fee tail, fief, scutage, seisin,* and *subinfeudation,* to name just a few, have passed from the legal lexicon into the history books. Conversely, legal terms generally retain their vitality as long as the concepts to which they refer remain current. Much property terminology, such as the hoary Law French terms *chattel, fee simple, easement, estate,* or *reverter,* have proven quite durable. As long as the concept remains part of the law, the corresponding words are unlikely to disappear. Though these words may be ancient, they are not obsolete.

Asylees, Escapees, and Tippees

Another example of linguistic innovation in legal language is the frequent addition of the suffix *-ee* to a verb, primarily to indicate the human object of an action. As discussed previously, this trait ultimately derives from Law French. Although the process itself has a long history, words formed in this matter can be very creative.

Otto Jespersen notes that although the process began with legal language, it spread into ordinary speech. He cites examples such as *lovee, gazee, staree, cursee, laughee, flirtee, floggee, wishee,* and *callee,* all attested in various literary writings.[25] Yet today, ordinary language has retained only a few of these terms, virtually all derived from legal usage: *employee, referee,* and *trustee,* for instance. In legal language, on the other hand, the process is still quite vibrant.

Many *-ee* forms function as direct objects to refer to the person who is acted upon: *acquittee, arrestee, conscriptee, detainee, expellee, inauguree, indictee, invitee,* and *shelteree* are some examples. If *V* represents the verb, these words have the meaning "the person who is *V*-ed." Each can be paraphrased as a person who is acquitted, arrested, or conscripted.

Formations with *-ee* can also refer to the indirect object of an action ("the person to whom something is *V-ed*"): *allocatee, covenantee, grantee, indorsee, lessee, patentee, payee, pledgee, referee,* and *trustee.* Here, the paraphrase must include the preposition *to:* someone *to whom* something is allocated, covenanted, and so on.

Other formations are more idiosyncratic: *asylee* (someone who seeks asylum, not the person who is "asyled"); *condemnee* (someone whose property has been condemned, not someone who has been condemned); *discriminatee* (a person discriminated against); *escapee* (someone who escapes, not the person who is escaped from); *tippee* (a person who is tipped off); *abortee* (a woman who has an abortion, not the aborted fetus); *optionee* (a person against whose interests someone else has an option).

All of these forms are attested in Bryan Garner's *Dictionary of Modern Legal Usage,* though they vary in acceptability, even within the profession. Yet they illustrate that while some legal language may be archaic, other usage is extremely innovative.

Frequently *-ee* words come in matched pairs: *mortgagor/mortgagee, trustor/trustee, bailor/bailee, employer/employee,* and so forth. The *-or* word typically indicates the actor, and hence has more of an active sense, while the *-ee* word refers to the recipient of the action, and thus has more of a passive sense. For example, the *mortgagor* is the person who mortgages property (i.e., the borrower of a loan), just as the *lessor* is the person who leases real estate to someone else (i.e., the landlady). In contrast, the *mortgagee* is the person to whom the property is mortgaged (i.e., the bank), and the *lessee* is the person to whom real estate is leased (i.e., the tenant). Obviously, a drawback to these sets of words is that people—including lawyers sometimes—find it hard to remember which is which. Just who is the *lessor* and who is the *lessee?*

Despite some stylistically questionable formations, words created with *-ee* are very functional. Being able to refer to the *assignee,* instead of having to say *the person to whom an obligation has been assigned,* promotes an economy of expression that justifies retaining this means of word formation. Of course, these words are mainly useful when they fill a lexical gap (as in *assignee,* for which there is no term in ordinary language). When ordinary English has a word for a concept, there is no need to create neologisms. Thus, the more common term *tenant* is preferable to *lessee,* especially when dealing with nonlawyers.

Occasionally the French *-ee* form (originally a past participle) is replaced by the English equivalent, as in *the insured.* In ordinary English such words typically have generic or collective reference and take a plural verb: *the insured are quite lucky these days.*[26] In legal usage, by contrast, *the insured* functions as a singular noun that refers to an individual (*the insured is required to give notice of any claim within 10 days*). In fact, legal usage allows such words to be pluralized (*the injureds*), and they can even be used as possessives. One case not too long ago commented on *an insured's right to rely on the provisions of this policy.*[27] Although they derive from past participles, therefore, these words now act as regular nouns. Other past participles that lawyers use as ordinary nouns include *the accused, the deceased,* and *the condemned.*

Legal language is an odd mixture of very archaic features, on the one hand, and quite innovative usage, on the other. To some it may seem rather schizophrenic. But perhaps this is no more odd than seeing conservatively dressed lawyers in a baroque courtroom, advancing highly creative and pathbreaking arguments about privacy on the World Wide Web.

Formal and Ritualistic Language

Formal and ritualistic language is another trait of the legal lexicon. Such language tends to be archaic as well, although it need not be.

In the courtroom, verbal formulas and ritualistic words put the audience on notice that this is a proceeding with important consequences. And as linguist Robin Lakoff has noted, the formality of the courtroom reminds participants that this is an adversarial setting. Furthermore, ritualistic language helps frame the proceeding, marking its beginning and end. Signaling the start of the session is the talismanic cry of the bailiff: *Oyez, oyez, oyez* or *Hear ye, hear ye, hear ye,* followed by an invocation for all to rise. The ritualistic administration of the oath to witnesses and jurors, and their placement in boxes that separate them from the outside world, only heightens this otherworldly impression. Lakoff concludes that we should not be too quick to abolish ceremony and formality, "since we *want* the courtroom to be hallowed, to be set aside."[28]

The architecture of courthouses reinforces the message of solemnity and significance. When Iceland recently built a new home for its Supreme Court in Reykjavik, the architects, Steve Christer and Margrét Harðardóttir, designed what must be one of the most modernistic courthouses in the world. Nonetheless, the interior of the building radiates "an imposing, solemn atmosphere." As the architects put it: "This is the final point in the Icelandic judicial system. Here people go free, pay a fine or go to jail. We designed a place that respected the scale of the seriousness, without using the ubiquitous dark mahogany."[29] Many courts still favor the wood paneling, but the message is the same.

The ritualistic language and ceremonies of the courtroom have much in common with a religious service, and serve much the same purpose. The rituals and archaic language indicate that this is a special occasion, quite different from ordinary discourse. The formal and unusual clothing of the main participants—the vestments of the priests, or the robes and wigs of the judges—reinforce the impression that this is a solemn occasion and add an aura of authority to the proceedings. The separation from everyday life is also stressed by the behavior of observers, who are expected to show the proper respect by remaining silent under most circumstances, and by wearing appropriate attire. Indeed, in a courthouse this respect can be enforced by the judge's contempt power.

Many written legal documents also have an extremely formal quality, an impression often intensified by archaic words and grammar. Pleadings to the court typically begin with the phrase *Comes now plaintiff. . . .* Likewise, such documents often end with equally ritualistic words, as when a complaint finishes with the prayer for relief: *Wherefore, plaintiff prays for relief as follows. . . .* When responding, the defendant may conclude with the words: *Wherefore, defendant prays that plaintiff take nothing by reason of his complaint.* An affidavit, even today, often ends with the formulaic phrase: *Further affiant sayeth not.*

As in the courtroom, the most formal or ritualistic parts of a legal document or speech event tend to occur at the start and the finish. This is consistent with their function of separating the ordinary from the legal. Once again, ritualistic language creates a frame around the document, marking its beginning and its end.[30]

Private legal documents may also be quite formal in tone. Perhaps the best example is a will, which stereotypically bears the redundant title *Last Will and Testament* and starts out with a ritualistic provision such as the following:

> I Arnold Johnson a resident of Mesa Arizona of Maricopa County, State of Arizona, being of sound and disposing mind and memory, do make, publish and declare this my last WILL AND TESTAMENT, hereby revoking and making null and void any and all other last Wills and Testaments heretofore by me made.[31]

The will typically ends on an equally formal note, with a signature and formal attestation by witnesses. A contemporary will can be found in appendix C.

The conspiracy theory would suggest that lawyers employ highly stilted, formal, and redundant legal prose to create the impression that drafting legal documents is far more complex than it really is. The apparent fear among lawyers is that clients would no longer purchase their services if they were aware that a perfectly valid will could start out with the simple sentence *I, Arnold Johnson, of Mesa, Arizona, declare that this is my will.* If necessary, Mr. Johnson could add *I revoke any previous will.* To quote Bentham (the ultimate conspiracy advocate with regard to legal language) if you strip away the jargon, "every simpleton is ready to say—What is there in all that? 'Tis just what I should have done myself."[32]

Yet while formal legal language is normally not essential for a valid legal document, it may nonetheless have a function. Many documents, especially when they are informal and written by the parties themselves, raise doubts about whether the person intended to make a binding legal commitment, or was instead expressing a vague intent to do so in the future. Consider Aunt Mable, who writes a letter to her nephew, stating that *I want you to have my antique dresser when I die,* and signs the letter. In many American jurisdictions, this could potentially be a valid holographic (handwritten) will. Yet courts would have serious concerns about whether Auntie had what is called **testamentary intent.** Did she really intend this letter to be a will? Or was she just informing her nephew that this is what she planned to do at a later date, when she consulted a lawyer to draw up her will?

As in the courtroom, formal and ritualistic language in wills and similar documents can signal to the parties that this is a legal act with significant consequences. Gulliver and Tilson have called this the **ritual function** of the formalities surrounding the execution of certain legal documents. As they put it:

> The formalities of transfer therefore generally require the performance of some ceremonial for the purpose of impressing the transferor with the significance of his statements and thus justifying the court in reaching the conclusion, if the ceremonial is performed, that they were deliberately intended to be operative.[33]

This is similar to Lon Fuller's **cautionary function.**[34]

Even though formal legal language may serve some purpose, we should ponder whether that goal might not be carried out just as well by some other means, one that does less injury to the goal of clear communication. After all, use of formal legal prose creates documents that those most affected—the testator or the parties to the contract—may not understand very well. The fact that something is an operative legal document can be signaled in a different way. To stay with the example of wills, the title of the document (*Last Will and Testament*) should give adequate warning that this is a legally binding document, especially after the testator has signed it in the presence of two witnesses. The same holds for documents with the words *contract* or *lease* at the top; anyone who signs one should not be surprised that it is a legally enforceable contract or lease.

Taken to extremes, the language of lawyers can be so formal as to become pretentious. When a judge declares to parties who have argued a motion that she will *take it under submission,* what she really means is *I'll think it over.* Similarly, American lawyers seem incapable of *telling* their clients anything. Invariably, they *advise* them that, for example, a deposition has been rescheduled to the next day. Maybe lawyers feel uncomfortable charging their clients for "telling" them things; they seem less inhibited about billing for "advice." In fact, American attorneys seldom *say* anything to anyone; they almost invariably *indicate* (*I indicated to opposing counsel that the settlement offer was inadequate*). Although the Latinate *indicate* has a fancy ring, it can refer to a wide variety of suggestions, insinuations, gestures, and so forth. Anglo-Saxon *say* is less pretentious and more accurate if the person actually *said* something.

Overall, the pompous tone of much legal language derives from the overuse of relatively unusual words, often of Latin origin, where a more common word would suffice: *approximately* for *around,* *commence* or *initiate* for *begin,* *desist* for *stop,* *employ* for *use,* *expedite* for *hasten,* *necessitate* for *require,* *present* for *give,* *prior* for *earlier,* *request* for *ask,* and *terminate* for *end,* to list just a small sampling.

As we will see later in this book, efforts have recently been made to reduce unnecessary formality and pompousness in legal documents. Yet not all lawyers have jumped on board. Some now have decided that rather than remedy the defect, they will simply disclose it. Thus, forms sold by a prominent American legal publisher suggest adding the following clause at the beginning of a will:

> I trust that the formal terminology in this Will and the absence of personal messages will not cause you to doubt my affection for you. You are well aware of that affection. A Will is a legal instrument, the purpose of which is to dispose of property. . . .[35]

As with any defective product, however, disclosure of a linguistic defect is no substitute for fixing the problem.

Do and Shall

Two of the more common words in the legal lexicon are the auxiliary verbs *do* and *shall*. Both are used in an unusual and somewhat archaic sense.

Ordinarily, *do* can function as a main verb (*do this for me*). It is used in certain types of questions (*do you want to go home?*) and negative sentences (*I do not understand you*). *Do* is occasionally used in declarative sentences, but typically only to add emphasis: *I DO like ice cream!* Furthermore, *do* in declarative sentences tends to implicitly contrast with the negative proposition that I *do not* like ice cream.

In legal writing, *do* often appears in declarative sentences, but not with the emphatic or contrastive sense that it has in ordinary speech. Rather, it frequently indicates that the following main verb creates or modifies legal institutions or relations. Consider the preamble to the United States Constitution:

> We the people of the United States . . . *do* ordain and establish this Constitution for the United States of America.

The same usage is reflected in many enactment clauses, which give legal force to the statute or statutes that follow them:

> The People of the State of California, represented in Senate and Assembly, *do* enact as follows. . . .

Do in cases such as these marks the verbs as being what are called **performatives.** It is similar to *hereby*, which also signifies that the following verb is actually performing an operative legal act. Performatives are quite common in legal language because they allow a person to create or modify a state of affairs simply by saying so. Thus, sincerely saying *I hereby promise* (or in legalese: *I do promise*) constitutes the act of promising. In contrast, saying *I promised him yesterday* (where it is impossible to add *hereby*) is simply talking about promising, not doing it. As J. L. Austin has written, *hereby* "is a useful criterion that the utterance is performative."[36] The same purpose is sometimes fulfilled in writing by the term *by these presents*, which is short for *by the present writing*.[37]

Thus, *do* (in the present tense) often fulfills the same function as *hereby*. When the legislature says or writes *we do enact* or *we hereby enact* (and assuming other aspects of the ritual are performed), it is actually enacting something into law merely by uttering those words. Out of caution or habit, lawyers sometimes use both markers of performativity:

> I *do hereby* nominate, constitute and appoint my husband, Vasil Pavlinko, as Executor of this my Last Will and Testament.[38]

Whether *do* (or even *hereby*) is necessary here is questionable. Normally, it should suffice to write: *I appoint my husband, Vasil Pavlinko, to be my executor.* Only where it is unclear that a verb is a performative does it make sense to add *hereby*.

Another feature of the legal lexicon is the modal verb *shall*. In ordinary English, *shall* typically expresses the future. It is traditionally used only in the first person (*I shall* and *we shall*); elsewhere, *will* is preferred (*you will, she will*). In American English, *shall* has become virtually obsolete, so that the sole future modal verb is *will*.

It is commonly asserted that in legal language, *shall* does not indicate futurity, but is instead employed to express a command or obligation, and can thus be paraphrased with *must*. To some extent this is true. Under California law, someone who qualifies as a sex offender *shall* register with the chief of police or sheriff within a specified time.[39] This use of *shall* is obviously not so much a prediction of a future event as the imposition of an obligation on the offender to register.

Yet *shall* is not restricted to commanding. It can also make declarations:

> This Act *shall* be known as The Penal Code of California. . . .[40]

It seems odd to say that the legislature is requiring that the populace *must* refer to this Act as *The Penal Code of California*. Could someone be thrown in prison for calling it the *California Penal Code* or even the *Criminal Code*? Clearly, this is not a command!

Nor is *shall* limited to legislation; it may, for instance, express the terms of a contract:

> The Publisher *shall* pay the Author . . . an advance . . . which *shall* be a charge against all sums accruing to the Author under this Agreement. . . .[41]

The first *shall* in this contract sets forth one of the mutual set of promises that the parties make to each other in the agreement. It is best paraphrased by *promises to* or *will*. The second *shall* is either part of that same promise, or perhaps a type of declaration. In any event, neither is a command.

It should be plain that *shall* does more than merely indicate obligation. Its function seems to depend on the type of document in which it occurs. Generally, however, *shall* indicates that the verb and phrase that follow are part of what is being enacted, promised, and so forth. Consequently, legal documents have at least one performative, express or implied, that indicates the overall force of the document: enacting (a statute), promising (a contract), and so forth. That which is being enacted or promised is indicated by *shall.* The overall structure of a publishing contract can be represented as follows:

> The Author and Publisher *hereby promise* each other the following:
>
> 1. the Author *shall prepare* and *deliver* . . .
> 2. the Publisher *shall publish* . . .
> 3. the Publisher *shall pay* . . .

Statutes work in roughly the same way.

Shall has another function: it unambiguously indicates that something is intended to be legally binding. As Frederick Bowers has noted, *shall* is generally "used as a kind of totem, to conjure up some flavour of the law."[42] That may be the real reason for its pervasiveness in legal language.

Jargon, Argot, and Technical Terms

Legal language contains a large number of words that are not used at all in ordinary speech, or are used in a different sense. Critics dismissively characterize most of this vocabulary as **argot** or **jargon,** both of which tend to have a negative connotation. Lawyers, in contrast, praise the many precise **terms of art** in their lexicon. While this might seem to be merely a question of semantics, the vocabulary of the law is actually a very important issue.

Several writers have claimed that the legal lexicon consists of a great deal of argot. One such writer is Mellinkoff, who uses the term to refer to a specialized language, or means of communication within a group, whether or not intended to exclude strangers.[43] Mellinkoff contrasts argot with technical terminology, which is far more precise. These days, linguists tend to use the term in a more restricted sense, referring to a secret language through which a group intends to obscure communication. This usage harks back to the origins of the word, which was first used in French sources to refer to the clandestine language of beggars and street merchants.[44]

In certain respects legal English is indeed an argot. The lengthy retention of Law French, as well as impenetrable legal English, was surely motivated in part to obscure communication, compelling clients to hire lawyers as translators. On the other hand, it is too cynical to conclude that the legal profession uses legal language *primarily* to make its conversations unintelligible to outsiders. Lack of comprehensibility seems more an incidental—albeit fortuitous—byproduct of other forces, as we saw in part 1.

Much of what Mellinkoff characterizes as argot is really what we would today call **jargon:** the vocabulary of a trade, occupation, or profession.[45] The phrase *technical term* (or *term of art*) and *jargon* are closely related, and often linguists use them interchangeably. One way of distinguishing them is to posit that a technical term or term of art should have a relatively precise meaning. I will use "jargon" as a broader category that encompasses more than precise technical terms. Any words or phrases that are commonly and fairly exclusively used by a profession or trade— even if relatively vague—can be labeled jargon. Examples of legal jargon that are probably not terms of art include *arguendo, black-letter law, boilerplate, case at bar, case on point* or *case on all fours, chilling effect, conclusory, decedent, grandfather clause, hypothetical* (used as a noun, as in *a good hypothetical is hard to find*), *instant case, judge-shopping, predecease, sidebar,* and numerous others. Some of this jargon is useful in providing a single word where otherwise an entire phrase would be necessary, or where there is no term at all. A good example is *conclusory,* in reference to an allegation or statement that suggests a particular conclusion without expressly justifying the result, or *judge-shopping* in the sense of trying to file a lawsuit with a judge who is likely to be sympathetic to your cause. Such terms are far too handy to abandon.

An interesting and utilitarian type of legal jargon is the tendency to refer to a rule or doctrine by the name of the case that established it. Consider an *Allen charge,* a *Mary Carter agreement,* a *Miranda warning,* a *Terry Stop,* or a *Totten trust.*[46] These examples show, once more, that the legal lexicon can be very creative when the need arises, and that it can greatly facilitate in-group communication.

Jargon is more objectionable when it serves mainly to suggest that the speaker or writer is a member of the legal fraternity. All too often, "talking like a lawyer" seems to be its only function. Some illustrations of useless jargon are *indicate* to mean "say" (*I indicated to the judge . . .*) or *implicate* for "relates to" or "invokes" (*Plaintiff's argument implicates the First Amendment*). In such cases, ordinary English would do just as well. Furthermore, when the audience consists of the lay public, jargon should be studiously avoided. What facilitates in-group communication necessarily impedes communication with others.

As noted above, jargon is closely related to **technical terms;** the distinction is mainly one of degree. One of the most striking features of legal English is its technical terminology. Such terms have an important function for any profession, of course. For one thing, a phrase like *cy pres* allows for more efficient communication by encapsuling in two short words what might otherwise take an entire paragraph to explain. And technical terms are useful because they often have a fairly precise definition. Even Mellinkoff, normally a stern critic of legal jargon, admitted that there is "a small area of relative precision in the language of the law—mostly terms of art."[47]

Some experts on legal language have suggested that, despite appearances, the law actually has very few real terms of art.[48] Yet these scholars probably have too narrow a view of the nature of a technical term. If a word or phrase is used exclusively by a particular trade or profession, or if the profession uses it in a way that differs from its normal meaning, and the term has a relatively well-defined sense, it should be considered a technical term. An absolutely fixed and precise meaning is not essential, nor is it usually attainable.

Anyone who wants an idea of the extent of legal terminology need only skim through a law dictionary. Bear in mind, however, that an unabridged legal dictionary contains an awful lot of obsolete vocabulary that is purely of interest to historians. How often does a modern lawyer have to look up Anglo-Saxon or feudal legal concepts, such as *frank-ferm* ("a species of estate held in socage")?[49] Still, even without archaisms, the legal vocabulary is substantial.

Not only does the law have many technical terms, but the legal subdisciplines have their own terminology, and sometimes a term can differ in meaning according to specialty. *Libel* in tort law refers to a type of defamation. The same word means something quite different in admiralty law: to bring an action against a ship. Thus, the meaning of *to libel a ship* could depend on whether it is being used in admiralty or tort.

As in many other fields, legal terms of art may arise through usage or convention. Of course, usage can change over time and from place to place. In fact, even at the same time and in the same place, lawyers may use legal terminology in slightly different ways. The result is that technical legal terms are not immune from the vagueness and ambiguity inherent in ordinary English. Incidentally, this was one of the justifications for the long retention of Law French. Because it was no longer a spoken language, it was felt to be resistant to vagaries in usage that beset every living language.

Although their terminology is not as exact as lawyers believe, critics tend to underestimate its usefulness and precision. It is unrealistic to expect the legal vocabulary to achieve the exactitude of the scientific lexicon. Scientific language is often quite precise because the concepts or categories themselves are well defined. The scientific community seems to agree, for the most part, on the definition of terms like *centimeter* and *photosynthesis*. Unfortunately, legal vocabulary tends to refer to legal and social institutions that change frequently, which results in the meaning of associated terminology changing as well. The content of a term like *negligence* will change depending on the era, the society, and the norms established by its legal system.

Furthermore, most exact sciences are international in scope, sharing common assumptions and vocabulary that transcend political borders. *Oxygen* can be directly translated into German as *Sauerstoff,* with minimal loss in meaning. Legal systems, by comparison, are highly parochial. Each of the fifty American states is a separate jurisdiction, with its own laws, court system, and bar. Precise language is possible only when there is a unified speech community that consistently uses a term in the same way. With such splintered jurisdictions, attaining agreement on the exact use of legal terminology is close to impossible. Because each jurisdiction has a somewhat different view of the law of negligence, the word *negligence* cannot have one absolutely precise meaning throughout the English-speaking world. Despite these difficulties, words like *negligence* are clearly technical legal terms, in my view. *Negligence* says in one word what it would take at least a paragraph to explain. And despite some variation, its general meaning is well established.

There is another way that technical legal terminology can arise, or change over time. The law differs from most other fields in the degree to which technical terms are created not through usage, but by authoritative pronouncements of courts or legislatures. For example, *income* is a highly technical concept for tax purposes, and its meaning in this context has been extensively refined by the courts over the years.

It might seem that judicial decisions and statutory definitions would make the meaning of legal terminology more precise, especially compared to terms whose meaning depends on usage. There is some truth to this. But judicial interpretations can also muddy the waters by deviating from accepted legal usage, or even from ordinary usage. Judges have been known to interpret *and* as *or* (and *or* as *and*), even though the distinction between *A and B* and *A or B* is normally fairly clear.[50] Surely such interpretations undermine whatever precision inheres in the terms *and* and *or*. Why would a court do so? Very often, because the "precise" or "literal" legal meaning could not possibly be what the writer of the document intended. But by giving effect to the deviant usage of the writer in a published opinion, a court undermines the established meaning of the term.

An illustration is the term *issue,* widely used in wills. When a testator leaves her estate to her *issue,* the ordinary meaning of the term is her descendants, or anyone to whom she has contributed genetic material. Now suppose that one of her children was adopted. Clearly, that child is not *issue* in the ordinary meaning of the word. Yet many judges have ruled in published opinions that the term includes adopted children, often relying on indications that this is what the testator would have wanted, or policy reasons.[51] While this seems like the right thing to do, it has completely undermined any precision that the term *issue* might once have had.

The moral of this tale is that it might be possible for the law to have extremely precise technical terms. Law schools could spend more time teaching legal vocabulary. To maintain the clear meaning of those terms, judges would refuse to deviate from them. Yet even if this goal could be achieved, it would elevate form over substance, and legal meaning over the intentions of the speaker. For people who use a legal term of art in a way that differs from its "precise" meaning, it is a very good thing indeed that judges are increasingly willing to deviate from the literal meaning of a word, even though validating the aberrant usage undermines the precision of the term. Ultimately, the legal profession will have to acknowledge that its terminology—while obviously very useful—can never be as exact as it might hope or believe.

Relationships among Words

Words do not exist in a vacuum; they are related to each other in a variety of ways. Although legal language is like ordinary English in having synonyms, homonyms, etc., it sometimes modifies these relationships among words in interesting ways.

Homonyms

Homonyms are words that sound the same, but have different meanings. Examples are *to, too,* and *two,* which are all pronounced alike despite their divergent spellings. Homonyms need not be spelled differently, of course. Consider *sound,* which can be a part of the ocean, or a noise, or can be an adjective, as in *safe and sound.* All of these should probably be considered separate words. Sometimes a word has several different but related meanings; it is generally viewed as one word that is *polysemous,* rather than several separate homonymous words. *Crown,* which has—*inter alia*—the senses of a physical head ornament and the symbolic authority of the sovereign, is one polysemous word because its meanings are so closely related. But the distinction between homonymy and polysemy is not always easy to make, which shows that even in fields besides law, technical terms are seldom as precise as one might like.

One of the reasons that homonymy and polysemy are of interest to the law is that there are many words that have a legal meaning very different from their ordinary significance. In other words, a great deal of legal vocabulary looks like ordinary language, but has quite a distinct meaning; I call these **legal homonyms,** and they can easily engender confusion. While a strictly legal phrase like *cy pres* is plainly a term of art, legal homonyms seem like ordinary words but are not. They are hence potentially quite confusing for the uninitiated. Consider the sentence *I intend to file a complaint.* In ordinary language, this would mean simply that I will write my grievance on a piece of paper and give it to the proper authority. Legally, of course, it means that I plan to begin a lawsuit, which is a vastly more serious and costly threat. Some other legal homonyms:

> *Action:* not a physical movement, but a lawsuit.
> *Aggravation:* in death penalty law, not merely something that annoys you, but a reason to sentence someone to death.
> *Brief:* a noun referring to a type of legal document, not an adjective, and despite the name, virtually never brief.
> *Continuance:* the postponement of a proceeding until a later date; if a judge continues a hearing, it will not continue, but will stop and start up again later.
> *Motion:* a request that a court issue an order or engage in some other act; the only thing that moves is the lawyer's lips.
> *Notice:* formally notifying a person of something, as in giving notice of (or "noticing") a claim against that person. It is legally effective, as a rule, regardless of whether anybody actually notices it.

Party: someone who is part of a lawsuit, which despite the name is usually not much fun. In any event, it often refers to a single person or entity, not a group.

Personal Property: property other than real property, including not only used clothing and furniture, but also automobiles and large trucks.

Plead: formally presenting one's case to a court, usually by way of complaint or answer. Actually pleading, in the sense of imploring or begging the court, is considered bad form.

Prayer: usually the last part of the pleading, in which the party requests the court to grant or deny the relief sought by the plaintiff. As with pleading, displays of emotion, as well as genuflection, should be avoided. On the other hand, subtly suggesting that the judge is omniscient has been known to work wonders.

Real property: land and the structures on it, as opposed to personal property (which—by implication—is not real).

Service: giving someone—usually the opposing party—a legal document, often to begin a lawsuit against that person. Serving a person in this sense is not really a service, so you should not expect a gratuity.

Strike: to delete something from the record, usually without physical force. The court reporter will put it in the record anyway, so the reader will know what was stricken.

This list is far from complete,[52] but despite its tongue-in-cheek nature, it should illustrate that legal homonyms can be confusing indeed. An amusing illustration occurred during a deposition:

Q: Mrs. Jones, is your appearance this morning pursuant to a deposition notice which I sent your attorney?
A: No, this is how I dress when I go to work.[53]

Unfortunately, other examples are less innocuous.

One of the great advantages of the continued use of French, especially after it died out as a living language in England, is that Law French terms were unambiguously legal. There would virtually never have been a serious dispute regarding whether a word was being used in a technical or ordinary sense. Now that the law is in English, courts are often confronted with the issue of whether a word should be given its ordinary or its technical legal meaning. Often it helps to consider, as some courts do, whether the document was written by a lawyer, in which case the technical legal usage should probably prevail, or by a layperson, who would most likely have intended the ordinary meaning.[54]

Synonyms

Synonyms are different words with the same meaning. For most speakers of English, the words *lawyer* and *attorney* mean exactly the same thing. Whether two words ever have completely identical meanings is debatable, of course; some people feel that *attorney* has a more prestigious ring to it than *lawyer*. My mother insists that I am an *attorney*, in contrast to *lawyers*, who—as everyone knows—chase after ambulances and fleece their clients.

The legal profession has a very schizophrenic attitude toward synonyms. On the one hand, legal language tends to avoid linguistic variety. In ordinary language, I might invite a guest into my humble *residence* and then ask what she thinks of my new *domicile*, using these terms synonymously. Yet in legal language, there is a principle that can be summarized as **same meaning, same form.** If a lawyer uses *residence* to refer to a particular concept or thing, she should consistently use the term *residence* thereafter, thus avoiding synonyms or near-synonyms like *domicile*. Legal drafters are expressly warned to avoid elegant variation.[55]

Yet the obsessive use of word lists by many lawyers seems to indicate a great love for synonyms, or at least, near-synonyms. Of course, there may be times when a long list of semantically related words may serve the useful function of "covering all the bases." In other situations, lawyers use lists of synonymous words for no good reason whatsoever, as in *rest, residue and remainder* and *give, devise and bequeath*. Additional illustrations include *aid and abet; due and owing; full faith and credit; goods and chattels; ordered, adjudged and decreed; mind and memory; null and void; possession, custody and control; right, title and interest; save and except; true and correct;* and so forth. Whatever subtle distinctions there may have been between these words at one time, those differences are irrelevant in today's legal world.

Some synonymous phrases of this kind, though redundant, have essentially become fixed expressions or idioms. The crucial issue is whether the idiom serves a function. Sometimes the idiom has come to acquire a meaning that the individual words do not. *Full faith and credit* is a technical term in American law that cannot be replaced by *full faith* or *full credit*. Others, such as *null and void*, might be justified as more emphatic than simply *void* (the same holds for *any and all* or *each and every*, as well as the oath to tell *the truth, the whole truth, and nothing but the truth*). In contrast, it is hard to imagine how *save and except* adds anything to *except*, or how *order, judge and decree* differs from simply *order*. These are, in the words of Mellinkoff, nothing more than "worthless doubling."[56]

Antonyms

Words may be semantically related in another way: as opposites. Words that have opposite meanings are generally called **antonyms.** To be more precise, antonyms have most semantic features in common, but typically differ in one critical respect. Thus, *black* and *white* are both adjectives that refer to color, and *hot* and *cold* both refer to temperature. These word pairs are closely related semantically, but they differ with respect to one property or feature. *Hot,* for example, refers to the presence of heat, and *cold* to its absence.

In legal usage many pairs of words are turned into antonyms, even though they have no such relationship in ordinary language. For example, the semantic fields of the words *speech* and *conduct* overlap to some extent in ordinary language, and they are certainly not antonyms. Indeed, *speech* may simply be a subset of *conduct*. Yet in legal language, especially when discussing the Free Speech Clause of the United States Constitution, courts distinguish between activities that are *speech* (which is protected by the Free Speech Clause) and *conduct* (which is not). In other words, the courts have turned *speech* and *conduct* into antonyms that no longer overlap.[57]

Another example from American constitutional law is the terms *taking* and *regulation*. If a government action regarding property is held to be a *taking*, then under the Fifth Amendment the government must provide compensation. If it is not a *taking*, it is deemed to be a mere *regulation* regarding the property, which does not require compensation. Although *taking* and *regulation* are hardly antonyms in ordinary speech, they have become so in this legal arena.

Conclusion

The legal lexicon differs in many ways from ordinary speech and writing. Each of these differences must promote the main goal of any language: clear and effective communication. Not surprisingly, archaic language is generally unnecessary and fails this test. Jargon and technical terminology are more problematic because they actually facilitate in-group communication while greatly reducing comprehension by the public. We will explore some solutions to this dilemma in part 4.

CHAPTER SEVEN

Interpretation and Meaning

Some of the most important questions in the law deal with meaning, especially the interpretation (or "construction") of documents like the Constitution, statutes, contracts, deeds, and wills. In many ways, interpreting a legal document is not that different from understanding any other writing. Yet there are some interesting, and very important, differences. This chapter addresses some of the ways in which legal and ordinary language interpretation differ.

Definitions

We normally think of definitions as the stuff of dictionaries. Yet the quest for precision, along with a desire to reduce the length of documents, has led to a growing dependence on definitions in legal drafting, especially in formal written texts.

To set the stage, it is helpful to know that at one time, dictionaries were viewed as providing guidance on how words *ought* to be used. Thus a verb like *intrigue* would be defined as "to engage in a covert plot," but would not contain the definition "to invoke interest," even though the latter definition is ubiquitous in actual speech and writing (as in *this article intrigues me*). The popular meaning did not appear in dictionaries because certain language experts considered it "wrong." Other commonly heard words and expressions, such as *ain't* or *finalize,* or words regarded as obscene, were not in the dictionary at all: these were simply not proper words of English. Such a dictionary is **prescriptive,** in that it attempts to prescribe or dictate language usage.

A more modern view of dictionaries is that they should be a repository of the knowledge that the speech community possesses about words. Such a dictionary is **descriptive,** because it describes actual usage by the speech community. This reflects the philosophy that the meaning of a term depends entirely upon how it is used, and cannot be dictated by an organization or the government.

The notion that usage determines meaning is hardly a novel concept in the legal world, at least in the United States. For instance, when Noah Webster approached Chief Justice John Marshall for an endorsement of his dictionary, Justice Marshall is reported to have refused, commenting that in America it was individuals rather than public bodies that dictate language use.[1] Similarly, in the English-speaking world, spelling is a matter of usage rather than legislation. No governmental agencies mandate how we ought to spell words, although there have been sporadic attempts to do so. President Theodore Roosevelt tried to have the Government Printing Office promote the simplified spelling of words like *tho, thru,* and *thoro,* but was rebuffed by Congress and finally limited his innovations to White House communications.[2] The law recognizes the importance of usage as well. The meaning of a contract term may depend on the **usage of the trade,** or on how the parties themselves used the term in the past (called **course of dealing** and **course of performance**).

Consistent with modern linguistic theory, current dictionaries do not try to dictate meaning; instead, they endeavor to describe how people actually use a word. This is the only sensible approach, of course. I mostly look up a word because I heard or read someone use it and do not know what she meant by it. I therefore need to know how people generally use the word, not how some self-proclaimed expert believes people *ought* to use it.

In contrast, a legal definition—for example, in a statute or contract—resembles the prescriptive practices of bygone eras, because it dictates how the word ought to be used in that statute or contract. The difference is that statutory definitions *are* authoritative. The editors of a dictionary do not have the power to tell me how to speak; they cannot mandate that I use the word *intrigue* in a particular sense. But a legislature does have the authority to declare that a specific term used in a piece of legislation shall be understood in a particular way. Thus, for purposes of the Consumer Legal Remedies Act, California law defines a *person* as "an individual, partnership, corporation, limited liability company, association, or other group, however organized."[3] From a descriptive standpoint, this is nonsense. No self-respecting lexicographer would deign to define *person* in these terms. Speakers normally use *person* to refer to an individual, which in certain respects is the exact opposite of a corporation, association, or group. Yet it would be futile for a lawyer to argue to a court that, based upon common usage, an association is not a *person* under this act. Although the legislature cannot change the ordinary meaning of *person,* it does have the power to define the term for purposes of its legislation. As some courts have put it: "The legislature may act as its own lexicographer."[4]

I will call this a **declaratory definition.** How the word is actually used is not dispositive and is arguably irrelevant. What matters is the meaning that is given to it by declaration, usually within a limited context.[5] "[C]ommon law and dictionary definitions must yield when the legislature, by express enactment, defines its own terms."[6]

While declaratory definitions are ubiquitous in statutes, they occur as well in contracts and other operative legal documents. Actually, declaratory definitions are found not just in legal texts, but can be part of ordinary speech as well. Just as a lawmaking body is entitled to declare how certain of its words are to be taken, a speaker of English can sometimes assert a degree of authority over her own language use, at least for limited purposes. Thus, someone who writes a book or makes a scholarly presentation could declare that when she uses the term *convention,* she is doing so in a very specific sense. Or a mathematician could define X to refer to a particular number. Nonetheless, few fields use declaratory definitions anywhere nearly as much as the law.

Many lawyers follow an informal convention that defined terms should thereafter be marked by capitalizing the first letter, or by printing the word in bold type, to warn readers that the term has been given an authoritative definition. In fact, one court—called upon to interpret the word *work* in an agreement—gave the word its ordinary meaning, ignoring arguments that *work* was specifically defined elsewhere in the document. It did so primarily because the relevant instance of *work* was not capitalized, and thus did not invoke the definition in the contract.[7]

Properly used, declaratory definitions may promote precision by making explicit which of various possible meanings a word has in a particular legal document. The above definition of *person* makes it plain that a legal meaning is intended, rather than the ordinary usage of the word. Similarly, the word *record* could refer to an account of a judicial proceeding, a disk containing music that can be played on a phonograph, and so forth. When this lexical item occurs in the California Information Practices Act of 1977, however, it is declared to have only one specific meaning:

> any file or grouping of information about an individual that is maintained by an agency by reference to an identifying particular such as the individual's name, photograph, finger or voice print, or a number or symbol assigned to the individual.[8]

Other logical meanings of the word, like "phonograph record" or "a record of a court proceeding," can thus be eliminated when interpreting this act.

Declaratory definitions furthermore can minimize problems caused by overly vague or flexible terms. We observed previously that the terms *indecent* and *obscene* are quite broad and relatively indeterminate. This can create problems if these words are contained in criminal statutes, which may be so vague that they fail to properly warn people how to comply or give law enforcement officers too much discretion in carrying out the law.[9] Such concerns must have inspired the highly contorted definition of *buttocks* in a Florida ordinance aimed at reducing the amount of exposed flesh in establishments featuring nude or nearly nude dancers. To require dancers to *cover* their *buttocks*, without more, would only invite them to skirt the rule by wearing the skimpiest covering possible, leaving virtually nothing to the imagination. The county thus deemed it prudent to define *buttocks* as precisely as possible:

> the area at the rear of the human body (sometimes referred to as the gluteus maximus) which lies between two imaginary lines running parallel to the ground when a person is standing, the first or top of such lines being one-half inch below the top of the vertical cleavage of the nates (i.e., the prominence formed by the muscles running from the back of the hip to the back of the leg) and the second or bottom line being one-half inch above the lowest point of the curvature of the fleshy protuberance (sometimes referred to as the gluteal fold), and between two imaginary lines, one on each side of the body (the outside lines), which outside lines are perpendicular to the ground and to the horizontal lines described above and which perpendicular outside lines pass through the outermost point(s) at which each nate meets the outer side of each leg. . . .[10]

The county may have had the best of intentions, but it is far from certain that this definition makes the ordinance easier to understand and obey. Done properly, however, definitions can at least reduce the indeterminacy of an otherwise vague term.

The *buttocks* example illustrates some of the hazards of definitions. A statute can be made to appear relatively short and simple through this means, as in *no person shall expose his or her buttocks in public*. Yet hidden within this deceptively straightforward statute may be a term with a horribly long and convoluted definition, without which the statute cannot be properly understood.

Legal definitions can, in addition, be misused or simply confusing.

This is especially problematic when words seem to have a plain meaning, but are aberrantly defined. Thus, the New Zealand Poultry Act of 1968 declared *day old poultry* to be "any poultry of an age of 72 hours or less"![11] Likewise, an American statute defines an *employer* as a "person . . . who has fifteen or more employees."[12] Someone who employs fourteen people is not an *employer* under this act! And Puerto Ricans might be pleasantly surprised—or outraged—to discover that their island has been defined as a "state" in a federal statute.[13] The British Parliament at one point coined its own word, *patrial,* and then defined it as a person with the right of abode in the United Kingdom.[14] A few intrepid courts have refused to follow a statutory definition that deviates too much from the ordinary meaning of the term, or that seems to contradict the evident purpose of the law,[15] but most seem to have no serious objections.

Another type of legal definition is what I will call **incorporating definitions.** These so-called "definitions" do not define a term at all. Nor do they necessarily promote precision. Rather, they allow the drafter to remove long portions of text from the operative part of the legal document and place it in a separate definitions section. To create the full text, the reader must find the definition and incorporate it into the operative language. Typically, incorporating definitions do not state that a term *means* this or that, but that it *includes* the listed items.

For instance, American lawyers often request documents from the other party, something they can do before a trial begins. They typically want to be as all-inclusive as possible, requesting everything that could conceivably contain writing, graphic images, or any other representation of speech or thought. Consequently, a formal request for documents (directed to an opposing party in litigation) may begin with a long and tedious definition of *document:*

> As used herein, the word "document" shall mean and include any and all letters, correspondence, memoranda, notes, working papers, bills, daily diaries, schedules, tape recordings, computer prints, any computer readable medium, reports, books, contracts, ledgers, logs, schedules, invoices, computations, projections, photographs, drawings, schematics, designs, tabulations, graphs, charts, drafts or revisions of any nature whatever, together with any attachments thereto or enclosures therewith, including the original, identical copies reproduced in any manner, and nonidentical copies thereof.

Incorporating definitions clearly shorten the actual document requests by eliminating the need to repeat this verbose list. The lawyer can now request another party to produce *any document* on subject A, *any document* on subject B, and so forth, rather than having to request *any letters, correspondence, memoranda, notes, working papers, bills,* etc., on subject A, *any letters, correspondence, memoranda, notes, working papers, bills,* etc., on subject B, ad nauseam. Bentham endorsed this function of definitions and "abbreviative words" as a remedy for long-windedness. He suggested that they be used in legal language like the variables x and y in mathematics.[16]

Of course, it is dangerous to bury too much of the substance of the text in the definition. It enables a legal document to become extremely long and complex, while appearing deceptively simple. And readers may not suspect that so much of the essence of a statute is contained in what appear to be innocuous definitions. The Canadian expert on statutory interpretation, E. A. Driedger, opposed the use of what I call incorporating definitions, arguing that definitions should not contain substantive matters of law, which tended to clutter them up and make the law hard to find.[17] Like so many other tools of the legal drafter, definitions are a powerful instrument that must be used with care.

With increasing reliance on computers, the issue of definitions may be greatly simplified. Computer programs and much information on the Internet currently use **hypertext** linking.[18] This allows a word or phrase to be linked to some other text in a different location. Like capitalizing defined terms, an item with a hypertext link appears on the screen in another color or font. The user accesses the linked information by clicking on the highlighted word. When statutes are authoritatively published in computerized form, it will be easy to mark all defined terms with a distinct font or color, and just as easy for the reader to access the definition through the click of a mouse. No doubt this will create its own unforeseen complications, but many of the present problems with definitions should disappear.

Reference

The distinction between **sense** and **reference** is attributed to the philosopher Gottlob Frege. *Sense* is roughly equivalent to *meaning*. Thus, using Frege's famous illustration, *the Morning Star* has a sense that can be paraphrased as "the star that appears in the morning." Its referent, on the other hand, is the planet Venus.[19]

Reference is critical in many areas of the law. The law of trademarks is largely about reference. To be effective, a trademark must refer unambiguously to the maker of a product. If I have a valid trademark for *Peter's*

Hamburger Shoppe, and a rival begins marketing the same product under the name *Pete's Burger Shop,* my loyal consumers may become confused. In other words, the referential link between my trademark and my product may become weak or ambiguous; to prevent this from occurring, I may be able to enjoin Pete's use of a confusingly similar name. In real life we often have to learn to live with the misunderstandings that arise when there are two Petes in the same group. Trademark law aims to avoid such referential confusion by allowing the first Pete to prevent anyone else from using the name.

Likewise, a will must refer as clearly as possible to the recipients of a testator's largesse, as well as to what each beneficiary should receive. A great deal of litigation arises from ambiguous referring expressions. In one case, for example, a man left a legacy to the *National Society for the Prevention of Cruelty to Children.*[20] Unfortunately, there were two different societies with essentially the same name, and the court was left to decide which one the will referred to.

At least with wills, courts seem aware of the distinction between sense and reference. Courts are traditionally hesitant to allow extrinsic evidence regarding the sense, or meaning, of a term in a will. Thus, if the issue is the meaning of the word *wife,* which seems to have a fairly well established, or "plain," meaning, courts may not allow evidence of whether the testator means "person to whom one is legally married" or instead the "person whom one treats as a wife." In an Ontario case, a court held that *wife* plainly means "legally married spouse" (whom the testator had abandoned), ignoring extrinsic evidence that the testator used the term in a looser sense for the person he factually treated as his wife.[21] On the other hand, courts more readily allow evidence on the reference of the term *wife;* in other words, if I give the remainder of my estate *to my wife,* without naming her, they will invariably look outside the will to determine who my wife is and give her the property.

Because ambiguity of reference can present serious problems, lawyers go out of their way to make it as precise as possible. Use of *said* and *aforesaid* is one such attempt; as we saw above, it simply does not promote more accurate reference. In contrast, what is called the "legal" description of real property, despite its terribly arcane language, almost certainly makes reference to plots of land relatively exact. References to people, who may share a name with someone else, are made more determinate by using as full a name as possible and adding ancillary information, such as the person's profession, age, and residence.

Legal documents also make frequent use of what I will call **declaratory**

reference, much like declaratory definitions. One can often refer to people and institutions by several different expressions. Indeed, we sometimes engage in elegant referential variation. A notorious example is Russian novels, which seem to switch almost randomly between calling a single character *Alexei* on one occasion, *Nikolayevich* on the next, and then *Romanov.* In a legal setting, this can be problematic when there are closely related but distinct entities, such as Hilda Garcia the individual, Hilda Garcia as general partner in the Hilda Garcia Partnership, and the Hilda Garcia Boutique, a retail establishment owned 51 percent by Hilda Garcia as an individual and 49 percent by the Hilda Garcia Partnership.

An older solution to this problem, at least in contracts, was to declare that one party was *the party of the first part,* another was *the party of the second part,* and so forth. This pompous habit was deliciously lampooned by the Marx Brothers in their film *A Night at the Opera.* Groucho, as Otis Driftwood, is trying to make a contract with Forelo (Chico), who represents an opera singer:

> Now, pay particular attention to this first clause because it's most important. Says the—uh—the party of the first part shall be known in this contract as the party of the first part. How do you like that? That's pretty neat, eh?[22]

Chico was not impressed, nor should we be. While intended to clarify reference, this system is horribly cumbersome. And some lawyers seem to feel that even this ponderous phrase is not sufficient, adding *said* for good measure (*the said party of the second part*).[23] Moreover, it is hard to remember which party is first, second, third, and so forth. Though they would seem a prime candidate for the trash heap of the law, Lawrence Solan reports that the terms *party of the first part, second part,* and so on, appeared in hundreds of contracts discussed in published legal opinions during the 1980s,[24] which almost certainly indicates that the phrases were actually used in many thousands of contracts in this period.

Much simpler is using names, which seems to be increasingly popular. But names can be ambiguous or confusing, as noted above, and names of businesses may be quite long. Hence the practice of *declaring* that Hilda Garcia, an individual residing in San Antonio, Texas, shall be referred to as *Garcia,* and that the Hilda Garcia Partnership shall be referred to as the *Garcia Partnership.* A shorter way of declaring reference is by parentheses: *Hilda Garcia, an individual ("Garcia")...*

Courts use declaratory reference for people and entities, as well as for case names. In judicial opinions parties may be "named" *Plaintiff* or *Defendant,* for example, with the result that these terms are used like names, without *the: Plaintiff sued Defendant for malicious prosecution.* Or a court may state that the lower court's opinion in *United States ex rel. Patterson v. Smith* will be known as *Smith I,* while the opinion of the appellate court in the same case will be *Smith II.*

Another issue with reference is that philosophers and linguists often distinguish between **referential** and **attributive** use of definite descriptions. Thus, *the fastest runner in Ohio* could refer to a specific, known individual, in which case the phrase would be used referentially. He could also be referred to as *John Smith* or—if his father is speaking—as *my son.* The same phrase can be used attributively: *the Fleet Feet Award is given annually to the fastest runner in Ohio.*[25] Here, *the fastest runner in Ohio* refers to whoever happens to meet the description at the relevant time.

This distinction is relevant to the law of wills. If I leave you *my car* in my will, am I referring to a specific car that I now own (referential), or whatever car I happen to own at my death (attributive)? It can make a big difference. If I am referring referentially to the specific car that I now own, and I later sell the car and buy a new one, you will get nothing when I die. At least in many common law jurisdictions, the gift of a particular car is a **specific legacy** that is **adeemed** (or **extinguished**) when I sell the car; in other words, the sale is treated as an implicit revocation of the gift. But if the reference is attributive, referring to whatever car I own at death, it is considered a **general legacy** that is not adeemed (or extinguished). In other words, you get my new car.[26] Similarly, do gifts to *my children* or *my secretary* refer specifically to my children or secretary at the time I write the will, or to whoever happens to fit those descriptions when I die? The type of reference is clearly quite significant.

Statutes are notable for their widespread use of attributive descriptions. Criminal laws are typically phrased to refer to *any person who does X* or *every person who does Y.* They apply to whoever comes within the description. Indeed, attributive descriptions seem to be almost inherent in public laws, which should apply evenly throughout the population, instead of singling out specific persons or groups for special treatment.[27]

Incidentally, a fascinating but highly dubious legislative trick occurs when a description in a statute is written to appear attributive but is in fact referential. For example, a legislator may have what seems to be a generally applicable tax bill enacted into law, whereas it actually turns out to benefit only one wealthy family that just happens to be one of his biggest contributors.[28]

Meaning

Meaning is obviously one of the most important issues in the law. A tremendous amount of judicial energy is devoted to interpreting the language of statutes, contracts, wills, and other legal documents. Meaning is also a central concern of linguists and other students of language. In this section we discuss how ordinary language interpretation, which is what linguists and philosophers study, relates to legal approaches to interpretation.

Experts on language have come to distinguish different types of meaning. One important kind is **word meaning.** Definitions concentrate on the meaning of words, based on how they are ordinarily used. For example, as speakers of English we know that *chair* often refers to an object for sitting on, is supported by four legs, and has a back rest. But it can also refer to objects that deviate from the prototypical chair; if it had five legs and a back rest, it would probably still be a chair, albeit an unusual one. Furthermore, *chair* is used in a figurative sense to refer to the head of a department or a committee, or to a particular type of professorship, among other possibilities.

Words can, of course, be combined into sentences, allowing us to speak of **sentence meaning.** To derive the sentence meaning, we consider the possible word meanings, as well as the grammatical relationships between the words. Often the context that a sentence provides allows us to provisionally eliminate some of the many possible word meanings. Thus, although *chair* can mean "chairman" in isolation, when it occurs in the sentence *Sandra sat on the chair,* its most likely interpretation is "something to sit on." On the other hand, in the sentence *the dean appointed Bill to be chair of the committee,* the meaning of *chair* is probably "chairman." By combining our knowledge of the possible meanings of the words with the linguistic rules for combining words into sentences, we can generally derive at least one—and often more—potential interpretation for any specific sentence. Very roughly speaking, the sentence meaning corresponds to what is called the **literal** meaning.

Yet what matters most is not the word or sentence meaning, but what the speaker intended to communicate by means of the utterance. This is called the **utterance meaning** or **speaker's meaning.**[29] When we speak of word or sentence meaning, we generally say that *this word/sentence means X.* On the other hand, with utterance or speaker's meaning, we would say that *Jane meant X in uttering this word or sentence.*

Of course, what Jane meant by the sentence—what she intended to communicate—is limited by the possible meanings of the words and the sentence. Without highly unusual circumstances, Jane cannot rationally intend to communicate "I bought a new typewriter" by saying *Sandra sat on the chair.*

To determine what Jane intends to communicate in saying *Sandra sat on the chair,* we begin by looking at the word and sentence meaning. But we also rely on the linguistic context, what we know about Jane and about Sandra and the chair, and any other information that might be relevant. If the conversation is about who sat where in a room with only one chair and a sofa, we will probably assume that Jane meant that Sandra rested her body on a type of furniture that had four legs and a backrest. On the other hand, suppose that the conversation is about a committee meeting that devolved into a fistfight, with Sandra knocking the chairman—Bill—to the floor. Now, if Jane tells us that *Sandra sat on the chair,* Jane might well mean that Sandra sat on Bill. Another scenario might involve a verbal slugfest in the committee, in which case Jane might well mean that Sandra metaphorically sat on the chairman, Bill, in the sense of figuratively overpowering him.

Assuming that language is mainly concerned with the communication of information and ideas, it should be evident that the ultimate question is the speaker's meaning. What matters is the speaker's communicative intentions, rather than just the meaning of her words and sentences. Word and sentence meaning are a means to an end—a way to figure out what the speaker intends to communicate.

Imagine that your friend Cheri gives you instructions on how to reach her house for a dinner engagement. The instructions state that after you pass Castillo Street, you are to *turn right at the next street.* You drive past Castillo street. The next possible turn to the right is a small lane going into a mobile home park, which provides access only to those mobile homes. Should you count this as the first *street,* or is it merely a *driveway?* The point is that the meaning of the word *street,* or the sentence *turn right at the next street,* will surely be helpful in deciding this question, but it is not the real issue. The ultimate issue is what Cheri meant by her instructions, because unless you figure this out, you will be late for the dinner party. Consequently, if you happen to know that Cheri has the eccentric habit of calling every little lane and driveway a *street,* you should count the lane into the mobile home park as the next street, because she probably meant it to be included. What she meant by her instructions is the only thing that matters if you wish to eat dinner before it turns stone cold.

Use of sarcasm or irony provides a similar illustration. Suppose that we go to an old Godzilla movie. You ask me afterwards what I thought of it, and I reply that *the special effects were terrific.* In fact, we are both well aware that the "special effects" consisted of enlarged shots of an ordinary lizard next to small plastic figures of people. Furthermore, I roll my eyes when making my comment. Obviously, the statement is ironic or sarcastic; what I really meant is the *opposite* of the literal meaning of the sentence. Again, the word or sentence meaning is only the beginning of the inquiry. If you want to know what I thought of the film, you have to determine the speaker's meaning: what I meant by my utterance.

Despite its prominence in ordinary communication, the role of the speaker's meaning is a problematic issue in legal interpretation. With private legal documents, like wills and contracts, it is well established that the intent of the testator or of the parties should govern the meaning. Thus, the speaker's meaning should prevail. Nonetheless, this general principle is undercut by severe limitations on the use of any evidence other than the words of the document itself, primarily imposed by the **plain meaning rule.** Although the rule has been stated in different ways over the centuries, it basically provides that if a document is plain or unambiguous, as determined solely from the language contained in the "four corners" of the document, a judge cannot refer to any outside ("extrinsic") evidence to decide what it means.[30] In other words, the sorts of factors that we would normally use to gauge the speaker's or writer's intent are inadmissible, and cannot be considered. The rule has the practical effect of focusing the court's attention on the meaning of words and sentences, rather than on the speaker's intent, even though that intent is legally what should decide the issue.

Similar questions arise with more public legal documents, such as statutes and constitutions. There is extensive debate in American courts on when, and to what extent, judges should consider legislative intent (the speaker's meaning) when interpreting statutes. Under the plain meaning rule, courts would look beyond the statutory language only when the text was ambiguous. There would, in other words, have to be more than one plausible sentence meaning before judges could look at evidence of the legislature's intent. In the words of Justice Holmes: "We do not inquire what the legislature meant; we ask only what the statute means."[31]

Over time, however, American judges began to refer almost routinely to evidence of legislative intent, including committee reports and speeches made on the floor. In other words, courts paid more attention to what the speaker—the legislature—meant by the words of a statute.

Recently, the pendulum may have begun to swing back. Justice Scalia of the United States Supreme Court has championed an approach called **textualism.** Scalia and others argue that legislative history should rarely be relevant, in essence advocating sentence meaning over speaker's meaning.[32] To be more exact, textualism claims that it does try to discover the intent of the legislature, but limits this inquiry to the text of the statute itself. Practically speaking, textualism must rely almost entirely on word and sentence meaning, which may explain why the Supreme Court so often consults dictionaries and why many of the canons of interpretation (like *expressio unius*) have been revived.[33] Only when the text is ambiguous will the textualist look to other indications of legislative intent. To a large extent, therefore, textualism is a revival of the traditional plain meaning rule.

For the plain meaning rule to operate properly, judges must be able to decide when the language of a legal document is, in fact, plain and unambiguous. Lawrence Solan has shown that this is quite difficult. Too often, a group of judges of the United States Supreme Court have concluded that a statutory provision "plainly" means *X,* while a substantial minority has argued just as fiercely that it "plainly" means *Y.*[34]

Furthermore, because interpretation tries to discover what a speaker meant by his words, excluding evidence that bears on the speaker's intent seems hard to justify. This is true even if the words appear plain on the surface. My comment on the Godzilla movie—that the special effects were terrific—seems as plain as day. Only with our shared background knowledge about the movie and your observation that I winked can you figure out that I really intended my utterance to be sarcastic.

Yet despite much valid criticism, the plain meaning rule is not irrational. To a large extent, the notion that legal language should be interpreted in isolation, without reference to the surrounding circumstances and other clues of the speaker's actual intent, is a product of the historic shift from speech to writing. As linguists like Wallace Chafe have pointed out, a speaker and listener have face-to-face contact. The listener can perceive nonverbal cues, like winking or laughing, that show that the speaker is joking or being ironic. The interlocutors almost always share knowledge of the circumstances and the environment of the conversation. In addition, the speaker can monitor the effect of what she is saying on the listener and explain something again in a slightly different way, or the listener can ask for clarification.[35]

In contrast, written language is more **autonomous.** At least in formal documents, the writer strives to include in the text itself everything that is needed to understand it. This is necessary because the writer and reader may be separated in time or space, and often in both. In fact, the writer may not even know who the readers will be and cannot assume that they share background information or knowledge of the circumstances that prompted the writing.[36]

Perhaps more than any other writers, lawyers drafting legal texts strive to make them as autonomous as possible. If all goes well, it should not be necessary years or decades later to ask the parties for clarification or amplification of the terms of a contract; it should all be there in the text itself. Indeed, with wills it is impossible for a deceased testator to explain what it means. And because nonverbal cues, such as pointing to an object, are lost in the process of writing, a legal document must use written words as a substitute. Furthermore, because of the seriousness of the topic, we can safely assume that humor, irony, figurative usage, and similar literary devices will be avoided. Finally, legal documents—like many other types of writing—are prepared with a fair amount of care, whereas speaking tends to be much more spontaneous.

In light of these factors, a judge interpreting a legal document can reasonably presume that the lawyer drafting it was successful in creating a carefully crafted and relatively complete and autonomous document. Barring indications that something went wrong, many judges assume that they should be able to figure out what the parties or legislators meant from the text of the document itself, without needing to burden themselves with large amounts of evidence on the surrounding circumstances. These presumptions, obviously, form the underpinnings of the plain meaning rule.

As an initial assumption that gives way when presented with evidence to the contrary, the plain meaning rule makes a great deal of sense. At the same time, courts need to keep in mind that in reality the legal drafter often fails to create the perfectly autonomous document. A certain amount of vagueness and ambiguity is inherent in language, and it becomes even more apparent when an opposing party wants to avoid a contract and can pay lawyers large sums of money to pick holes in it. As an ironclad principle, the plain meaning rule is unjustifiable. What is clear, however, is that the law will always have a greater respect for the text than is usual in most ordinary language.

Besides the plain meaning rule, there is another reason that legal interpretation places less emphasis on the speaker's actual meaning: collective authorship. A will is typically drafted by one person, so that only the intent of a single person matters when there is an ambiguity. Contracts are drafted by two parties and "speak" on behalf of both. This plainly complicates the problem of determining the "speaker's" intent. The problem is compounded many times over with legislation, where there may have been hundreds of legislators who were somehow involved in a statute's drafting, or at least voted for it; in a sense, all of the legislators who vote for a statute are "speaking" through it. There may hence be many speakers, each of whom is likely to have a somewhat different intended meaning.

Further complicating the matter is that the speaker or speakers may long since have died, raising questions about whether the intent of legislators who lived generations ago should have any bearing on how to govern a nation that has changed drastically in the meantime. Even if we agree to be bound by the intent of previous generations, there may be very little evidence available regarding the actual intent of the drafter of a will, or of a legislature. The lawyer who drafted the will may herself have died without leaving any record of what the testator told her when the will was drafted. In the same vein, many state legislatures preserve virtually no record of debates and other evidence of legislative history. Consequently, with only the written text as evidence of the speaker's intent, courts may have no choice but to concentrate on the meaning of the words themselves.

Courts and lawyers may face a further obstacle that is far less an issue in ordinary conversation: gaps. Despite lawyers' best efforts to be as comprehensive as possible, legislation often fails to foresee and deal with every possible contingency. When such a gap becomes apparent, there is simply no text to be interpreted. In the words of John Chipman Gray, "the legislature . . . had no meaning at all," so that the job of the judge is "not to determine what the legislature did mean on a point which was present to its mind, but to guess what it would have intended on a point not present to its mind."[37]

In ordinary speech—for example, if a boss leaves an employee incomplete instructions—the employee can usually call the boss for amplification. Courts, however, do not have the option of calling the legislature and asking what it meant, so they must find some other way to deal with the problem.

When there is insufficient evidence of what the speaker meant by a legal document, or where there are various speakers or authors who attach divergent meanings to a collectively-produced utterance or written text, or if the text contains a gap, ordinary language interpretation has reached its limits. Courts must find other devices to resolve the problem. For instance, if a statute could be interpreted in two ways, only one of which is constitutional, courts may invoke the rule that they will interpret it in such a fashion as to make it constitutional. There are several similar principles.[38] They do not involve interpretation, for the most part. Rather, they are nonlinguistic ways of resolving an ambiguity or of filling a gap.

It should be clear from this discussion that legal "interpretation" involves more than what linguists or philosophers typically mean by that term. Of course, courts generally begin by trying to figure out what the speaker meant by a word or sentence in a legal text. This is ordinary language interpretation. But if there is no text to interpret (a gap), or if there is insufficient evidence of the speaker's intent to resolve an ambiguity, courts can no longer really **interpret** the text. In that case, judges must **construct** meaning.[39] It is interesting, in fact, that at least in the past, courts frequently spoke of judicial *construction* of a statute, rather than *interpretation.*

When courts engage in construction, they provide meaning where there was none before. They do so because they are in the business of deciding disputes, which often turn on whether a contract has been breached, or a statute violated. The only alternative is for the courts to refuse to decide the lawsuit because they cannot resolve the ambiguity or fill the gap.

The position of the courts is very much like a group of people who play a new board game for the first time. They follow the written instructions to the letter, until they become stuck when they encounter an uncertainty in the rules. They could just stop. But mostly, people—like courts—want to continue playing. To do so, they must decide how the rules should be interpreted. They could proceed on the basis of what they believe the game's inventors would have done if they had thought about it. Or they might use their own ideas about how the game ought to be played. Somehow, they must fill the gap or resolve the ambiguity by formulating an additional rule of their own. They may even write down their new rule, creating a written precedent for the next time they play the game.

Judges are like these gameplayers; they cannot stop a lawsuit in midcourse and let cases linger interminably. When interpretation fails, they need to construct meaning in order to continue resolving disputes. Thus, in our system it is virtually inevitable that judges engage in some construction. As Benjamin Cardozo stated, "[t]he power to declare the law carries with it the power, and within limits the duty, to make law when none exists."[40]

Another way in which legal interpretation differs from how we understand ordinary language is found in the symbiotic relationship between rules that govern speaking or writing (how the speaker/writer *encodes* something) and interpretation (how the hearer/reader *decodes* it). A simple illustration is that if a speaker wants to refer to more than one *cat,* she uses the English rule that most words can be pluralized by adding an *s* to the end, producing *cats.* When the hearer or reader encounters *cats,* he uses that same rule to decode or interpret this word as being the plural of *cat.*

To the extent that the legal profession uses distinct rules or conventions to encode information, the legal interpreter must apply those same rules or conventions to decode what the utterance or writing means. For example, we have seen that in ordinary conversation a speaker avoids repeating a noun in a single discourse; the second occurrence of the noun is replaced by a pronoun. We therefore say *John kissed his girlfriend,* not *John kissed John's girlfriend.* If the speaker does choose to repeat the noun, as in the second example, we are inclined to infer that there may be a second *John,* and that it was his girlfriend who was kissed by the first John.[41] In contrast, legal language avoids pronouns, preferring to repeat the noun. In legal interpretation, therefore, the reader should *not* infer that there is a second John merely from the fact that the noun was repeated. In fact, the inference from repetition of a noun ought to be that it systematically refers to exactly the same person or thing.

A closely related rule for encoding legal texts is the **same meaning, same form** principle. We saw previously that this rule requires lawyers to avoid elegant variation. Instead, they should consistently use one word if they mean the same thing. In ordinary language, variation of expression is accepted, or at least tolerated. If I invite you to visit me at my *residence,* and then welcome you to enter my humble *domicile,* you will assume that both of these words refer to my house. On the other hand, if a statute refers on one occasion to *domicile* and on another to *residence,* legal professionals will infer that those terms do *not* mean the same thing, despite their near semantic identity.[42]

Of course, lawyers are human beings who do not always apply legal drafting principles. The maxims of interpretation, such as *expressio unius* and *ejusdem generis,* are not consistently applied by either drafters or judges. Indeed, as Karl Llewellyn famously showed, the maxims often contradict each other.[43] Despite these problems, to the extent that legal drafters try to apply rules and conventions such as these, interpreters of their words must use them as well.

When interpreting a legal text, we must therefore keep in mind the nature of the document. Ideally, it was prepared with a certain amount of care and was written in a relatively autonomous manner. We should respect the text and try to interpret it based upon the words contained within it. If prepared by professional legal drafters, we should be aware of the linguistic conventions that they used to create the document, and we should use those conventions to decode it. On the other hand, we should never forget the limitations of the text. Many proponents of textualism tend to overrate the ability of legal texts to regulate human affairs. Virtually all documents are susceptible to ambiguities and gaps. When these occur, we have gone as far as the language of the text can take us.

CHAPTER EIGHT

Variation

So far, most of the discussion has attempted to describe legal English as a unitary system. In reality, it is far from uniform. Certainly when we look at the actual use of language by the profession, there is a great deal of variation. In this section, we explore some of that variety.

Legal Dialects

Virtually every language has different dialects. Historically speaking, dialects normally arise because languages spread out geographically, creating subcommunities of speakers who may become fairly isolated from each other. Language is always changing, so over time, these groups of speakers will begin to speak differently (because the language of each group will change in different ways). Eventually, the distinctions between dialects can become great enough that they are treated as separate languages.

Although the situation is actually more complicated, the English settlements in places like Australia, New Zealand, and North America provide an example of a speech community that spread out over time. The English language in each of these places gradually changed, and changed differently in the disparate areas. As a consequence, even though it has been a mere two hundred years or so, the British, Americans, New Zealanders, and Australians all speak distinct dialects of English. And each of these countries has dialect differences of its own. This is especially true of Britain, where regional varieties have had hundreds of years to develop. Of course, with modern mass communication and the standardizing influence of education, speech communities are far less isolated. Consequently, dialect differentiation in English is likely to slow down and may even be reversed.

Dialects can differ in many ways from each other and from the standard language. Everyone knows that words are pronounced differently in Australia, Britain, or the United States; in fact, this is probably the most salient distinguishing feature of English dialects. But there may be variation in other aspects of the grammar also. The British use a plural with nouns like Parliament (*Parliament have decided*), while Americans use a singular (*Congress has decided*). And there are many lexical variations. British say *lorry* where Americans say *truck*, to name just one example. Finally, dialects may have a word that has different shades of meaning. *Dear* may mean "expensive" in British, a sense Americans do not share.

Lawyers in the various English-speaking countries clearly speak different dialects of legal English. One obvious cause is that the legal systems themselves—like the language—have undergone distinct changes. British lawyers may be *solicitors* or *barristers*. This distinction is unknown in the United States, and those words are not part of American legal English (except when referring to the English system, of course).

Sometimes one word has different meanings in various jurisdictions. In American legal English, a *judgment* is the disposition or outcome of a case. In England, *judgment* also refers to the statement of reasons for the disposition, something that American lawyers call an *opinion*. An appellate court *affirms* or *reverses* a lower court's judgment in the United States, while it *allows* the appeal or *dismisses* it in England. A *brief* is an argument to the court in the United States, while it is a written case summary for the guidance of a barrister in England. *Corporate law* in America is *company law* in England. Legal idioms may also differ from place to place. An American lawyer is *admitted to the bar,* while a British barrister is *called to the bar* and may eventually *take silk* (become a Queen's Counsel).

In contrast to the United States, the dialects of legal English spoken in the other former British colonies, such as Australia, Canada, New Zealand, and Singapore, to name a few, do not diverge as much from British usage because they separated from the English at a later date. Nonetheless, each system has its distinctive linguistic features.

One reason that legal English differs from place to place is that it may have to deal with indigenous laws and customs. In India, for example, law reports from the higher courts are often in legal English. Many passages in a case report from the state of Rajasthan could have been written by a judge in England: *original orders have not been produced along with the writ petition except a copy of such order was filed. . . .*[1] But other passages from the same case have a distinctly Indian flavor: *he had paid revenue to the State since Samwat Year 2025 and his name was also recorded in the Khasra Record of Samwat Year 2029.*[2] Similarly, an Indian will begins as follows:

> We, Pandit Kunwar Lal, Son of Pandit Bhagwan Singh and
> Mst. Ram Pyari *alias* Chandra Prabha, wife of Pandit Kunwar Lal
> aforesaid, caste Brahman, resident of qasba Firozabad, district
> Agra, do declare as follows. . . .[3]

Just as ordinary English has acquired distinctive accents and vocabulary around the world, legal English has shown itself to be quite adaptable to local circumstances.

Spoken versus Written Legal Language

Another type of variation is that between spoken and written language. In theory, we should expect writing to be very similar or even identical to spoken language. Writing is, after all, nothing more than a way of representing speech. Of course, certain aspects of speech—intonation comes to mind—are not conveyed very well by our writing system. Yet even if writing could be made to reflect all the nuances of speech, oral and written communication would still differ in some very interesting ways.

We saw previously that the shift from speaking to writing had some very significant consequences for legal English. Written documents tend to resist change and exert a conservatizing influence on the language of the law. And once written legal texts came to be regarded as authoritative, lawyers began to fixate more on the text and less on the speaker's intended meaning. Finally, we discussed the plain meaning rule, and observed that it seems to have largely resulted from the fact that writing tends to be more autonomous than speech. Writing something down, especially in authoritative form, can have significant consequences for how it is interpreted.

Whether something is spoken or written has other implications. Perhaps because it generally leaves no permanent record and is more spontaneous, oral communication tends to be less formal than written language. This applies to legal language also. Archaic, formal and ritualistic language is primarily found in lawyers' documents; it is far less common in their speech.

Furthermore, written language tends to be more syntactically complex and lexically dense than speech. Again, the reasons are fairly obvious: writing can occur over an extended period of time, which allows an opportunity for reflection and editing. The permanence of the written record motivates people to choose their words carefully. And because the reader can go over dense written material several times, if need be, writing can be far more complex than speech. The complexity, density, and formality of legal language is thus closely related to the fact that legal language is predominantly written.

Most of the characteristics of legal language that were discussed in this part are less true of spoken legal English. This is especially so with the syntactic and stylistic features; convoluted and lengthy sentences that run into the hundreds of words would be virtually impossible to construct when speaking. On the other hand, technical vocabulary remains, even when lawyers are speaking fairly informally. An American lawyer might tell opposing counsel to *shove that demurrer up your ass*. This is very ordinary, albeit pithy English, but the technical vocabulary (*demurrer*) remains. Indeed, technical vocabulary and jargon is probably the only constant characteristic of every genre and variety of legal language.

Because legal language is so closely associated with writing, there has been relatively less analysis of the spoken language of the profession. As with written legal language, there is a continuum of oral language use by lawyers, ranging from very formal spoken legal English (including a great deal of technical vocabulary and distinctive legal style) to colloquial English and slang. This topic will be discussed more thoroughly in part 3, which deals with language in the courtroom.

Telegraphic Speech

A less usual variety of legal language is **telegraphic speech.**[4] It is called "telegraphic" because it resembles the language of telegrams, in which clients pay per word and have a strong incentive to leave out any excess or predictable verbiage. Newspaper headlines are typically also telegraphic: *Smith Guilty!* in place of the full sentence *The Jury Finds Smith Guilty!*

Telegraphic speech occasionally occurs in written legal language. An illustration is the order (such as *appeal allowed* or *remanded*) that follows the written opinion of a court. It is more commonly used by lawyers and judges during trial, especially when making and ruling on objections during testimony:

> Counsel for defendant: *Objection! Hearsay.*
> Prosecutor: *Not offered for the truth of the matter.*
> Judge: *Overruled.*

Telegraphic speech, though it comes across as informal, is a quick and efficient way to communicate standard messages, especially when the content is so predictable that any deleted words can easily be recovered. Its use for making objections no doubt results from the reluctance of courts to tolerate long interruptions. In any event, it vividly shows that judges and lawyers are quite capable of cutting out excess verbiage and getting directly to the point when it suits their purpose.

Legal Slang

Another type of legal English is highly informal language, or **slang.** Like jargon, slang tends to refer mainly to individual lexical items or phrases. While some slang is known by the entire speech community, social subgroups often have their own slang, which promotes group solidarity and makes it harder for outsiders to understand certain topics. Teenagers, for example, have an ever-changing vocabulary for subjects, like sex and drugs, that they prefer to keep private from adults. In this function, therefore, slang resembles an argot.

Despite the notion that legal English is formal and stilted, there is a fair amount of lawyerly slang. Most of it seems geared primarily towards efficiency by shortening words or phrases, or by creating novel terms for which there is no formal equivalent. An example of the latter is the term *wobbler,* which in California refers to a crime that can be charged either as a misdemeanor or as a felony. Slang here provides a word where there is no formal equivalent, and it allows a point to be made more succinctly.

One of the best ways to shorten terms is through **clipping.** When first introduced, clippings are normally viewed as slang. Yet many shortened forms have become accepted in the standard language. Thus, a baseball *fan* (from *fanatic*) is probably no longer slang, nor are clippings like *bike, cab* (*cabriolet*), *exam, memo, mob* (*mobile vulgus*), *perks* (*perquisites*), or *pub* (*public house*).

Lawyers use a fair number of clipped terms, including *depo* (*deposition*), *hypo* (*hypothetical example*), *punies* (*punitive damages*), *in pro per* (*in propria persona*) and *rogs* (*interrogatories*). While these examples are quite informal, others, like *pro tem* (*pro tempore*), are acceptable even in fairly formal legal language.

Acronyms are another way to shorten legal phrases. An acronym consists of the initial letters of several words. Acronyms are common in many trades and professions, and the law is no exception. A few American examples are *TRO* (*temporary restraining order*), *TSC* (*trial setting conference*), *JNOV* (*judgment non obstante veredicto*), *P's and A's* (*memorandum of points and authorities*), and *UCC* (*Uniform Commercial Code*). Even though lawyers frequently use acronyms, they are still felt to be somewhat informal. In a brief to a court, for instance, careful attorneys generally write the phrases out in full.

Sometimes an acronym can be pronounced as a word. Some, in fact, have become ordinary lexical items, including *radar* (radio detecting and ranging) and *scuba* (self-contained underwater breathing apparatus). At least in the United States, several pronounceable acronyms come from the titles of legislation: *RICO* from the *Racketeer Influenced and Corrupt Organizations Act,* and *ERISA* from the *Employee Retirement Income Security Act.* A recently coined acronym, which has quickly become accepted legal usage in California, is a *SLAPP* suit (*strategic lawsuit against public participation*), a tool invented by real estate developers to intimidate environmental groups that oppose their projects.[5]

Although most slang consists of individual words, there are also legal idioms that should probably be viewed as slang. Examples are *grant cert* (grant a writ of certiorari), *cop a plea* (plead guilty), or to *paper a judge* (peremptorily challenge a judge, based in California on section 170.6 of the Code of Civil Procedure). An alternative in California to "papering" a judge is to *170.6 a judge.* This last example shows that a common type of legal slang is to use section numbers of statutes to refer to their substantive or procedural provisions.

A different way to shorten a phrase is to replace an adjective and noun combination with an adjective that functions by itself as a noun. Bordering on slang are the terms *incidentals, consequentials,* and *punitives* for *incidental damages, consequential damages,* and *punitive damages.* (Oddly, *expectation damages* or *general damages* seldom become *expectations* or *generals,* perhaps because these words are existing nouns with other meanings.) Consider also *a hypothetical* (from *hypothetical example* or *hypothetical case*), although this word is fairly accepted jargon, rather than slang. Likewise, *precedent* must originally have been an adjective (*a precedent case*) but is now used as a noun by itself (*a precedent*).

Of course, informal legal language and legal slang is appropriate only in limited circumstances. We will see in part 3 that it is a familiar element of the courtroom. Not surprisingly, it is also common in law offices and in meetings of lawyers, where it can facilitate communication and create group solidarity. When speaking to clients, it is less appropriate; unlike teenagers obscuring discussion of sex or alcohol so that their parents will not understand them, lawyers should have nothing to hide from their clients. And like all slang, legal slang is relatively rare in writing. Overall, informal varieties of legal language, such as slang and telegraphic speech, can be a fast and functional means of communication under the proper circumstances.

Variation and Genre

It should be evident by now that there is great variation in legal language, depending on geographical location, degree of formality, speaking versus writing, and related factors. The language and style of lawyers also differs substantially from one genre of writing to another. Basically, a **genre** refers to a category of composition; the members of the category usually share a particular structure as well as level of formality.

Some of the more common legal genres are pleadings, petitions, orders and statutes, and private legal documents like contracts and wills. As a class, these can be called **operative legal documents,** in that they create or modify legal relations. In linguistic terminology, they all contain **legal performatives.** Operative documents tend to have not only very formal and formulaic legal language, but they traditionally adhere to a very rigid structure. The most notorious attributes of legal English tend to occur in operative documents.

Another general class can be called **expository documents.** These typically delve into one or more points of law with a relatively objective tone. An office memorandum explaining a legal matter or letter to a client are examples of this category. Expository genres tend to conform to a traditional structure, but it is usually less rigid than that of operative documents. The style resembles formal everyday language, although use of legal terminology is almost unavoidable. One study supports the observation that expository documents, specifically letters from corporate counsel to clients, are normally not all that complex linguistically, being similar to Camus's *The Plague,* Mark Twain's *Innocents Abroad,* or C. S. Lewis's *Out of the Silent Planet.* They were less complex than *The Great Gatsby* or *Walden.*[6]

Judicial opinions are also expository, to the extent that the judge expresses what the law is (opinions typically also contain a judgment or order at the end that constitutes the actual disposition of the case; such an order is operative, of course). Most modern opinions have a relatively formal tone, but the language is largely standard English rather than legalese. Of course, even though a judicial opinion is supposedly "objective" rather than "persuasive," a judge actually aims to persuade the reader that her decision was correct, but the objective tone suggests that the outcome is the only rational conclusion in light of the law and the facts.[7]

Perhaps because of the power of the judges who write them, some judicial opinions have recently exhibited substantial freedom in tone and form. One from Michigan was composed in verse:

> We thought that we would never see
> A suit to compensate a tree.
>
> A suit whose claim in tort is prest
> Upon a mangled tree's behest;
>
> A tree whose battered trunk was prest
> Against a Chevy's crumpled crest;
>
> A tree that faces each new day
> With bark and limb in disarray;
>
> A tree that may forever bear
> A lasting need for tender care.
>
> Flora lovers though we three,
> We must uphold the court's decree.[8]

Another opinion, involving the right to use the trademark "Pig Sandwich," was filled with porcine puns, including "this little piggie went to see his lawyer"; appellant "went to hog heaven"; and "though not entirely kosher, Hard Rock's actions were not sufficiently swinish to bring this case to the 'exceptional' level required for an award of attorney's fees."[9]

Overall, however, most judges tend to feel that poetry, humor, and similar literary flourishes are inappropriate to the seriousness of their subject matter. In the words of William Prosser: "Judicial humor is a dreadful thing."[10]

A literary device that is more acceptable and effective in opinions is metaphor. For example, with regard to the Free Speech Clause of the United States Constitution, courts commonly discuss how freedom of expression fosters a "marketplace of ideas." Likewise, speech directed at a "captive audience" may give the government greater leeway to regulate it.[11]

Judges give themselves more stylistic latitude in dissenting opinions. In the Supreme Court case declaring that the act of burning the American flag was protected free speech, Chief Justice Rehnquist figuratively burst into song, reciting the first verse of the national anthem in his dissent.[12] In a case that held that Henry Miller's *Tropic of Cancer* was not legally obscene, Justice Musmanno of the Pennsylvania Supreme Court, a famous and often acerbic dissenter, had this to say about the majority's opinion:

> "Cancer" is not a book. It is a cesspool, an open sewer, a pit of putrification, a slimy gathering of all that is rotten in the debris

of human depravity. And in the center of all this waste and stench, besmearing himself with its foulest defilement, splashes, leaps, cavorts and wallows a bifurcated specimen that responds to the name of Henry Miller. . . . From Pittsburgh to Philadelphia, from Dan to Beersheba, and from the Ramparts of the Bible to Samuel Eliot Morison's *Oxford History of the American People*, I dissent.[13]

The structure of judicial opinions, like other legal genres but to a greater extent, can differ substantially from jurisdiction to jurisdiction. English appellate courts sometimes still issue *seriatim* opinions, in which the judges pronounce their opinions (or "judgments") one after the other. In civil law countries such as France, opinions of courts like the Cour de Cassation adhere to a very rigid style and compact format that is virtually inscrutable to outsiders.[14]

A final general category of legal genres is **persuasive documents.** This class includes briefs that are submitted to courts and memoranda of points and authorities. Like expository documents, they tend not to be especially formulaic or legalistic in language, although they do use fairly formal standard English.

Clearly, legal language is not monolithic. Even if we limit ourselves to the written variety, there is substantial variation among different genres of documents. Generally speaking, operative documents have by far the most legalese, as compared to persuasive and expository documents.

It is highly ironic that documents with the most legalese (like contracts, wills, deeds, and statutes) are also most likely to be read by clients and directly affect their interests. In contrast, those documents with the least legalese (like legal memoranda, briefs, and opinions) tend to be written for judges and other lawyers. One possible reason is that operative documents tend to have direct and highly significant consequences; ritualistic legalese helps warn clients that they should exercise caution before signing them. On the other hand, the conspiracy theorist would point out that serving gobbledygook to clients enables lawyers to justify their fees and preserve their monopoly, but that lawyers cynically shift to more ordinary English when it serves their interest to communicate clearly. Whether this strategy is intentional or not, the distinction surely provides food for thought.

So What Is Legal Language Exactly?

The preceding chapters have illustrated some of the many ways in which legal language differs from ordinary speech. This may leave readers wondering: what is legal language exactly? A separate language? A dialect? Jargon? Argot? A style?[15]

By now it should be obvious that none of these concepts, by itself, is sufficient. When lawyers first used Anglo-French in the English courts, they were simply speaking a variety of French, a living language among the aristocracy, rather than their own exclusive language. Once Anglo-French died out, the Law French that survived in the courts might indeed be characterized as a distinct language, spoken only by the profession. Of course, whether it was truly a language, in light of its simplified structure and vocabulary, is questionable. The same holds for legal English today. If we isolate what is distinctive in legal English, leaving out features of ordinary speech, what remains is far too incomplete to function as a language.[16] To a large extent, modern legal English is a set of linguistic features that are superimposed on everyday speech.

As noted previously, legal language is not a **dialect,** a concept that is traditionally associated with geography, although there are several dialects of legal English. Nor can legal language be characterized merely as **jargon.** This term relates primarily to vocabulary. We have seen in this part that the language of lawyers encompasses much more. We have also observed that **argot** normally refers to the speech of an insular group, with overtones of secrecy and perhaps even illegality. While there may be those who depict the legal profession and its language as secretive and criminal, the term argot is too restrictive and loaded a term to describe the language of the profession.

The notion of **style** is more promising but also problematic, in part because linguists do not agree on what this term means exactly.[17] Crystal and Davy use "style" to refer to the language habits of a person, or a group of people.[18] As we saw earlier, the language habits of the profession cause lawyers to frequently choose one means of expression, such as the passive construction or word lists, over other possibilities. There is clearly a fairly distinct legal style. This does not mean that legal language is solely a matter of style, however. Many of its features, including unusual vocabulary, divergent morphology and syntax, and use of *shall,* involve not just a preference of one means of expression over others, but the use of words and structures that are not really part of the repertoire of ordinary English.

More recently, some linguists have begun to analyze certain language varieties in terms of **sublanguages.** One definition of this term is a "language used in a body of texts dealing with a circumscribed subject area . . . in which the authors of the documents share a common vocabulary and common habits of word usage."[19] Sublanguages have been described for communications within various disciplines or activities, such as medicine, aviation hydraulics, stock market reports, weather reports, and so forth.[20] The term carries with it the idea that the sublanguage is a subset, or part, of the language as a whole.[21] Critically, each sublanguage has its own "specialized grammar."[22]

Some other characteristics that have been attributed to sublanguages include (1) they have a limited subject matter; (2) they contain lexical, syntactic, and semantic restrictions; (3) they allow "deviant" rules of grammar that are not acceptable in the standard language; and (4) certain constructions are unusually frequent.[23] Most of these features seem to apply to legal language, and some scholars have indeed suggested that the language of the law is a sublanguage of English.[24] Certainly the notion of a sublanguage suggests that legal language differs from ordinary speech not merely lexically, but also in terms of morphology, syntax, semantics, and the various other features that have been the topic of the preceding chapters.

Whatever term we use to describe legal language, it needs to encompass the very complex linguistic habits of an ancient and diverse profession that uses words more than almost any other and has learned to use them in a very strategic way. Much more could be and has been written about this topic. But it is time to shift our focus from the nature of legal language to how the profession uses it to accomplish its aims, especially in the courtroom.

PART THREE

In the Courtroom

The discussion so far has largely centered on the written language of the law. In the courtroom, however, the profession engages in a great deal of spoken communication. Not only does courtroom practice allow us to look at oral usage more closely, but it gives us a chance to observe legal language in its most dramatic setting.

In examining the linguistic behavior of lawyers in the courtroom, we will encounter many of the characteristics that have been noted previously. Nonetheless, it will become evident that when lawyers are sufficiently motivated, they quickly abandon legalese in favor of clear and comprehensible communication.

CHAPTER NINE

Pleadings: Constructing the Legal Narrative

Trials are very much about stories or narratives. A lawsuit typically begins after a series of events has caused something wrong or illegal to happen to someone, and for which the injured person seeks a remedy. The person asking the court for a remedy therefore comes telling a tale. Before continuing with a description of how the plaintiff's story unfolds during the course of the trial, we set the stage by briefly considering the structure of narratives.

Narratives

In one sense, *narrative* is a fancy word for a story. As opposed to some other types of discourse, a narrative is normally told by one person; it contrasts with a conversation, which consists of turn-taking (sequences of speech) by two or more participants. Furthermore, the narrative typically deals with events, real or imagined, that took place in the past.

There is no single type of narrative, because people tell stories in numerous ways.[1] A very basic structure, sufficient for our purposes, begins by providing some background information, often introducing the characters or the setting. Thus, a fairy tale may start by relating that once upon a time, there was a girl called Little Red Riding Hood (or Little Red-Cap). After this introduction, the narrative continues by presenting a sequence of events, usually in chronological order. In the version of the Grimm brothers, the fairy tale recounts how Little Red Riding Hood went through the forest to visit her grandmother, talked to the wolf, picked some flowers, and finally arrived at her grandmother's house only to find the wolf in her grandmother's bed, having devoured grandma. Typically, the recitation of events leads to a crisis or problem. In this case, the problem arises when the wolf proceeded to eat Little Red Riding Hood. Narratives of this kind usually end with a resolution of the problem. Fortunately for Little Red Riding Hood, a hunter happened to pass along and found the wolf, suspected that it might have eaten someone, cut open the wolf's stomach, and rescued both Little Red Riding Hood and her grandmother.[2] A basic narrative type thus begins with an introduction that supplies some background information, continues with a chronological sequence of events, builds to a crisis or problem, and ends by offering a resolution.

Pleadings

The pleading stage, which formally begins a lawsuit, is where the plaintiff first tells his story to the court. The pleading that contains the plaintiff's story is typically called the **complaint,** at least in civil cases. But the story that the plaintiff tells through the complaint differs from our basic narrative structure in at least two important ways.

An ordinary story is normally **asserted** as truth, even if it is fictional. This means that the speaker expressly or impliedly represents the story as being true. In contrast, the story told in a complaint is **alleged** to be true; its truth remains to be established at trial. Admittedly, an allegation is quite similar to an assertion: both present facts that the speaker believes to be true, or at least has some basis for believing. The distinction is that the allegation makes a weaker claim to the truth, while indicating that the speaker will produce, or at least has available, evidence to support his claim. Allegations thus tell a story in a more tentative way, recognizing that the actual truth, for legal purposes, must await the outcome of the trial. Often the tentative nature of the complaint is unavoidable because the plaintiff may not know exactly what happened. Elsewhere, the plaintiff may be absolutely sure that his story is accurate, but presents it in the form of unproven allegations because this is the conventional format for pleadings, perhaps in deference to the court's role as determiner of the truth.

The complaint differs from the basic narrative in another way: at the pleading stage, the story is still incomplete. This is so because there has not yet been a resolution of the problem or crisis; the outcome depends upon whether the facts alleged in the complaint can be proven at trial, as well as the judgment that the court decides to enter.

The basic structure of pleadings has been a fairly constant element of trials for many hundreds of years. In fact, medieval lawyers were well aware that much of their task revolved around alleging and proving the stories of clients. As early as 1230 there are references to pleaders who appeared in court, called *narratores* in Latin.[3] The story that the *narrator* told was—logically enough—a *narratio*. Incidentally, the Law French verb for telling a story was *counter,* a meaning which has survived in the words *account* and *recount.* Thus pleaders were known as *counters,* and the narratives that they told were called *counts,* a term still used today.[4]

The following example is an action for trespass from 1341. It first identified the parties and recited that the defendants had been attached to answer by writ (which brought them under the jurisdiction of the court). The record continues by presenting the plaintiff's story, which was made orally in court by her lawyer, and was recorded in Latin by the clerk:

> And thereupon the same Isot, by Simon of Kegworth her attorney, complains that the aforesaid John son of John of Clavering and the others, together with the said Robert the Ironmonger of Mimms and the others, on the Saturday [6 Nov. 1339] next after the feast of All Saints in the thirteenth year of the reign of the present King Edward, with force and arms, namely with swords etc., took and led away thirty-one cows, eight bullocks and ten heifers of the selfsame Isot's, worth thirty pounds, found at Ramsden Bellhouse, against the peace [of the lord king]. Whereby she says she is the worse and has damage to the extent of sixty pounds. And thereof she produces suit etc.[5]

Like the basic narrative, this complaint begins with certain background information, describing the parties and where they reside. It next gives a chronology of events. This sequence of events caused a problem or crisis. Unlike the basic narrative, however, the complaint does not resolve the crisis. Instead, it requests that the court do so by granting a remedy: payment of sixty pounds.

Today, over half a millennium later, the basic structure of the complaint is remarkably similar. One major change is that pleadings are now drafted by lawyers and presented to the court in writing. The following is a fairly routine complaint for personal injury filed in the 1980s:

> The plaintiff Anne Rasmussen, by her attorney, William S. Hart . . . alleges:
> 1. That on or about December 30, 1980, at a point on United States Highway No. 40 approximately 15 miles West of Steamboat Springs, Colorado, in the County of Routt and State of Colorado, the defendant Paula Graham did so negligently and carelessly operate a motor vehicle in which the plaintiff Anne Rasmussen was a passenger that said motor vehicle struck a snowplow and caused severe injuries to said plaintiff.
> 2. That as a direct and proximate result of the negligence and carelessness of the defendant as aforesaid, the plaintiff Anne Rasmussen sustained numerous and severe permanent and dis-

abling injuries including, but not limited to, lacerations, contu-
sions, and fractures of the bones of the head, face and jaw. . . .
   WHEREFORE, plaintiff Anne Rasmussen demands judgment
against the defendant Paula Graham in the total sum of One
Hundred Thirty-Four Thousand Seven Hundred Seven Hundred Ninety One Dollars and 40/100 ($134,791.40), together
with her costs, interest from the date of filing the Complaint
herein, and for such other and further relief as the Court deems
proper.[6]

In medieval times the exact words in a pleading could be critical; one
slip was sometimes fatal. The modern example illustrates that pleadings
continue to be phrased in legalese, including much formulaic and ritualistic language, although it is safe to say that currently the content has
become far more important than the form. The ritualistic language of
pleadings signals that something significant and different from ordinary
life is about to commence. In fact, because *complaint* is a legal homonym
(with both an ordinary and legal meaning), the legalistic language helps
make it clear to the defendant that this is not merely a grievance, which
is the ordinary meaning of the word *complaint.* Rather, this is a *complaint*
in the legal sense: an important legal document that puts into gear the
machinery of the law. It suggests to her that perhaps she should consult
an attorney.

   Of course, the kinds of stories that can be told in a pleading are also
greatly affected by the substantive law. For various reasons, the law limits
itself to addressing only certain categories of problems or crises. If your
problem is that your neighbors have converted their house into a loud
factory that disturbs your sleep, the legal system will probably offer a
remedy. On the other hand, a complaint that your neighbors have added
a second story to their house may fall on deaf ears, even though it may
precipitate a crisis for you by blocking your view, depriving you of sun-
light, and invading the privacy of your back yard. The fact that the judicial system addresses only certain types of stories and problems is expressed in modern legal terms by the requirement that you have a **cause
of action.** Another requirement is that you tell your story to the right
person: someone endowed with the authority to offer a resolution. This
is technically known as **jurisdiction.**

   The defendant can respond to the complaint in various ways. One
strategy is to contest the legal adequacy of the complaint, alleging that
the plaintiff has no valid cause of action, or that the court has no jurisdiction. Another option is to admit that the story is legally adequate in
theory, but to challenge its truth by denying the facts. Or the defendant

can offer a counternarrative that—if found to be true—would require the court to resolve the dispute in the defendant's favor. Finally, the defendant can admit that the plaintiff's narrative is both legally adequate and true, but offer an excuse or justification for her behavior. Often an excuse or justification fills factual gaps in the plaintiff's story. Thus, the defendant might admit that she struck and injured the plaintiff, as alleged in the complaint, but might supplement the plaintiff's story by adding that she did so only after the plaintiff threatened her with a knife.

If the court decides that the plaintiff's story is legally adequate, the trial—to determine its truth—can begin.

CHAPTER TEN

Testimony and Truth

After the pleading stage has been completed, the search for the truth commences. In the American system there are extensive proceedings before trial during which each side has the right to obtain information about the other's case, a process called **discovery.** The discovery process—especially in civil cases—can include taking live testimony of potential witnesses (**depositions**), posing written questions (**interrogatories**), or obtaining documentary evidence (**requests for documents**). In theory, each side should learn the details of the other's story and the strength of the evidence to support that story. In the vast majority of cases, the situation becomes clear enough that a trial is deemed unnecessary, or is considered too risky or costly, and the parties settle the case.

In criminal proceedings the settlement negotiations are known as **plea bargaining.** Typically, the prosecution will offer the accused a less severe penalty if she forgoes trial and pleads guilty, often to a reduced charge. In the United States, most criminal cases are disposed of by plea bargaining; the process has become routine for many prosecutors and defense attorneys. Not surprisingly, they have developed their own slang to facilitate the process, as revealed by this exchange recorded in a study of plea bargaining by Douglas Maynard:

> DEFENSE ATTORNEY: Is there an offer in that case?
> PROSECUTOR: Yeah, a reckless with a deuce dispo.[1]

The *reckless* is presumably "reckless driving," *deuce* refers to "drunk driving," and *dispo* must be "disposition." Other terms from California criminal law practice include *auto burg* (automobile burglary), *cop to* (admit, confess, plead guilty), *mal mish* (malicious mischief), *plead* (plead guilty), and *priors* (prior convictions).[2] The time-saving benefits of such slang in the high-paced atmosphere of plea bargaining are evident. Furthermore, a shared speech variety creates group cohesion. It is interesting that even though these lawyers are officially adversaries, on another level they are members of the same community who converse with each other in a common language and have a shared goal: processing cases as expeditiously as possible. Furthermore, it is a language that their clients do not share. In fact, the lawyers may purposely speak an unintelligible code to discourage their clients from interfering in the process and slowing it down.[3] Incidentally, this is a subvariety of legal language, peculiar to the criminal bar. Even other lawyers have trouble understanding it.

Where a case does not settle, it necessarily proceeds to trial. As observed previously, the trial begins with several formalities that emphasize the seriousness of the proceeding, its separateness from ordinary life, and the venerable and authoritative character of the court. Some of these rituals are verbal, including the triple incantation of *hear ye* or *oyez* and the formal language of the proceedings. Sessions of the United States Supreme Court begin as follows:

> Oyez! Oyez! Oyez! All persons having business before the Honorable, the Supreme Court of the United States, are admonished to draw near and give their attention, for the Court is now sitting. God save the United States and this Honorable Court![4]

Other formalities are nonverbal but nonetheless conventionally communicate the same message. These include the distinctive clothing of the judge (and in some systems, the lawyers as well), the central position and elevation of the judge's bench, insignia of power and authority (seals, coats of arms, flags), and the silence and respect that observers are expected to maintain.

The truth of the plaintiff's story can be determined either by the judge or by the jury. Assuming that it is a jury trial, the people who comprise the jury must first be selected. This process is often called by the Law French term *voir dire*. Many people suppose that this term means something like "see them speak," based on modern French *voir* "see" and *dire* "say, speak." In fact, *voier* meant "true" in Law French; the term *voir dire* referred to an oath to speak truthfully when examined.[5] After the jury is selected, the search for truth can begin.

Chapter 1 discussed some of the ways that the medieval English legal system tried to determine the truth of stories, including ordeal and trial by battle. Today we search for truth mainly via the sworn testimony of witnesses. Testimony is not the only type of evidence—documents, photographs, and many other kinds of proof are equally acceptable—but it remains extremely important.

We often say that a witness *gives* testimony. In reality, the legal system *takes* it. In the rest of this chapter we discuss how lawyers use language to elicit the testimony of witnesses. We will see that how questions are asked can potentially influence the answer. Furthermore, now that we have sworn off hot irons and dunking chairs, how can the fact finder decide whether a witness is telling the truth? It turns out that linguistic cues provide part of the answer. Finally, we will return to an earlier theme—how speech differs from writing—to discuss the effect of converting what the witness says into a written transcript that becomes the authoritative version of what transpired at trial.

Most of the examples in the next two chapters will be drawn from two actual murder cases. One is the Jackson trial, which is used because much of the testimony, as well as background information and documentary materials, is readily available in one convenient source.[6] Though the names and places have been changed, the events are real. In 1970, a young woman named Sandra Jackson moved out of her conservative family's home and into an apartment, where she lived with her boyfriend and other "hippies." Her father eventually tracked her down. While they were sleeping, he shot and killed not only Sandra, but her boyfriend and two other residents of the building. He was tried and convicted of manslaughter of his daughter and second-degree murder of the others.

The other trial is that of Orenthal James (O. J.) Simpson, a former football player who was accused of stabbing to death his divorced wife, Nicole, and a young man who was accompanying her. The proceeding took place in Los Angeles shortly after the racially-tinged trials of four white police officers who beat a black motorist after his refusal to stop when they pursued him; their acquittal led to serious race riots. Simpson, an African American celebrity, was tried for the murder of his former wife, who was white; his trial also came to have serious racial undercurrents. The analysis here is based mainly on official transcripts and, to a lesser extent, videotapes of the live television coverage of the trial.[7]

Simpson was acquitted, despite strong evidence that he was guilty. Some may suggest that his trial was a fluke because of his celebrity, and that we should hesitate to draw lessons from such an unusual occurrence. Of course, there is no single explanation for why the jury acquitted Simpson. I will argue, however, that his lawyers' clever use of language was an important reason for the jury's decision.

Language Variation and Code-Switching in the Courtroom

We saw in chapter 8 that there is a great deal of variation in legal language. In written communications, lawyers tend to be quite formal. Furthermore, the amount of legalese typically depends on the nature of the document (operative, expository, or persuasive) that the lawyer is drafting.

There is similar variation in the spoken language of lawyers. A study of North Carolina courts by William O'Barr and his colleagues revealed that lawyers and other participants use a range of language varieties in court, including formal legal language, Standard English, colloquial English, and the local dialect.[8] What is most interesting, however, is not merely that this language variation exists, but by whom each style or variety is used, the purpose for which it is used, and the effect that it has on the hearer.

People who can speak more than one language, or more than one variety of a language, may choose to speak one variety on a certain occasion and a different one on another. We noted previously that this is called **code-switching,** and that during the late Middle Ages, English lawyers engaged in code-switching between Latin, Law French, and English. In written legal language, switching seems to have been dictated almost entirely by custom: court records were traditionally kept in Latin, for instance. Unfortunately, we have less information on when the legal profession used one language or the other in spoken courtroom discourse.

Code-switching is virtually never random; speakers will alternate between varieties of language depending on a number of factors. One factor is the *topic* of the discussion. When speaking about the law, it is natural for lawyers to switch to legal language, and particularly to employ technical terminology. This is true for other professions as well; doctors discussing a patient's ailment will do so in medical language. On the other hand, it would be silly to use legal language to talk about the weather during a cocktail party, even if it is part of a bar association function. No serious lawyer, discussing bad weather that might disrupt a planned barbecue with another lawyer, would ponder aloud whether *said storm may disrupt, impede, hinder, or delay the aforesaid event, to wit, the barbecue.* Yet she might have no qualms about placing such language in a contract or complaint.

The hearer's ability to understand the code is another important factor in code-switching. Effective communication requires speaking to someone in language that the person will best understand. When addressing a lay person, the lawyer will—or certainly should—use ordinary language. A lawyer advising a client on the financial implications of a change in the tax laws should thus switch from legalese to ordinary English. If a lawyer tries to communicate with a client in legalese, one can only conclude that she just does not know how to translate legal concepts into ordinary language, or that she does not really want to communicate with the client. In either case, the client is not well served.

The situation is complicated by a third factor: the type of language a speaker uses is closely related to his social and economic position, and thus greatly influences how others view him. Typically, speakers of standard English (as spoken by newscasters on television, for example) are considered to be more highly educated and are felt to have a higher status than those who speak regional varieties. Conversely, speakers of some varieties of English (such as Brooklynese, Black Vernacular or "Ebonics," Cockney) are stigmatized by the mainstream culture, which assumes they are less well educated and have lower socioeconomic status.[9]

The other side of the coin is that language is a powerful device for maintaining group cohesion. An African American who speaks both standard English and Black English can signal that he is part of the black community by speaking Black English to his "brothers," while he can distance himself by speaking standard English, "like a white man." The choice of one variety over the other can thus be used strategically, depending on the impression that the speaker wishes to make on a particular audience.

Like other members of our society, lawyers are well aware of the social implications of code-switching. They learn early in their careers to identify themselves as members of the profession by "talking like lawyers." In the courtroom, however, other considerations may prevail. Most litigators avoid unnecessary legalese because they realize that jurors will not understand it, and it may actually antagonize them. Lawyers therefore mostly speak standard English in court. Those who are concerned with appearing competent and intelligent will use more formal language, but still ordinary English. Thus, the North Carolina lawyer who is handling an intellectual property case before a well-educated jury in the state capital will almost certainly use fairly formal standard English, although perhaps with a slight Southern accent. On the other hand, if that same attorney is in a rural town representing a local mom-and-pop company in a contract dispute with a huge multinational corporation based in New York, the lawyer might well choose to emphasize group cohesion by his use of language. By speaking a more regional variety, he would subtly be communicating to the jurors that he—and his clients—are part of the local community, perhaps even "good ole boys," in stark contrast to those big-city lawyers in their fancy pin-striped suits.

When code-switching is a deliberate mechanism to appeal to the sympathy or even the prejudices of the jurors, it raises ethical questions. Arguably, there is little harm in speaking formal standard English to appear competent and intelligent. Yet language variation is more problematic when it tries to appeal subtly to values or attitudes that could not be invoked expressly. An ugly example comes from a South Carolina case in 1947, in which a black man suspected of murder was killed by a white mob. The case received much attention from the Northern news media, and the prosecution of the black man's alleged killers was perceived locally as an attempt to force Northern values on a Southern community. Lawyers for the defendants reportedly appealed to the prejudices of the local community by loading their delivery to the jury with a heavy Southern accent.[10] The covert message was clear: ignore the evidence of guilt, uphold (white) Southern values, and send these carpetbaggers packing. Language is obviously a very powerful tool, and like all tools, it can be used for evil as well as good.

Questioning of Witnesses

Because the plaintiff has the burden of proof, it is his lawyer's job to prove the facts of the story alleged in the complaint. One of the primary ways to do so is to call witnesses to testify. Typically, these witnesses have their own stories to tell, which we might call **subnarratives;** each of them forms part of the larger narrative that is in dispute.

After jury selection and some other preliminaries, each side presents its case, beginning with the plaintiff. Before actually calling witnesses, counsel for the parties make an **opening statement,** in which they outline the evidence and how it will prove their client's case. The importance of keeping the client's story in mind is emphasized by trial manuals, such as one that comments that "[e]ffective opening statements are usually based on good storytelling."[11] Although traditionally they should limit themselves to outlining the facts that they intend to prove, most lawyers try to use the opening statement strategically, not only outlining the story they will tell through the evidence, but attempting to persuade the jury that the story is true. Consequently, lawyers have a strong incentive to be as clear as possible when addressing the jury. They realize intuitively that convoluted legalese does not communicate very well, so the opening statement is normally made in ordinary, albeit fairly formal, English.

After the opening statement, each side presents the evidence that supports its story. As noted, every witness should have a story to tell—or at least, part of a story. Yet witnesses are usually not permitted to testify in narrative form. Rather, most of the examination of witnesses occurs in a rigid question-and-answer format. This is a critical point; with a narrative, the story-teller herself decides how to tell her tale, while a question-and-answer format allocates control to the questioner (in this case, the examining lawyer).

Direct Examination

In a traditional court, examination of witnesses follows the question-and-answer format, with limited opportunity to give answers in narrative style. This is often frustrating for witnesses. In an English trial in 1682, a certain Lord Grey had been accused of corrupting the morals of Lady Henrietta Berkeley, apparently because he had helped the young woman run away from her tyrannical parents and secretly marry. Lady Henrietta took the stand. In response to questions, she testified that she had left home voluntarily. She was then told to sit down. "Will you not give me leave to tell the reason why I left my father's house?" she begged the court. "Will you not give me leave to speak for myself?" One of the judges retorted: "You are, madam, to answer only such questions as are asked you pertinent to the issue that the jury are to try; and if the counsel will ask you no questions, you are not to tell any story of yourself."[12] In terms of questioning strategies, little has changed in the intervening three centuries.

The side that called the witness engages in **direct examination.** Not surprisingly, the testimony of each witness begins with very ritualistic language as the witness is sworn in:

> THE CLERK: Please raise your right hand.
> Do you solemnly swear that the testimony you may give in the cause now pending before this court, shall be the truth, the whole truth and nothing but the truth, so help you God.
> THE WITNESS: Yes, I do.[13]

A typical pattern for questioning during direct examination is to begin by allowing the witness to give a brief narrative answer, but limited to

the topic that the lawyer's question raises. The following is an example
from the Jackson murder trial:

> Q: Would you tell the ladies and gentlemen of the jury what
> you observed when you entered apartment 9?
> A: As we entered the apartment, we walked into the kitchen
> area . . . and I walked through the kitchen to the right into the
> living room, where I observed a white male, approximately
> twenty-four years old, lying face up on the davenport. He was
> covered partially with a blanket, and there was blood gushing
> from his mouth.[14]

Questions like these are not so much requests for information as they
are polite commands to tell a mini-narrative. In fact, the "question" is
functionally more like an imperative: *Please tell the jury what you saw.*

After allowing the witness to tell his mini-narrative, the examining
lawyer asks a series of follow-up questions to clarify or expand on the
testimony, or to focus on particular points. The broadest of such questions are **wh-questions,** which begin with a question word like *why, when,*
or *how.* Although this type of question could theoretically allow for a
long narrative response, lawyers phrase them in such a way as to limit
the answer to a brief reply:

> Q: With respect to the white young man, where was he when
> you first observed him?
> A: He was lying next to a white female.[15]

Another common category of questions during direct examination
allows only a *yes* or *no* answer (these are sometimes called **yes/no questions**):[16]

> Q: Did he appear to you to be deceased?
> A: Yes, he did.[17]

A similar type is the **disjunctive question;** here, the question likewise
restricts the answer to two choices, but the choices are explicitly presented in the question:

> Q: Who was closer to the door that you entered, the young
> man or the young lady?
> A: The young man.[18]

During direct examination, there is consequently a progression from
open-ended questions, or requests to tell a brief narrative, to increasingly coercive or controlling questions that give the witness very little

leeway, as when lawyers force the witness to choose between two options by asking yes/no and disjunctive questions.

There are various reasons why lawyers maintain such rigid control over their questioning. No doubt the most important is strategic—to advance the client's case. For the plaintiff's counsel, this means producing persuasive evidence to support the critical elements of his client's story. Defense counsel must offer factual support for the defendant's counternarrative or defense. Lawyers accomplish these aims by steering the testimony of witnesses, to the extent it is legally and ethically permissible, in very specific directions.

The effectiveness of this strategy is demonstrated by the work of Conley and O'Barr on small claims courts in North Carolina and Colorado. In such informal settings, litigants are allowed to tell their own stories in largely narrative style. Conley and O'Barr found that litigants were far more satisfied with their courtroom experience when they could tell their own stories directly to a person in a position of authority. The drawback, however, was that the stories were frequently inadequate from a legal standpoint. Sometimes, for instance, the storytellers recited their narratives using passive or other impersonal constructions that failed to identify the actor who was responsible for their problems:

> The rent started falling behind.
> The tools got stolen.
> I got injured.

Overall, the storytellers tended to avoid expressly addressing issues of blame, responsibility, and agency.[19] Obviously, a legally adequate narrative must explain why the defendant should be held accountable for the injustice or injury that the plaintiff suffered. The traditional question-and-answer format, though frustrating for witnesses, allows lawyers to focus testimony on such legally relevant issues and to ensure that every element of their case receives factual support.

The strong legal preference for questions and answers over narratives is especially problematic for witnesses not accustomed to this unusual format. For example, Aboriginals who testify in Australian courts find the coercive question-and-answer format very alien. They are prone to say *yes* to many questions simply to please authority figures or to appear cooperative.[20] In such a situation, there is a danger that the person asking the questions may impose his own story on the witness, since it is the questioner who controls the direction of the conversation. Distortions are far less likely when a witness is able to tell her own story as a narrative.

Of course, lawyers could allow witnesses to use the narrative format more often, especially because witnesses themselves seem to prefer it. Yet from the lawyer's perspective, the danger that lurks in narrative testimony is that the witness could say too much. Irrelevant information would be annoying and time-consuming enough. Even more devastating is when a witness gratuitously volunteers information that damages the client's case. Thus, a lawyer typically allows for narrative testimony mainly from his own client, who should be well aware of what to say and what not to say, as well as expert witnesses, who are paid by the client and should be experienced enough to say only what will enhance their employer's case. Other witnesses are kept on a shorter leash. One of the worst things that can happen to a lawyer during trial is to lose control of a witness.

A further reason for tight control over testimony is the goal of precise communication. Lawyers often use questioning to clarify vague or ambiguous answers, or confirm exactly what the witness said, as in this illustration from the defense examination of a witness in the Jackson case. The witness has just testified that she went to a concert:

Q: Well was it like a rock or pop festival?
A: It was a free concert.
Q: It was "a freak"?
A: Free.
Q: Oh, a free. Excuse me.[21]

Naturally, even confirmatory questions like the above can be used strategically. Did the lawyer really hear *freak*? Or was he covertly suggesting to the jury that the victims were all countercultural "freaks" and that the father was somehow justified in rescuing his daughter from the "hippie commune" she had joined?

In addition, the question-and-answer format can produce more precise testimony by ensuring that technical terms are properly defined. Despite the profession's penchant for overusing legal terminology, lawyers realize that normally such terms need to be explained or translated. In the Jackson trial, a pathologist had used the medical term *aorta:*

Q: What is the aorta?
A: The largest artery—artery that carries blood from the heart through the entire system.

Most likely, the examining lawyer knew the meaning of the term but wished to have it explained to the jurors.

Lawyers also realize that some terminology is used within certain groups of people, and that nonmembers of the group (such as the jurors) may not understand it; this is especially true of argot or slang:

> Q: Well, among your age group, Mr. Richardson, does the term *stoned* or *to be stoned* have some particular significance?
> A: Yes, sir.
> Q: What is the significance of that term.
> A: It means to be high.
> . . .
> Q: But it's a term that is specifically used ordinarily among your peer group to refer to people who are high as a result of ingestion of either a narcotic drug or a dangerous drug?
> A: Yes, sir.[22]

Clearly, arguments that legal language cannot be translated into ordinary English are belied by the ability of litigators to accomplish this task when their strategic interests during trial demand it.

As we saw previously, lawyers sometimes use broad or general words, followed by a list of more precise elements that are included within the general term (as in *any X, including a, b, and c*). Often this combination of the general and the specific communicates more clearly than just a general term or a list. In testimony, when a witness uses a broad or general term, the lawyer may try to achieve this aim by eliciting a list of specific items included within the general language. In the Jackson murder case, a pathologist mentioned that she had tested the body of one of the victims for *narcotics*, which is a fairly broad category:

> Q: What narcotics?
> A: Basic drugs would include all opiates and derivatives.
> Q: Morphine and derivatives?
> A: All narcotics.
> Q: Morphine and narcotics, is that not correct?
> A: Yes, morphine, that's in the same category.
> . . .
> Q: What about LSD?
> A: We have not had much luck in the office of the medical examiner to have a reliable test for hallucinogens such as marijuana and LSD.[23]

In fact, opposing counsel can object to vague or overbroad questioning, forcing the examining lawyer to be more precise. During the Simpson trial, prosecutor Darden was asking a witness whether he had ever had *intimate and personal* conversations with the defendant. The judge sustained defense counsel's objection. Darden then resumed by asking about several more precise types of intimate conversations, including whether the witness had ever discussed his health, his relations with his wife, and Simpson's relations with his own wife.[24] In a written document, the lawyers might have asked the witness whether he had ever had *intimate and personal conversations with the defendant, including but not limited to discussions of your health, your relations with your wife, and Simpson's relations with his wife.* Via this questioning strategy they reach the same result orally.

Cross-examination

After a lawyer questions her own witness, the opposing side has a chance to cross-examine. Sometimes the cross-examining lawyer simply seeks information from the witness, as on direct examination, to support his client's narrative or counter-narrative. Yet a common strategy is not to bolster your own case, but to damage that of the opposition. In a sense, the cross-examining lawyer wishes to undermine what the witness communicated during direct examination. The lawyer aims to take the apparently clear communications made during direct examination and render them as uncertain, vague, and ambiguous as possible. The goal of the cross-examining lawyer is often befuddlement, rather than clarity. Not only do cross-examiners aim to muddy the message, but they may also try to drag the messengers through the mud by assailing their credibility or even accusing them of lying.

To accomplish these objectives, lawyers can utilize a more controlling and coercive method: **leading questions.**[25] A leading question suggests that there is only one correct answer, and in essence tries to "lead" the witness to that answer.[26] Leading questions are not directly tied to any particular linguistic form. In the words of McCormick, "the mere form of a question does not indicate whether it is leading. . . . The whole issue is whether an ordinary man would get the impression that the questioner desired one answer rather than another."[27]

Nonetheless, there are three common ways to ask a leading question. One is to use a negative yes/no question:

> Didn't you eat broccoli last night?

This question expects a positive response, although the expectation created by negative yes/no questions is sometimes rather complicated.[28]

Leading questions are also formed by making a statement, followed by what linguists call a **tag:**

> You ate broccoli last night, didn't you?
> You ate broccoli last night, isn't that correct?
> It is true, isn't it, that you ate broccoli last night?

Notice that although the tag is typically at the end, it can occur in the middle of the sentence, as in the last of the three examples. Finally, a common form of leading question is simply to make a statement with question intonation:

> You ate broccoli last night?

In many ways, "leading questions" are less requests for information than assertions of fact or accusations for which the examining lawyer seeks agreement. This is most clear in the last example, which is not really a question, but rather an assertion with interrogatory (rising) intonation. As a book on trial techniques points out, the cross-examiner should strive to make the assertions and statements of fact; the witness should simply be asked to agree with them.[29]

Although not all cross-examination consists of leading questions, research confirms that they are indeed very common.[30] They can be quite effective in undermining the accuracy or precision of a witness's testimony. For instance, Detective Mark Fuhrman testified in the Simpson case that he had found a glove (apparently worn by the killer) at the scene of the murder and another one at Simpson's estate. During his cross-examination, he was quizzed about his earlier testimony during a preliminary hearing, which the examining lawyer read from the transcript:

> Q: (*Reading from transcript of preliminary hearing on July 5*) "Question: When did you first observe [the glove]? Answer: We had flashlights. We were looking at the female victim. We looked at the male victim. I noticed the glove when I walked around to the—after I exited the residence the first time and walked around to the side or the north side, north perimeter of Bundy of 875 Bundy, there is an iron fence and through that iron fence you can get very close to the male victim, and looking there I could see them at his feet."
> Did you use the word "them" in your answer on July 5th?
> A: Yes, sir. Yes, sir.

Q: And was the last item to which "them" could have applied in your narrative the word "glove"?
A: Singular, yes.
Q: I'm simply asking whether glove, line 14, was the item you were talking about just prior to saying "I saw them at his feet"?
A: "Them," I was referring to the knit cap, the glove.
Q: Show me anywhere on that page where the knit cap is mentioned? Can you?
A: That page, no.
Q: All right. All right.
Do you see anything on the prior page, Detective Fuhrman, about the knit cap?
. . .
A: I do not.[31]

Not only did this cross-examination undermine the perceived accuracy and effect of the original testimony, but it cast doubt on the reliability and truthfulness of the witness. The questioning was meant to raise the suspicion in the jurors' minds that Fuhrman had actually found both gloves at the scene of the crime and had transported one of them to Simpson's estate in an attempt to frame him for the murder.

In another sequence, lawyer F. Lee Bailey used leading questions to attack Detective Fuhrman's credibility more directly. Fuhrman had denied ever saying the word *nigger* during the prior ten years:

Q: Are you therefore saying that you have not used that word in the past ten years, Detective Fuhrman?
A: Yes, that is what I'm saying.
Q: And you say under oath that you have not addressed any black person as a nigger or spoken about black people as niggers in the past ten years, Detective Fuhrman?
A: That's what I'm saying, sir.
Q: So that anyone who comes to this court and quotes you as using that word in dealing with African Americans would be a liar, would they not, Detective Fuhrman?
A: Yes, they would.
Q: All of them, correct?
A: All of them.[32]

Here, the point is not to muddy the waters at all. Instead, Bailey tried to obtain a clear and precise statement under oath ("I never used *nigger* during the past ten years") that could then be contrasted with evidence that Fuhrman had, in fact, used that slur. Once it became clear that he had used the "N-word" routinely during the past decade, it was evident that *Fuhrman* was the liar, and his credibility was completely destroyed.

Defense attorney Johnnie Cochran drove this point home to the jury during his closing argument. After quoting Fuhrman's denial that he had used the "n-word," Cochran continued: "That's what he told you under oath in this case. Did he lie? Did he lie? Did he lie under oath? Did this key prosecution witness lie under oath?"[33] The answer could not have been plainer.

Cross-examination is quite coercive. This may not be a serious problem for educated or affluent witnesses, who may be fairly well equipped to deal with the pressure of such "questions." Here is an exchange during the cross-examination of a pathologist in the Jackson case, who manages to resist the questioning lawyer:

> Q: In other words, you just made no effort at the morgue to determine whether there had been any recent ingestion of any hallucinatory or narcotic drug?
> A: It wouldn't be fair to answer you with a yes or no. We perform examinations when they are indicated. And under these circumstances, we didn't feel as though they were indicated.[34]

Indeed, although lawyers have a great deal of power over the questioning process, witnesses often refuse to play the role of hapless victim. Witnesses can and do resist attempts by the cross-examining lawyer to pin them down to statements that are not accurate.[35] And, of course, opposing counsel can object to "badgering" of the witness.

On the other hand, less confident witnesses, such as children or people who are not members of mainstream culture, might be quite intimidated by such questioning, and might begin to equivocate.[36] That, of course, is frequently the main point of cross-examination: to undermine the testimony that the witness gave on direct examination. Yet it is troubling that this strategy is most likely to be effective with the socially and economically weakest members of society. One would hope that judges are aware of the problem and use their power as neutral arbiters to minimize its impact.

The Language of Questioning

Even though on the surface the lawyer and witness are engaged in a kind of conversation, the question-and-answer format differs from ordinary conversations in some interesting ways. In a sense, the jurors (or judge, if there is no jury) seem to be little more than eavesdroppers in a discussion between lawyer and witness. Actually, of course, both participants in the conversation are well aware that they are really addressing the jury, not each other. Occasionally, witnesses will even turn to the jury when giving an answer.

What this means is that once again—as happens so often in the law—we find lawyers speaking for others. In a very real sense, the witness is speaking to the jurors, but for the most part, jurors cannot ask the questions. This must be enormously frustrating for many jurors. Fortunately, some judges now allow jurors to pose their own questions, although they must normally be submitted in writing to the judge, who reviews the question before asking it.[37]

The "conversation" between the lawyer and witness is also unusual in that it consists of virtually nothing but questions and answers. Most conversations have far more variety. And only the attorney has the right to ask questions; the witness can only answer (and under many circumstances, *must* answer).[38] There are thus severe constraints on how this conversation can proceed. The question-and-answer process is unnatural in another way: the response is supposed to directly answer the question, and only answer the question. Normally, if I were to ask you, *Do you remember what you had for breakfast this morning?*, you can infer that this is really just a polite way of asking what you had for breakfast, not a test of your memory. Thus, you will probably respond: *I had coffee and granola.* Only people with a bad sense of humor would answer with *yes.* But in court, the same question would be answered much more literally:

> Q: Do you remember what you had for breakfast this morning?
> A: Yes.
> Q: What did you eat?
> A: Coffee and granola.
> Q: You mean to say that you ate granola and drank coffee, is that correct?
> A: Yes, sir.

In ordinary conversation, we can leave out information that is pragmatically obvious; in courtroom questioning, these logical steps tend to be made explicit. Furthermore, the witness can only answer the question that is posed. She cannot turn to the lawyer and ask what *he* had for breakfast. Virtually the only time that a witness can pose a question is when the original question was unclear; in that case, it is legitimate for the witness to ask the lawyer for clarification.

When lawyers question witnesses, they are well aware that if they wish to communicate effectively, they must use ordinary English, rather than legalese. At the same time, they tend to speak fairly formally. Here are some of the questions posed by a lawyer in the Jackson murder trial:

> Now, what if any effort was made on your part or on the part of Dr. Weatherall, Doctor, to determine whether this young man immediately prior to his death had ingested any heroin?
>
> Now, at the time that you began to live at 4330 Lincoln, did you hold some title in connection with that structure?
>
> During your lifetime, Mr. Richardson, have you ever been convicted of any crime?
>
> So I gather then from your answer, you didn't undertake any kind of gainful employment?[39]

Not only is the vocabulary formal and even stilted, but there are many redundant and wordy expressions, such as *on the part of Dr. Weatherall* for *by Dr. Weatherall, at the time that* for *when,* and the unnecessary *during your lifetime.* One explanation is that the setting itself is quite formal. And, of course, because we tend to associate more formal language with higher prestige and better education, lawyers prefer to speak what is felt to be a more prestigious variety of English.

Still, litigators can and do vary the formality of their speech during questioning, often for strategic reasons. A lawyer may use colloquial English to subtly criticize an expert witness for trying to obscure a simple matter by using big words, or on the other hand, consciously use very formal language with a lesser educated witness as a way to emphasize her lack of education.[40]

At times, courtroom language may be quite casual, especially the pedestrian administrative or procedural discussions that occur between bench and bar during a trial. In chapter 8 we mentioned **telegraphic speech,** which is truncated language stripped of all predictable elements and used for maximally efficient in-group communication. It is extremely common at trials for making objections (*objection!*) and ruling on them (*sustained*) without seriously interrupting the flow of testimony. Similarly, when prosecutor Christopher Darden in the Simpson case wished to approach the bench for a side-bar conference (a brief session between the lawyers and judge out of hearing of the jury), he simply asked *May I approach?*[41] The rest of the request was fully predictable and could safely be truncated.

Slang has the similar function of shortening communication, as we saw with the plea bargaining process. The following is an excerpt from the Simpson trial, taken from a side-bar conference in which prosecutor

Darden is explaining what his witness's testimony is going to be and
whether it is admissible:

> THE COURT: All right. We are at the side bar. Mr. Darden,
> where we going with this?
> MR. DARDEN: I'm just trying to establish the closeness of
> their relationship, that's all. He is not going to jump out and
> say he had sex with another woman or used drugs, you know,
> the usual things guys talk about.
> THE COURT: What is he going to say?
> MR. DARDEN: And he is going to say that he discussed an
> incident that apparently happened on January 1, 1989, and
> that is where we are headed. So you know, I don't think any
> bombs are about to fall on them.
> THE COURT: Mr. Douglas.
> . . .
> MR. DOUGLAS: [Y]our honor, the court has different inci-
> dents that the court has ruled inadmissible and I want to
> make sure we are talking about things that are cool.[42]

Sidebars during the Simpson trial were sometimes so casual that Judge
Ito called the attorneys by their first names, and they replied using *you*
rather than a third person form:

> THE COURT: All right. We are over at the side bar.
> Marcia, this guy has said, hey, my best recollection is 10:50.
> He said this four times now. Johnnie has got him to say, yeah,
> I told the police it was sometime between 10:50 and 11:00.
> He said four times now my best recollection now is 10:50.
>   How many times are we going to go over this? Just a ques-
> tion.
> MS. CLARK: You are right.
> MR. COCHRAN: You are right. Thank you, your honor.
> MS. CLARK: Okay.[43]

Even though trials are quite adversarial (and the Simpson trial was probably more antagonistic than most), lawyerly use of slang, as well as occasional joking, subtly reminds the participants that they are members of
the same profession and need to maintain a certain level of collegiality.

Implications of the Questioning Process

So far, we have viewed questioning as a transparent process designed to
elicit information. Of course, the legal system lets lawyers control witnesses to some degree, but this is justified as a way to discover the truth
as efficiently as possible. The system is not naive; it recognizes that each

side will try to elicit only information that is strategically valuable. This is felt to be remedied, however, by the adversarial nature of the proceedings, in which the opposing side is given an opportunity to cross-examine each witness and to offer its own evidence. In theory, truth and justice will triumph.

Yet the questioning process is not merely a neutral mechanism for arriving at the truth. The language of the questioning process itself can affect both the content of the testimony of the witness and her perceived credibility.

We have seen that there is a dramatic difference between the narrative style of testifying and the more fragmented style characteristic of the question-and-answer format. Psychological studies have shown that when someone witnesses an event and is later asked to recite as many details as she can remember in narrative format, the person will mention fewer details than when she is specifically questioned about them. But significantly, the details that she provides in the narrative are more likely to be accurate. Conversely, the question-and-answer format produces more information, but of lower quality.[44]

The way in which questions are worded, and the type of question used, may also have an impact on the witness's testimony. A well-known study by Elizabeth Loftus and John Palmer showed test subjects a film of an automobile accident. The subjects were later asked some questions to test their recall. Some of them were asked how fast the cars were going when they *smashed* into each other; others were asked how fast the cars were going when they *hit* each other. Although all subjects saw the same film, those with the *smashed* version of the question reported substantially higher speeds. Equally interesting is that these effects persisted. When asked a week later whether they had seen any broken glass in the film (it showed none), subjects with the *smashed* question reported far more often that they had indeed seen glass.[45]

Another study asked one group of people whether they got headaches *frequently*, and if so, how often. The group reported an average of 2.2 headaches per week. An equivalent group was asked: *Do you get headaches occasionally, and if so, how often?* This group reported having an average of only 0.7 headaches per week.[46]

Research confirms that the specific type of question can likewise distort the recall of witnesses. In one experiment 140 subjects watched short films. One film contained a bicycle. When later asked a neutral question, *Did you see a bicycle?*, 51 percent of the viewers responded that they had. But a different group that saw the same film was asked a leading question: *You did see a bicycle, didn't you?* Now, 74 percent said *yes.*[47] This is convincing evidence that the legal system's restrictions on the use of leading questions are quite justified.

Results such as these are not likely to surprise many litigators, who for centuries have framed their questions with the hope of influencing the response. Nonetheless, such research highlights the importance of minimizing the distorting effects of questioning. To some extent, the legal system itself keeps the problem within bounds. For one thing, lawyers are aware that using overtly coercive or manipulative questions will not go over well with the jury. If jurors get the impression that an examining lawyer is trying to lead or manipulate the witness, they will give far less credence to her testimony. For this reason, many trial manuals recommend asking open-ended questions during direct examination, thus allowing for a narrative response that avoids the impression of putting words in the witness's mouth. Only afterwards should the lawyer pose more specific questions.[48]

Actually, lawyers should make even greater use of narrative in the courtroom. No less a figure than John Henry Wigmore, a leading figure in evidence law, pointed out that the question-and-answer format had been taken to "absurd excesses." He urged that narrative, the "natural method" of giving testimony, should become the more usual way.[49]

Another limitation on manipulative questions comes from the adversarial nature of the proceedings, and specifically, the opposing attorney's right to object. If a lawyer were to ask an eyewitness how fast a car was driving when it *smashed* into another, counsel for the driver ought to object that the question is argumentative or assumes facts not in evidence, both objections that a competent judge would probably sustain. More subtle suggestive questioning, however, may not be noticed by opposing counsel, or the judge may not find it objectionable.

Perhaps a more troubling point is one raised by Richard Wydick, who observes that lawyers routinely interview witnesses and may rehearse the questioning process with them before trial.[50] Here, there is no opposing counsel to object to suggestive questions, nor are there jurors to keep the examination overtly neutral. Though the practice is ethically dubious, many lawyers are tempted to covertly shape the testimony of friendly witnesses by means of suggestive questioning, hoping that it will permanently alter their recall of an event and that they can then elicit more favorable testimony at trial through an overtly neutral question. An English barrister has illustrated this strategy, with the lawyer interviewing the client as follows before trial:

Q: When Bloggs came into the pub, did he have a knife in his hand?
A: I don't remember.
Q: Did you see him clearly?
A: Yes.
Q: Do people in that neighborhood often walk into pubs with knives in their hands?
A: No, certainly not.
Q: If you had seen Bloggs with a knife in his hand, would you remember that?
A: Yes, of course.
Q: And you don't remember any knife?
A: No, I don't remember any knife.

What started out as *I don't remember* may come out at trial as follows:

Q: When Bloggs came into the pub, did he have a knife in his hand?
A: No, he did not.[51]

The legal system should therefore remain alert to the potential implications of the wording of a question. Language is never really neutral. This is especially true in an adversarial system, where each side uses language strategically, its sole aim being to win the case.

The language and style of questioning not only influence the content of testimony but also the jury's assessment of its value. Specifically, the language of a witness can influence the jury's perception of whether that witness is telling the truth. Because a trial virtually always involves conflicting narratives, determining the truth depends not only on the amount of evidence that each side can offer, but also its quality. Naturally, the more competent and believable a witness seems to be, the more weight the jury will give to her testimony.

An extensive study of the language of witnesses was undertaken by the Language and Law Project at Duke University during the 1970s.[52] The researchers, who looked at actual criminal trials in North Carolina, found that the speech style of witnesses had a significant impact on how hearers assessed the testimony. For example, many witnesses were found to speak in a **powerless** style. This is characterized by the following features:

1. Abundant use of **hedges** (expressions of uncertainty, such as *I think* or *sort of*).
2. **Hesitation forms** (words with no meaning that are used to fill pauses and gaps, such as *uh* or *well*).

   3. **Question intonation** (giving an answer with rising intonation, another indication of uncertainty).
   4. **Intensifiers** (words that increase the force of an utterance,
such as *very* or *surely*).

If asked how long he was at the scene of an accident before an ambulance arrived, a powerless speaker might testify: *Oh, it seems like it was
about, uh, twenty minutes.* A more powerful speaker would just say: *Twenty
minutes.*[53]

Linguists had previously associated this speech style with women, but
the Duke study showed that at least in the courtroom, it was characteristic of some men as well. In particular, the powerless style was common
with both men and women of lower socioeconomic status. Witnesses who
had higher social status and were better educated used far fewer of these
features, thus speaking in a more powerful style.[54]

To determine the effects of the different speech styles, the research
team produced audio tapes in which the same speakers gave testimony
in both powerful and powerless styles. These tapes were then played to
groups of subjects, each group receiving a different style but the same
content. When asked to rate the testimony, the subjects found that witnesses who used the powerful style were significantly more convincing,
truthful, competent, intelligent, and trustworthy.[55]

The formality of a witness's language is also significant. The Duke
project found that witnesses who could successfully use formal language
were evaluated as being more convincing, competent, qualified, and intelligent than those who could not.[56] Several other studies have confirmed that correct use of standard English heightens credibility; in fact,
there is evidence that criminal defendants who use polite forms and
speak in complete sentences are more likely to be acquitted.[57]

Given that a more formal style of language is associated in the popular
mind with greater credibility, intelligence, and other positive evalua-
tions, the desire of lawyers to enhance their prestige through the use of
formal and even archaic language clearly has a strong basis in social
reality. This explains why the courtroom speech of lawyers—though
largely ordinary English—tends to be fairly formal, especially in the presence of the jury. Lawyers use a "higher" variety of language not merely
because they want to appear well educated and of good social standing,
but also for the strategic reason that they hope the respect given to the
lawyer will rub off on the client.

The speech of witnesses is more problematic. Unlike lawyers, witnesses
may not be able to switch to formal standard English. Especially people

who have less education and belong to the lower socioeconomic strata may normally speak a regional variety of English, or in the case of African Americans, what is called **Black English** or **Ebonics**. As we have seen, many regional and social dialects are stigmatized among the general population. When speakers of these language varieties testify, they may be judged less competent, intelligent, and truthful simply because of how they speak. Lawyers are aware of this problem and will almost always advise such clients to try to speak "proper" English. Yet the clients may not be able to do so very well, finding themselves judged less competent and intelligent despite their best efforts to use the rules and pronunciation of standard English. Unfortunately, because this is a social fact that is to a large extent subconscious, it may be virtually impossible to remedy the problem.

Ironically, the profession is becoming aware of the research regarding its language and style and is now attempting to apply that research strategically as well. For instance, an article in a trial litigation manual published by a division of the American Bar Association refers specifically to the research of Elizabeth Loftus and her finding that the questions that are asked about an event influence the way a witness remembers it. The article concludes:

> The lesson could not be more clear. Completely neutral questions are rare indeed. Questions which will influence the answers—at least statistically—can be framed so they will not run afoul of the rule against leading. If the words in question are going to influence the answers, they should be carefully thought out in advance.[58]

Thus, the very research that served as a warning about the dangers of the questioning process is being exploited by the profession to make the process even more effective! In a system where lawyers are under an obligation to do everything legally and ethically permissible to further the interests of their clients, this is exactly what one would expect. Still, one wonders whether this is what the researchers set out to accomplish.

Creating a Written Record

The testimony of witnesses, as well as most other proceedings, is transcribed by a court reporter. Even though this is supposed to be a *verbatim* transcript, the written record is seldom a real word-for-word transcription of the oral event. One reason, of course, is that the reporter inevitably makes mistakes. In addition, nonverbal or paralinguistic features, such as hesitation or pauses, gesturing, and intonation, are not reported all that well, if at all. Mostly, this results from the fact that writing is an imperfect means of representing speech. It is a significant point: we have seen that people make judgments of credibility on the basis of such non-verbal cues. This explains why courts of appeal, which must rely solely on the written record, defer to the factual findings made during trial by the judge or jury, who were able to observe the nonverbal behavior of witnesses.

Judges and lawyers do sometimes attempt to have the record reflect the more important nonverbal events that occur during trial. Judge Ito in the Simpson case was always quite careful to state for the record who was present in the courtroom or that they were at sidebar. And lawyers may have an interest in ensuring that the record contains certain nonverbal information. An example of the incompleteness of the written record is reported by Clark Cunningham. He describes an actual case, where he and some law students were representing a young man stopped for a traffic infraction. They asserted that the police may have been racially motivated when they stopped and questioned their client. At this juncture the judge interrupted:

> THE COURT: Maybe for the record, when we got into this bigot and racial thing, maybe for the record we should indicate that Mr. Dujon Johnson is a black American.[59]

The judge's (or lawyer's) statement to the record helps fill in gaps and ambiguities that would otherwise occur in the written transcript.

More disturbing than the inherent failures of the transcription process are some of the other practices of the court reporting profession, as pointed out by Anne Graffam Walker, a former court reporter with linguistic training. Walker observes that many reporters correct grammatical errors and eliminate false starts, especially in the speech of lawyers and judges. This is justified on the basis that only sworn testimony by witnesses is evidence, and thus inviolate. In fact, it appears that the reporting profession actually encourages its members to make changes to the speech of judges, allowing "the change or transposition of a few words" to avoid a judge's "crude and blundering expression."[60]

Obviously, these changes have much to do with the legal profession's aspirations towards elegance and prestige, which are enhanced by the use of erudite, grammatically correct language. Because the reporters are de facto employed by lawyers and judges, they are under some pressure to accommodate them by eliminating the many false starts and errors that inevitably occur in unscripted speech. Perhaps this is harmless enough in most circumstances, but it becomes cause for concern if the reporter covers for an abusive judge.

The transcript of proceedings is also interesting because, as noted, it becomes the definitive record of what occurred. In this sense, the transcript is like the authoritative written texts discussed in earlier chapters. For example, it was seen that one consequence of creating an authoritative text is that what was actually said—the oral basis for the text—becomes irrelevant. All that matters is what is contained in the text. This is largely true of trial transcripts as well.

The consequences of turning oral testimony into an authoritative written record are most striking when it involves interpretation of testimony by a witness speaking another language. A witness who speaks Spanish on the stand will have that testimony translated into English by an interpreter. It is the English translation that is transcribed and that becomes the official record of what the witness said. Not only does the original testimony in Spanish become irrelevant for purposes of subsequent proceedings, but it is considered erroneous for Spanish-speaking jurors to rely on it at trial.

This practice led to a rather perverse result in the United States Supreme Court case of *Hernandez v. New York*.[61] The Court there held that when a trial was slated to involve Spanish-language testimony, the prosecutor could legitimately exclude Spanish speakers from the jury if he believed that they might follow the witness's actual testimony, rather than listening only to the English translation. Essentially, jurors are supposed to treat the original oral testimony in such cases as though it does not exist. Of course, with English testimony jurors rely very much on what the witness said, and how she said it. I can think of no conceivable reason why Spanish speakers should not be allowed to do the same.

As with other legal documents, the trial transcript tends to be interpreted as an autonomous text. In the discussion on interpretation in chapter 7, we saw that courts generally presume that legal documents have been drafted in such a way that they can be interpreted "autonomously," without having to refer to information outside the text. Recall that lawyers, in their questioning of witnesses, also strive to create a clear and complete record. In a sense, this can be viewed as trying to convert the oral testimony into an autonomous written text.

A consequence is that judges tend to interpret the transcript as though it is an authoritative text, rather than being merely as a record of spoken language. Thus the trial transcript, like a contract, statute, or will, tends to be interpreted very literally. This is perhaps most evident in perjury prosecutions, where courts fixate on the written language in the transcript to determine whether a witness made a false statement in an earlier trial, rather than interpreting the earlier testimony as ordinary spoken language.

An illustration comes from *Bronston v. United States*.[62] Samuel Bronston was president of a movie production company that petitioned for bankruptcy. At a hearing, the company's creditors were trying to locate his personal and company bank accounts in various European countries. The transcript contained the following exchange between the lawyer for a creditor and Mr. Bronston:

> Q: Do you have any bank accounts in Swiss banks, Mr. Bronston?
> A: No, sir.
> Q: Have you ever?
> A: The company had an account there for about six months, in Zurich.[63]

In fact, Bronston had also had a large personal bank account in Switzerland for five years, where he had deposited and drawn checks for over $180,000.

Mr. Bronston was convicted of perjury. The prosecution's theory was that by addressing his second answer to the *company's* assets, Bronston falsely implied that he had never had a *personal* Swiss bank account. In a normal spoken conversation, this is exactly how people would understand his response. The reason, roughly speaking, is that when we request information, we normally assume that the response we receive is relatively complete, something the philosopher Paul Grice called the **maxim of quantity**.[64] Consider this exchange:

> Q: Have you ever had any children?
> A: I have a son, Paul, and a daughter, Tracy.

The implication of this answer is that the respondent has no other children. Thus, if the respondent actually had another daughter, Susan, who is presently in the penitentiary, most people would conclude that he had not been entirely truthful, or at least had been intentionally misleading.[65]

Nonetheless, the Supreme Court unanimously reversed Bronston's perjury conviction. The Court recognized that in ordinary conversation the hearer could reasonably infer from Bronston's answer that he had never had a personal bank account in Switzerland. But it emphasized that the answer was literally true. Even though a witness's testimony might be misleading, it is the responsibility of the questioning lawyer to probe further. In other words, the Court interpreted the testimony more like authoritative written text than as speech. Even though Bronston probably intended to lead his questioner astray by cleverly manipulating his answer, it was the duty of the examining attorney to ensure the creation of an autonomous text that could be interpreted literally, without the use of inferences. Instead of assuming that Bronston's response was a relatively complete answer to the question, the lawyer should have clarified the matter by specifically asking whether the response was, in fact, complete. This explains why many litigators almost compulsively follow an answer like that of Bronston by asking: *Is that all?* or *Is there anything else?*

Creating a written record in the form of a trial transcript therefore involves much more than mechanically converting speech into writing, even when complete accuracy is achieved. Lawyers always have the record in the back of their minds, aiming not only to make it complete, accurate, and autonomous, but also hoping to have it present all the facts—and only the facts—that will support their client's story. And courts tend to interpret the record quite literally, as written language, and with the assumption that the lawyers and court reporter were successful in creating a complete, accurate, and autonomous document.

Much of this may change when more modern methods of recording speech, such as tape and video recorders, are utilized more widely in the courtroom. Many courts are experimenting with such devices, especially because they can save a great deal of money. The irony is that if a decision is appealed, a court reporter must still create a written version from the tape recording or video, because appellate courts generally require a transcript of the proceedings. At least for now, the written record continues to reign supreme.

CHAPTER ELEVEN

Completing the Story

After the lawyers have produced evidence to prove or negate the plaintiff's story, they make their **summation** or **closing argument.** In closing, the plaintiff's attorney must weave together a complete narrative out of the fragments that were presented by the witnesses at trial. Then she must persuade the jury (or the judge in a bench trial) that it is true. If it is a jury trial, the judge must instruct the jury on how they are to proceed, and the rules of law that they are to apply to the case. The jury "retires" to deliberate, reaches a verdict, and reports the verdict to the court. This process determines the truth of the plaintiff's story, at least for legal purposes. If the story is found to be true, the judge enters a judgment on the basis of the verdict, typically offering the plaintiff some kind of remedy, and thus resolving the crisis or problem that precipitated the case originally. The narrative that began with the pleadings will then have been completed.

Closing Arguments

One function of closing argument is to weave together the subnarratives of the various witnesses into a complete and coherent story. Especially in a factually complex trial, the plaintiff's story emerges in a very fragmented fashion.[1] Suppose that the plaintiff (in criminal cases, the prosecution) alleges that the defendant robbed a bank at 10 o'clock in the morning. The defendant's roommate might be called to testify that the defendant left the house at 9:30 with a gun, that he did not return until late at night, and that three days later the defendant bought an expensive new car with a wad of cash. Parts or all of the roommate's story will be retold on cross-examination. A neighbor might then testify that she saw the defendant get into his car at 9:35 on the day of the crime and drive off in the direction of the bank. A week later she discovered some blood spots in the driveway next to his car. Obviously, it would be virtually impossible to present even this simple story in chronological order during trial, because the witnesses cannot be expected to return to the stand to testify over and over; rather, they generally relate all they know in one appearance, even though their stories overlap chronologically. From the jury's perspective, this results in testimony that skips back and forth in time and is thus very disorganized. It is the lawyer's job, mainly during closing argument, to weave it all together. In this sense, the lawyer is much like a film editor. A movie might begin in the desert, continue in Los Angeles, and then end back in the desert. Obviously, a director will normally film all the scenes in the desert at one time, rather than shuttling the crew out to the desert, back to Los Angeles, and then out to the desert again for the final scene. The film editor puts those scenes in their proper location in the film. This is quite similar to what the lawyer does for the jury.

The other major purpose of the closing arguments, of course, is to persuade the jury or judge that the party's version of the story is true. There is a tremendous amount that has been written about the persuasive use of language. To some extent, persuasion depends more on the *content* of what is said than on its *form,* and thus exceeds the scope of this book. I will concentrate here on some linguistic features that are commonly used to persuade.

Of course, the distinction between form and content is not always easy to draw, and the two are usually intertwined. An example is that words may be very similar in meaning; we discussed such **synonyms** in chapter 6 and saw that lawyers are prone to use long lists of them in written legal language. Yet though words can be very similar, they are arguably never identical. At the least, there will be subtle differences in connotation. In oral argument, lawyers avoid long lists of synonyms. Instead, they carefully choose only those words that convey a sense or connotation that favors their strategic interest. For instance, Brenda Danet studied the trial of a doctor accused of performing an illegal abortion. She found that participants used at least forty words and phrases to refer to the "subject" of the abortion, including *fetus, child, unborn child, product of conception, specimen, baby, the deceased, person, body, human being, offspring, embryo, victim, blob, neonate, individual, member of the human race,* and *loved one.*[2] Not surprisingly, the prosecutor gravitated towards words that emphasized the potential of the fetus to become a human being, including *baby* and *child.* The defense attorney preferred *fetus* or *embryo,* both cold, scientific terms.

Lawyers also use **antonyms** quite persuasively, especially to create rhetorical contrast. In the abortion case, lawyers not only chose terms that favored their position, but contrasted their own preferred terms with those of their adversary. The prosecutor mentioned during argument to the jury that the doctor had testified that he removed the *fetus—the subject*. He continued: "Take a look at the picture of the subject. Is it just a subject? Is it just a specimen?" The defense, in turn, noted that the indictment referred to the killing of a *baby boy,* emphasizing that "no baby boy was ever killed."[3] Thus, relationships among words can be used quite effectively during a trial.

Another linguistic feature of closing argument is the variety of language spoken by the lawyer. In the majority of cases, the lawyer wants to communicate as clearly as possible. So, she will generally avoid legalese and other aspects of legal language that impede comprehension. And as mentioned above, the lawyer can speak a particular language variety to project a desired image of herself, just as she chooses her clothing to enhance that image.

The prosecutor in the Jackson case used his language variety quite effectively. He wished to convey a sense of outrage to the jury and to mock the defendant's claim of insanity. Clearly, outrage or mockery are not expressed very well in stiff, formal language. So, his tone is quite casual:

> And then he came home at 1:40 A.M.
> And what does he do?
> Just like always, Mr. Jackson has a glass of milk.
> Is this insanity, legal insanity?
> Doing just as he had always done, he had his glass of milk.
> . . .
> He has his glass of milk, and then he proceeds to arm himself to the teeth.[4]

The closing argument of the defense counsel, in contrast, was in very formal English. After flattering the jury by praising their attentiveness, he continued:

> Therefore, this afternoon, with your indulgence, I will endeavor to respond—to respond to and comment upon, not only what Mr. Gilman did say to you in the course of his remarks in the morning, but I will endeavor to address myself as well to some of the significant areas that I find he neglected to bring to your attention.[5]

Perhaps the reason for this stilted tone is that the defense was relying on expert testimony that Mr. Jackson was legally insane; the lawyer's attempt to project an image of intelligence and education would be consistent with that theme. Formal language would also foster a sense of detachment, perhaps intended to encourage the jury to rationally analyze the mental state of a father who murdered his own daughter. At the same time, this style does not communicate all that clearly and forcefully, and it fails to involve the jury emotionally with the defense case.

The divergent styles of these two lawyers is most strikingly revealed by how they ask the jury not to accept their opponent's argument. Defense counsel told the jury that *what they say is not worthy of your credence.*[6] In stark contrast, the prosecution made the same point by rhetorically asking: *Are you kidding me?*[7] Ultimately, Mr. Jackson was found sane and convicted of manslaughter for the death of his daughter, and second-degree murder for the other victims. Readers may draw their own conclusions regarding the effectiveness of these disparate styles, but it is worth mentioning that trial manuals almost universally recommend avoiding excessively formal or legalistic speech in closing arguments. They stress the importance of presenting the client's story in simple, direct, conversational English.[8]

The research confirms these impressions. In her study of the abortion trial, Danet observed that the prosecutor used active verbs that were monosyllabic and vivid during his closing argument; he, of course, wanted to emphasize the actor. In contrast, the defense lawyer used nominalizations and passives, as well as Latinate, obfuscatory verbs.[9] The doctor was convicted. A linguistic investigation of a civil trial in Indiana likewise suggests that a more informal, conversational style tends to be most effective in the average case.[10]

Anecdotal evidence confirms this impression. A newspaper article recently related how Thomas Girardi, a Los Angeles lawyer, won a stunning settlement of $333 million for his clients. Asked the reason for his success, a fellow attorney explained: "He can take a complex set of facts and reduce it to a highly understandable situation for a jury. The average jury loves Tom Girardi because he doesn't talk like a lawyer."[11]

In the Simpson trial, prosecutor Clark began her closing argument on a very personal note. After opening with a stereotypical greeting (*Good morning, ladies and gentlemen*), she referred to her own emotions in very informal language, empathized with the jurors, and tried to negate the rather stiff and combative image that she had projected during most of the trial:

> I want to sit down and talk to you and tell you, "What do you want to know? What do you want to talk about?" Because that

way I don't have to talk about stuff you don't want to hear, stuff that you don't want explained, stuff that you are not interested in, and I can't, and I always have a sense of frustration.

So I'm sorry if I say things that you don't need to hear or I explain things that are already clear to you. Please bear with me because I am not a mind reader and I don't know.[12]

The sentences are short and simple, not the long and convoluted prose that characterizes much written legal language. Formal language would have highlighted the social distance between Clark, the representative of the state, and the jurors. Her clothing reinforced her desired image: she was dressed in a plain, light-colored suit and wore no flashy jewelry.[13] And her tone was relaxed and friendly.

Nonetheless, Clark had difficulties connecting with the jurors, perhaps because she was white and most of the jurors were black. In fact, eight out of the twelve were black females. To bond with these jurors, she would have to do so as a woman. She seems to have hoped that the prosecution would benefit from female sympathy with the main victim, Nicole Simpson, a woman who had been abused by her husband and alleged killer. Clark thus seems to have tried to create a bond with the jury by positioning herself as a woman, someone who is not afraid of revealing her emotions, and who is concerned about the well-being of the jurors.[14]

A common device in closing is the use of rhetorical questions.[15] Clark's closing argument—like many others—used such questions, which are very different from the questions used to examine witnesses. Obviously, closing argument should *answer* questions, not ask them. This is especially true with the prosecution, for whom unanswered questions can be fatal because they lead to reasonable doubt. Thus, the only type of question one is likely to hear at this time is rhetorical, those with an obvious answer. Clark used rhetorical questions, but with a twist. Unsure that the mainly African American jurors would agree with her that the answers were self-evident, Clark not only asked the questions, but answered them:

Let me come back to Mark Fuhrman for a minute.
Just so it is clear. Did he lie when he testified here in this courtroom saying that he did not use racial epithets in the last ten years?
Yes.
Is he a racist?
Yes.

> Is he the worst LAPD [Los Angeles Police Department] has
> to offer?
> Yes.
> Do we wish that this person was never hired by LAPD?
> Yes.
> Should LAPD have ever hired him?
> No.
> Should such a person be a police officer?
> No.
> In fact, do we wish there were no such person on the planet?
> Yes.
> But the fact that Mark Fuhrman is a racist and lied about it
> on the witness stand does not mean that we haven't proven the
> defendant guilty beyond a reasonable doubt.[16]

After going over the applicable law, Clark gave jurors a chronology of the murder, piecing together a story from the testimony at trial. She also extensively discussed the forensic evidence.

Co-counsel Christopher Darden hammered away at many of the themes that Clark had raised, again trying to arouse the indignation of the mainly female jury. For example, he pointed out that Simpson had insulted his wife while she was pregnant with his child, calling her a *fat pig.*[17]

One of his most effective uses of language involved a different topic: the fact that Nicole had left several items in a safe deposit box. These included letters from Simpson in which he tried to reconcile with her following marital difficulties, some photographs that documented his beating of her, and her will:

> Okay. She put those things there for a reason. I mean, they're
> just letters and they're just pictures. But if you are going to have
> a safe deposit box, you'd think that the things you put in that
> box are the things that you think are important.
> Now, I don't know how you want to interpret that conduct.
> You can interpret it any way you want. But let me suggest to you
> that you should interpret it this way. She is leaving you a road
> map to let you know who it is who will eventually kill her. She
> knew in 1989. She knew it and she wants you to know it. She
> knew who was going to do it to her, but she didn't know when.
> But whenever that event actually came, she wanted you to know
> who did it.[18]

This is an almost eerie use of the pronoun *you* to refer to the jurors. When Darden says *she wants you to know it,* he uses the present tense, intimating that Nicole herself is speaking to them from the grave and is pointing an accusing finger at her former husband. When Clark later made the final closing argument for the prosecution, she followed up on this theme:

> Usually I feel like I'm the only one left to speak for the victims. But in this case, Ron and Nicole are speaking to you. They're speaking to you and they're telling you who murdered them . . . and they both are telling you who did it with their hair, their clothes, their bodies, their blood. They tell you he did it. He did it. Mr. Simpson, Orenthal Simpson, he did it.
>
> They told you in the only way they can. Will you hear them or will you ignore their plea for justice?[19]

Darden also alluded to the deteriorating relationship between O. J. and Nicole. He remarked on a letter that O. J. sent her sometime after she moved out of his house, reading it to the jury:

> And this letter begins:
>
> "On the advice of legal counsel and because of the change in our circumstances I'm compelled to put you on written notice that you [do] not have my permission to use my address at Rockingham as your residence or mailing address for any purpose, including but not limited to information and tax returns filed with any taxing entity."
>
> Well what is this? What does this letter mean? How is this letter helpful to you? How many times do we break up with someone and then send them a letter a few days later or two weeks later in legalese?[20]

Clearly, few things could be more indicative of a failed and loveless relationship than to receive a letter from one's partner in emotionless legal language. What began as a relationship of love had become a relationship of law.

Both Clark and Darden consistently depersonalized Simpson by referring to him as *the defendant,* while personalizing the victims, whom they called by their first names, *Ron* and *Nicole.*[21] Consider this example from Darden's part of the closing argument:

> And this defendant, he was jealous and he was out of control and he was consumed with passion for Nicole and he was obsessive because in April of 1992, he is peeking through windows. He has already beaten her. He has already beaten up her car. And he does some other things.[22]

In contrast to written legal language, there are few passives and nominalizations in Darden's argument: he wanted to point clearly to Simpson

as the murderer, rather than obscuring the actor. Overall, the two prosecutors spoke relatively plainly and mostly in standard English.[23]

The primary closing argument for the defense was made by Johnnie
Cochran. One of the first things Cochran did was to subtly invite the
jury to compare his defense of Simpson to the Civil Rights Movement.
He quoted Abraham Lincoln and Frederick Douglas. He called the defense a *journey toward justice*. He emphasized not only that the jurors
ought to do the right thing, but that they were *empowered* to do justice.
By implication, they should ignore the law if they felt it was unjust.

Cochran then tried to personalize and dignify Mr. Simpson:

> Now, in this case, you're aware that we represent Mr. Orenthal
> James Simpson. The prosecution never calls him Mr. Orenthal
> James Simpson. They call him defendant. . . .
> You will determine the facts of whether or not he's set free
> to walk out those doors or whether he spends the rest of his life
> in prison. But he's Orenthal James Simpson. He's not just the
> defendant, and we on the defense are proud, consider it a privi-
> lege to have been part of representing him in this exercise and
> this journey towards justice, make no mistake about it.[24]

Cochran quite successfully negated the prosecution's strategy of deper-
sonalizing Simpson. Furthermore, he intimated that the jurors should
bear in mind that O. J. was not merely a celebrity, but an important
symbol for the African American community.

As opposed to the prosecution, which tries to unequivocally identify
the defendant as the perpetrator, the defense is often interested in obscuring the actor. We have seen one way to accomplish this: use of constructions like passives or nominalizations. Cochran used a different
strategy. He deflected attention from Simpson as the actor by focusing
on another actor, the Los Angeles Police Department:

> . . . your verdict talks about justice in America and it talks about
> the police and whether they're above the law. . . .[25]

The alleged malfeasance and racism of the Police Department remained
a theme throughout, particularly the roles of Detective Fuhrman and
another officer, whom Cochran called *twin devils of deception*.[26]

Cochran made quite effective use of poetic devices to imprint his
themes on the minds of the jurors, just as those devices were utilized in
Anglo-Saxon times to reinforce memory. Two important themes, already
mentioned, were the alliterative *journey toward justice* and the role of the
devils of deception. Cochran contended that the time had come to put a

stop to the *folly and fantasy* of the prosecution's theories. And he argued that the physical evidence collected by the police had been *compromised, contaminated and corrupted.*[27] The next day, Barry Scheck's further argument for the defense added another alliterative word to the list:

> there is a fourth C that goes along with how these things happened that relates to this testimony, and the fourth C has to do with cover-up. . . .[28]

Cochran at one point alluded to what he called the "defining moment" of the trial: when the prosecution had asked O. J. to try on the gloves found at the scene of the murder. In a dramatic display before the jury, O. J. seemed unable to fit the gloves on his hands. Cochran then introduced the leitmotif of his argument: *If it doesn't fit, you must acquit.* Later, he referred to the prosecution's theory that O. J. had worn a knit cap to disguise himself. He ridiculed the idea that O.J. could have concealed his identity just by putting on a cap. I represent his next words in verse form to emphasize their poetic nature:

> It's no disguise.
> It's no disguise.
>
> It makes no sense.
> It doesn't fit.
>
> If it doesn't fit,
> You must acquit.[29]

Cochran used not only rhyme, but iambic meter (unstressed-stressed) as well. Although such devices can backfire by appearing too "cute" or even condescending, these poetic effects seem to have met with remarkable success. Cochran repeated the line (*if it doesn't fit, you must acquit*) again and again to invoke the image of O. J. vainly trying to "fit" the glove on his hand, as well as to pound home the defense message that the evidence did not "fit" the prosecution's story.

Previous chapters discussed how legal language is replete with unnecessary redundancies and conjoined phrases. At the same time, we recognized that repetition and parallelism (as in *any and all* or *cease and desist*) can be useful for emphasis. Cochran used these devices to drive home a critical point about the evidence collected by the Los Angeles Police Department:

> You can't trust this evidence. You can't trust the messenger. You can't trust the message.[30]

While the prosecution tends to pose only rhetorical questions with an evident answer, a standard defense strategy is to create reasonable doubt. In contrast to the prosecution, the defense wants to emphasize questions to which the answer is *not* obvious. Cochran ended his argument by listing fifteen such questions. He put the prosecution on the defensive by informing the jury that he had written the questions down and given them to Marcia Clark, suggesting that if she could not answer all the questions to the jury's satisfaction during her final argument the next day, they should find Simpson not guilty.

As an African American representing a black defendant, Cochran—like Clark—shared a characteristic with most of the jurors, although it was a racial bond rather than shared gender. Of course, it would have seemed out of place for him to address the jury in Black English Vernacular or "Ebonics," even if it could be assumed that they all spoke it at home.[31] Furthermore, it would have been so flagrant an attempt to garner the jury's favor that it might have backfired. In reality, Cochran's style was relatively formal, sometimes even using foreign phrases and literary analogies:

> And here may be the coup de grace. All of these things are supposedly for motive, to show how somebody might have acted on June 12th.
> Interesting, isn't it. Again in the words of Shakespeare, they are hoisted by their own pitard [*sic*].[32]

Cochran's language was grammatical standard English, for the most part. With all the scientific evidence arrayed against his client, Cochran was well served by appearing intelligent and competent in his effort to undermine that evidence.

At the same time, Cochran carefully chose his language to subtly bond with the jury. In contrast to the impersonal nature of legal writing, lawyers during closing argument strive to involve the jury personally; they thus avoid the third person and commonly address jurors with the pronoun *you*. Moreover, they turn to the jurors and speak to them directly during the summation in a way that they typically cannot do during questioning. Cochran employed these strategies well. He frequently addressed the jurors in an almost personal sense, recalling that one juror was from Missouri, known as the "Show Me" State:

> One of you is from Missouri, and he reminded you—who's from Missouri here—saying to the prosecution, you show us.[33]

Cochran's use of the pronoun *we* was even more effective. Linguists distinguish between the **inclusive** and **exclusive** use of *we*.[34] If my wife and I meet you at the local farmers' market and I say that *we* are happy to see you, I am using *we* exclusively—it excludes you, the addressee. But if I then suggest that *we* all have coffee at the Earthling Cafe, I use *we* inclusively, because you—the addressee—are included. Clearly, the inclusive sense of *we* can be used to create group solidarity, a feeling of *us* versus *them*. In the following, Cochran had just pointed out that the prosecution represents and has at its disposal the power of the state. He continued:

> We are not going to let them get their way. We're not going to turn the Constitution on its head in this case. We are not going to allow it.[35]

To whom does *we* refer? On one level, *we* was used in an exclusive sense to refer solely to the defense team, while *they* referred to the prosecution. Yet surely Cochran wanted the jury to understand it in an inclusive sense, in which they would join him in the collective enterprise of defeating the power of the state and what he suggested was a racist conspiracy by members of the police department to "frame" his client. The inclusive *we* appeared again after Cochran told the jurors that they should not rely on any evidence that might have been tainted by Detective Fuhrman:

> This man cannot be trusted. He is sinful to the prosecution, and for them to say he's not important is untrue and you will not fall for it, because as guardians of justice here, we can't let it happen.[36]

Later, the inclusive sense becomes overt:

> But you and I, fighting for freedom and ideals and for justice for all, must continue to fight to expose hate and genocidal racism and these tendencies.[37]

Note also the religious and civil rights rhetoric in these excerpts, which recurred throughout the argument, and which may be especially likely to appeal to an African American audience.

Although Cochran spoke an educated and fairly formal style of standard English, he did so with some mild characteristics of Black English or Ebonics. One of the most salient characteristics of the speech of many African Americans is the simplification of final consonant clusters, so that *world* and *understand* are pronounced more like *worl* and *understan*. Cochran did not drop the final consonants in these words, but pronounced them fairly weakly. Another feature of Black English Vernacular concerns the diphthong *ai* (as in *crime*, pronounced to rhyme with *eye* in standard English). African Americans, as well as Southern Americans in general, tend to pronounce this with the pure vowel *ah*, producing something like *krahm*. Again, Cochran's pronunciation of these words struck me as hovering between the standard diphthong *ai* and the Black English *ah*. These features were very subtle, and they might be Cochran's ordinary speech. But cumulatively they strengthened the impression that he was a well-educated and competent lawyer who despite his accomplishments had not forsaken his African American roots.

Christopher Darden, when arguing for the prosecution, may have tried to convey a similar image, but less successfully. Darden several times used the word *ain't*, which is also common in Black English. But unlike Cochran's subtleties of articulation, *ain't* is immediately obvious and quite stigmatized in standard English. The jurors may well have perceived it as an incongruous attempt by a government lawyer to "talk down" to them.

It has been observed that with his white shirt collar and the cross on his lapel, Cochran looked more like a preacher than a lawyer.[38] He also talked like one. His rhythm and cadences were similar to the style of black ministers in particular. Obviously, Cochran was taking advantage of the fact that African Americans tend to be more religious than the American population as a whole and attend church services more often.[39]

Co-counsel Barry Scheck addressed the scientific evidence. He spoke standard English, with at most a slight trace of his New York background. Just as Cochran was the ideal person to argue racism, Scheck—a white male professor—fit stereotypical perceptions about who was most competent to convince the jury that the scientific evidence was invalid. Two factors that have been identified as particularly important in persuasion are the *trustworthiness* and *expertness* of the speaker.[40] Here, Cochran invoked trust through his language, and Scheck conveyed a sense of expertise.

Lawyers typically end their argument with admonitions to the jury to do the right thing and return a particular verdict. After Scheck finished reviewing the scientific evidence, Johnnie Cochran made his final remarks. He used archaic language and invoked sacred texts, thereby conveying to the jury a sense of authority and eternal truth. He quoted from the Book of Proverbs that *he that speaketh lies shall not escape*. And he recited one of his favorite poems, by James Russell Lowell, who wrote that *beyond the dim unknown standeth God within the shadows, keeping watch above his own.* Like a pastor warning his flock to stay on the straight and narrow way, Cochran's parting words to the jury were that *God . . . will watch you in your decision . . . God bless you.*[41]

Instructing the Jury

After the arguments of counsel, the jury must decide the truth of the plaintiff's story. To some degree, the jury must also decide whether the story is legally adequate. Judges tell the jury how to go about this task by means of **jury instructions.**[42]

In most American states, the bulk of the instructions are no longer drafted individually for each case. To save time and to reduce the possibility of legal error, most states now use what are called **standard** or **pattern instructions.** These are normally drafted by a committee of lawyers and judges, and are often taken verbatim from the text of a statute or judicial decision. Of course, where there is no pattern instruction, the judge will have to write an ad hoc instruction for the case at bar.[43]

Some of the instructions are purely procedural, informing jurors that they are to select a foreperson, or press a buzzer when they have reached a verdict. Others instruct jurors on how to evaluate the evidence. Here is one such instruction from the Simpson case:

> Discrepancies in a witness' testimony, or between his or her testimony and that of others, if there were any, do not necessarily mean that the witness should be discredited. Failure of recollection is a common experience and innocent misrecollection is not uncommon. It is also a fact that two persons witnessing an incident or transaction often will see or hear it differently. Whether a discrepancy pertains to a fact of importance or only to a trivial detail should be considered in weighing its significance.[44]

Note, first of all, the extremely formal language and the many literary, educated and unusual words, including *discrepancies, recollection,* and *transaction.* In fact, *misrecollection* is not even in my dictionary. And *discredit* is used in an unusual sense: as "not believe," rather than in its more common meaning of "lose face." The instruction also has several nominalizations, including *failure, recollection,* and *misrecollection.* It has passive constructions (*be discredited* and *be considered*) that fail to state who should do the discrediting and considering. (A more complete version of the Simpson jury instructions can be found in appendix D.)

Surely, this highly abstract and formal style is a poor means of communicating with an ordinary jury. Any lawyer who spoke in such language during trial would alienate herself from the jurors and stand a good chance of losing her case. As we saw in the analysis of closing arguments, good lawyers try to connect with the jurors and address them in terms they will understand.

Why is it that in sharp contrast to earlier phases of the trial, the legal profession abruptly refuses to speak clearly to jurors during the instruction phase, especially when very important rights and issues are at stake? Admittedly, the legal concepts contained in the instructions may be rather complicated. But even complex topics can be explained in simpler terms. The law is no more complicated than many topics that expert witnesses manage to explain in ordinary language. Instead of informing jurors that *failure of recollection is a common experience,* the judge could just say that *people often forget things,* with absolutely no loss in meaning.

One explanation for this sudden shift to extremely formal language must be that judges are now speaking. Presumably, most judges *want* to maintain a certain distance, as opposed to the lawyers, who do their best to bond with the jurors. The distancing effect of elevated language is reinforced by the judge's location, which is physically above the fray and separated by an empty space (the "well") from the other participants in the trial. The formal and archaic language, along with the physical elevation of the judge, endows the instructions with a sense of authority. And the judge's physical isolation reinforces the notion that the law, as embodied in the judge, is "detached" and therefore objective. Furthermore, judges are no different from ordinary lawyers; most prefer to speak formally because it suggests they are intelligent and competent. As a result, a certain level of formality may be inevitable. Still, judges should not forget their audience, and the fact that ultimately, what counts most is clear, concise, and comprehensible communication.

Other instructions are meant to educate the jurors on the law that they must apply. In a criminal case, the most critical instruction may be the requirement that the prosecution must prove the defendant guilty *beyond a reasonable doubt.* During closing argument in the Simpson case, the defense followed the conventional strategy of arguing that there was reasonable doubt. Here is how Judge Ito defined the concept for the jurors:

> Reasonable doubt is defined as follows:
>   It is not a mere possible doubt, because everything relating to human affairs is open to some possible or imaginary doubt.

> It is that state of the case which, after the entire comparison and consideration of all the evidence, leaves the mind of the jurors in that condition that they cannot say they feel an abiding conviction of the truth of the charge.[45]

As with most California instructions, this is hardly a model of clear communication. It never addresses the jurors as *you,* and is phrased in the negative. Furthermore, the pivotal term *abiding conviction* is likely to be quite obscure to the average juror. *Abide* is a literary word that is seldom heard in ordinary speech. And *conviction,* in the sense of "belief," is also fairly literary. *Conviction* is most commonly used as the nominalization of *convict,* not *convince.*

To some extent, the obscurity of this and the other instructions results from the fact that they are composed as written legal text. As we saw previously, written language tends to be lexically more dense and syntactically more complex than speech. Furthermore, when something is written down, it tends to resist change. Especially if it has been approved by a judge or legislature, it becomes authoritative text that the legal profession is even more reluctant to modernize. Because they are so distant from oral language, therefore, jury instructions are hard to follow. Furthermore, as Bernard Jackson has observed, there is an inherent difficulty in communicating by speech what was conceived in a written form of discourse.[46] It is bad enough to ask ordinary people to decipher dense written legal language. It is even worse to read it to them and then refuse—as many courts do—to provide them with the written copy.

California's reasonable doubt instruction illustrates these problems. The instruction tracks the language of California Penal Code section 1096. The statutory language, in turn, was adopted virtually verbatim from an 1850 Massachusetts case, *Commonwealth v. Webster.*[47] As noted by Justice Stanley Mosk of the California Supreme Court, the language of *Webster* was "already obsolete" when California adopted it in 1927, and is "hopelessly superannuated" today.[48] Yet it continues to be approved by California courts, and the United States Supreme Court somewhat grudgingly upheld the instruction in *Victor v. Nebraska.*[49] The prospect of changing it strikes fear in the hearts of most lawyers and judges.

Nonetheless, jurors are continually confused about the meaning of this instruction, as evidenced by *People v. Ruge,* a quite recent case from California.[50] The jury in *Ruge* had been instructed in the language of Penal Code section 1096, using the traditional phraseology that Judge Ito read in the Simpson case. Not surprisingly, reciting this language to the jurors did not enlighten them very much. Before long, they trooped back into the courtroom to inquire: "[W]e would like to know what constitutes reasonable doubt. . . . We read the instructions over and over. We want you to tell us."[51]

The judge cautioned them that "greater minds than mine have tried to better the instruction, and about all they get is reversed or they mess it up or somebody up in the Court of Appeal or the Supreme Court says, 'No, that's not quite it. You blew it.' " She then bravely tried to translate the concept into ordinary English that the jurors might actually be able to fathom. But her intuitions were right: she blew it, at least according to the court of appeal: "It was error for the court to attempt to embellish the concept of reasonable doubt."[52] The moral: "Thou shalt honor the sacred text, and in no wise alter it, that thy days may be long upon the bench."

With appellate decisions like this one, it is not surprising that many judges are extremely reluctant to explain any aspect of the instructions. When asked about the meaning of an instruction by the jury, many judges just reread it verbatim.[53] Others refuse to answer.[54] In fact, in a survey of fifteen judges in California with respect to jury requests for assistance, one judge replied that he tried to explain questions in plain English, a few provided a written copy or tape recording of the original instructions, and some would not explain or reiterate them at all. The majority simply reread the original instructions.[55] As one judge said when he referred a confused jury back to the original instructions, he wished he could be of more help. The foreperson responded, "We also wish you could be more help."[56]

The instruction ritual typically concludes with some final admonitions on how to conduct deliberations. The jurors are told of the possible verdicts that they can reach, and how to fill out and sign the verdict form. They then "retire" to the jury room to deliberate.

Resolving the Conflict

Although little is known with certainty about how jurors reach verdicts, it seems likely that—like lawyers who construct a narrative during the course of the trial—jurors also create possible stories to explain the evidence.[57] They may adopt the stories presented by the parties or construct a narrative of their own. Ultimately, they will have to choose one story over the others. In doing so, factors such as the credibility, intelligence, and competence of witnesses, and the persuasiveness of counsel, all of which are heavily influenced by the language that they used, will play a major role.

The jurors must not only construct a plausible story, but more practically, they need to reach a verdict. Typically, the verdict forms ask jurors one or more questions, such as whether the defendant was guilty of murder, or—if not—whether he was guilty of manslaughter. Jurors are thus like witnesses who are asked relatively coercive questions: they are allowed only two choices: *guilty* or *not guilty*. To be honest, modern juries do have other options. If they are unable to agree, they fail to answer the question and produce a "hung jury." In any event, a narrative response is not acceptable, even though the jury might prefer to return to court and explain that most of them believe that the defendant is probably guilty, but that they feel sorry for her, believe she will not commit the same crime again, and would prefer to sentence her to probation for two years. It is the legal system that poses the questions, and it requires that jurors respond in terms of technical legal categories, based on the law contained in their instructions.

Because the instructions are so hard to understand, however, it is uncertain how well jurors actually follow the law in reaching a verdict, even when they sincerely want to. As early as 1314, a jury was asked to determine whether a piece of land was *free alms* or *lay fee*. The jurors complained to the judge, "We be no lawyers." Rather than clarify the matter, the judge replied: "Good people, say what you think."[58] Few judges today would tell the jury to forget about the law and do what they think is right. But when instructions are incomprehensible, the effect is the same. As a former juror remarked:

> A number of years ago, I served in a state court where the Judge instructed us in language none of us understood. It was involved and tedious and long, and so full of whereases and therewiths that he lost us halfway through. . . . [W]e proceeded to consider the case according to our rough sense of justice without much regard for the law.[59]

However they make decisions, jurors normally do reach a verdict. Once they have done so, the closing rituals of the trial can begin. In the *Simpson* case, the jury returned its verdict in a remarkably short period of time: less than a day.[60] Mr. Simpson and the various lawyers were given some time to return to court for the reading of the verdict and to bring closure to a saga that had taken over a year of their lives.

In a dramatic moment broadcast live to an audience of millions of television viewers, Simpson rose to face the jury. The court clerk then read the verdicts.

In the matter of People of the State of California versus Orenthal James Simpson, case number BA097211. We, the jury, in
the above-entitled action, find the defendant, Orenthal James
Simpson, not guilty of the crime of murder in violation of Penal
Code section 187(a), a felony, upon Nicole Brown Simpson, a
human being, as charged in count I of the information.[61]

After reading all the verdicts in this fashion, each juror was quizzed individually whether this was his or her verdict, and each responded *yes*. The
judge then excused the jurors. And he ordered the defendant "released
forthwith." Because the jurors apparently decided that the story told by
the state was not true, the state was not entitled to a remedy.

If a jury declares that the plaintiff's story is true, the judge is now in
a position to offer a resolution by means of her judgment. In a criminal
case, she might sentence the defendant to prison. Or, if the dispute is
civil, she might award monetary compensation to the plaintiff. In either
event, the unfinished narrative in the complaint has now been completed.

Conclusion

Much more can and has been written about how lawyers use language
during trial. Obviously, lawyers can use language very effectively. One
of the interesting aspects of the Simpson case is that most Americans
believe that he was actually guilty. How, then, can we account for the
fact that the jury found him not guilty in a matter of hours? There are
many plausible reasons for the verdict. But I have no doubt that Cochran's extremely effective use of language during his closing argument
was a very important factor.

It should be evident that when lawyers are sufficiently motivated, they
are quite capable of communicating with the jury in a clear and comprehensible way. Given the ability of lawyers to communicate clearly, why do
they not do so more often? If they are able to explain difficult technical
concepts to ordinary jurors, why should they not be able to do the same
when drafting a contract or a will? Why should legislators not be able
to pass statutes that are written in plain English? That is the topic of the
rest of this book.

PART FOUR

Reforming the Language of the Law

We have seen that members of the public have long expressed frustration with legal language. Even within the profession, critics have excoriated the wordy, archaic, and ponderous nature of the language used by their colleagues. Recall the case of *Mylward v. Weldon,* one of the earliest and most famous examples of internal criticism, dating from 1596. The plaintiff, represented by his son, managed to produce a written pleading totaling 120 pages, even though "all the matter thereof which is pertinent" could have been stated in sixteen. The judge was so annoyed by the son's verbosity that he ordered the Warden of the Fleet to cut a hole in the offending document, place the man's head through it, and lead him "round about Westminster Hall, whilst the Courts are sitting, and shall shew him at the bar of every of the three Courts within the Hall."[1] Around the same time, Sir Francis Bacon promulgated Chancery Ordinance 55, which provided that if any bill or other pleading was of "an immoderate length, both the party and the counsel under whose hand it passeth shall be fined."[2]

Recall also that the lawyer and philosopher Jeremy Bentham was a stern critic of legal language at the end of the eighteenth century and the beginning of the next. He lambasted the language of lawyers as "excrementitious matter" and "literary garbage."[3] Bentham was a strong advocate of **codification,** in which all of the law would be systematically divided into codes on various topics. Individual parts of each code should be small enough for people to remember, and written clearly enough that citizens would know the "exact idea of the will of the legislator."[4] He may have been one of the first to argue that plain, comprehensible legal language is essential in a state that claims to serve the interests of the people. "Until, therefore, the nomenclature and language of law shall be improved, the great end of good government cannot be fully attained."[5]

On the other side of the Atlantic, the United States actually proved more receptive to codification than Bentham's native England. In 1837 a report by Joseph Story suggested that codification would give the law "certainty, clearness, and facility of reference," noting that it is "desirable . . . that the laws, which govern the rights, duties, relations, and business of the people, should . . . be accessible to them for daily use or consultation."[6] While codification did promote facility of reference for lawyers, it has been far less successful in making the law clear and accessible to ordinary people.

Although there were similar murmurs of protest from time to time,[7] it is fair to say that a truly vigorous movement to reform legal English is the product of the past three decades or so. Professor David Mellinkoff's book, *The Language of the Law,* published in 1963, showed quite convincingly that many of the attributes of traditional legal language could not be justified as more precise than ordinary speech. A substantial debate on the virtues and vices of legal language followed.[8]

Traditional legalese is especially problematic when the audience is the lay public. All too often, ordinary citizens have at best a dim notion of the laws that govern their rights and obligations. Nor do they fully comprehend the contracts, deeds, and wills that are drafted on their behalf. And although the legal system relies on jurors to reach a reasoned verdict based on the law, the instructions that the judge reads to them are typically phrased in highly convoluted legal language. How are jurors to apply the law fairly if they scarcely understand it?

Given the need for reform, there are two quite different approaches that the profession could undertake. One avenue is **simplification,** which involves making legal language identical to ordinary English, to the extent feasible. While a few technical terms might have to be retained, an extreme version of this approach would try to eliminate virtually all of the characteristics of legal language that were outlined in this book. Of course, less far-reaching reform is also possible, and may indeed be necessary if complete simplification turns out to be impossible. It might be more realistic to rid legal language merely of its most archaic and incomprehensible attributes. Naturally, such a compromise would leave many objectionable features intact.

The alternative approach is **translation.** This solution to the problem, in its most extreme form, would not change legal language at all. Instead, it would urge (and train) legal professionals to be better translators when dealing with the lay public. Rather than simplifying, the translation approach accepts the existence of both legal and ordinary language, but it acknowledges the difficulties that legalese creates for the "monolingual" public. Although the problem could be solved by teaching everyone to be "bilingual" in legal and ordinary language, such a solution would be too time-consuming and expensive to be practical; we simply cannot train everyone to be a lawyer. Instead, the comprehension difficulties are solved by teaching lawyers to be better translators. This is doubtless the solution that many members of the legal profession would prefer: it leaves legal language—and the profession—largely intact.

Translation differs philosophically from simplification in an important way: translation assumes that legal language must—or should—remain quite distinct from ordinary speech. Simplification obviously rejects that assumption. To a large extent, the choice between these two methods will depend on whether it is, in fact, possible and practical to render all legal concepts in ordinary, comprehensible English. Ultimately, it seems likely that we will end up with a combination of both approaches. As far as possible, we should simplify legal language, especially when it is directed at the ordinary public. People should understand the tax forms that they are required to fill out. On the other hand, it is probably unrealistic to expect that the Internal Revenue Code of the United States could be made so simple that the proverbial man (or woman) on the street could pick up a copy and comprehend every detail. Even lawyers struggle to understand it. Here, translation and explanation by a tax lawyer or other expert is a virtual necessity.

Although the exact approach may vary, the overall goal should always be to make legal language as clear as possible for its intended audience. In the following chapters, we discuss how this goal has been implemented in the past few decades, as well as the unfinished business that remains to be done in the future.

CHAPTER TWELVE

What Makes Legal Language Difficult to Understand?

If legal language is to become a clearer and more efficient means of communication, we need to identify the features that are most likely to impede comprehension. Some aspects present greater difficulties than others. Furthermore, comprehension can be impaired by linguistic features that are not specifically legal. In the following discussion, we highlight some of the more common traits of legal English that have been found to reduce comprehension.[1]

Technical Vocabulary

No doubt one of the things that makes legal language hardest to understand is its unusual vocabulary. Although some technical terms are relatively well known (*defendant, judge, jury*), others are at best vaguely familiar to many people (*beyond a reasonable doubt, negligence* or *wrongful imprisonment*). Further terms—legal homonyms—seem familiar but have an unexpected meaning for the average person (as in *aggravation* or *file a complaint*). Still other vocabulary is a complete mystery to nonlawyers, including words like *estoppel, lis pendens, per stirpes, testator,* and *tortfeasor*.

Some of the best evidence that people have trouble with legal terminology comes from the fact that jurors, after they have received their instructions, all too often turn to dictionaries for enlightenment. Jurors do this even though the rules prohibit them from consulting any outside source (which includes dictionaries). A survey of American decisional law found many cases in which jurors have been accused of misconduct for looking up words, including *assault, battery, culpable, custody, entrapment, inference, insanity, legal cause, malice, malpractice, motive, murder, negligent, possession, premeditate, preponderance, proximate, prudent, rape, reasonable, undue, utter* (as in *utter a forged check*), and *wanton*.[2] One could hardly wish for more convincing evidence that jurors have genuine problems deciding what these terms mean.

Identifying the problem is relatively easy; finding a solution is another matter. As we saw in chapter 6, technical words and jargon arise precisely because they facilitate communication within a profession. Where would a field like linguistics be without terms of art like *ergativity, grammaticalization, illocutionary force indicating device,* or *markedness?* What would woodworkers do without terms like *bevel miter cut* or *dowel-scoring jig?* If linguistics or carpentry is entitled to promote internal communication by developing its own technical terms and jargon, surely the legal profession should be permitted to do so also.

The problem, of course, is communication with the public. What may be useful shorthand to a lawyer is impenetrable gobbledygook to the layman. Linguists (fortunately!) do not have to explain *phonemic representation* or *universal grammar* to the public, and the vast majority of humanity gets along perfectly well in a state of ignorant bliss.

In contrast, people *do* have the right to know the meaning of the contracts that they sign and for which they will be held legally responsible. When people are entitled to understand a legal document, it should be as free as possible of technical terms and jargon. If technical terms are unavoidable, they should at least be explained in ordinary language.

Archaic, Formal, and Unusual Words

Not surprisingly, archaic, formal, and unusual vocabulary and syntactic constructions are also problematic for lay persons, even if they sometimes serve a useful function. The idiosyncratic legal uses of *(afore)said, same,* and *such,* to mention a few anachronisms, are no longer part of ordinary language and thus reduce understanding. The same holds for forms composed of *here-, there-,* and *where-,* such as *hereof, therewith,* and *wherein.*

Formal or highly literate vocabulary also causes comprehension difficulties. Not everyone knows what *initiate* or *terminate* means, but virtually any speaker of English understands *begin* and *end.* Many people have limited exposure in their daily lives to highly literate vocabulary. Because we mostly learn the meanings of words by hearing them used, many people simply do not know what learned or literary terminology means. Lawyers, of course, hear such terms much more often and are better educated than the average person, so they may not realize the extent of the problem. Especially if the audience for a document is nonlawyers, vocabulary that is rare in ordinary speech should be avoided.

Impersonal Constructions

Research suggests that the profession's frequent reliance on impersonal constructions, often using nouns in place of pronouns like *I* and *you,* is another factor that makes legal documents harder to understand.[3] Consider a contract of sale in which a consumer buys an automobile; the contract might provide that *vendor shall have the right to modify this clause with thirty day's notice to vendee.* As the buyer, can I modify the clause? Am I the vendor or the vendee? It is clearer, of course, if the more ordinary terms *buyer* and *seller* are used. But clearest of all is to personalize it by stating that *we have the right to modify this clause after giving you thirty day's notice.*

Of course, in theory a contract "speaks" for at least two parties. We saw earlier that this is a reason for using the third person; otherwise, it is unclear which party is *I* and which is *you.* This is a valid argument when a contract exists between two businesses, or two parties of equal bargaining power. Here, the contract is indeed a type of two-way communication in which each party speaks to the other, each promising to do certain things.

Yet the typical consumer contract is not a two-way conversation; it is really a one-way manifesto from the business to the consumer. There is no negotiation, and the consumer is not involved in drafting it. Instead, it is handed to the consumer on a take-it-or-leave-it basis, something called a **contract of adhesion** in legal parlance.[4] It is truly *I* or *we*—the business—that is doing all the "speaking" and dictating of terms, and *you*—the consumer—that is doing the listening. Rather than hiding this reality, consumer contracts ought to be written using the first and second person.

Statutes are likewise always in the third person. At least part of the reason, as discussed in chapter 4, is that they are not just commands addressed to the public, but are also directed at law enforcement, at judges, and other officials. It would therefore be problematic to phrase them in the second person. On the other hand, laws are often publicized in order to notify the population at large that a particular activity is prohibited. Here, the third person is more difficult to justify. Consider signs like *no person shall obstruct this passageway.* It would be more effective to simply state *do not obstruct this passageway* (which has an understood *you*). Furthermore, there is evidence that impersonal phrases imposing obligation (*it is your duty to . . .*, *it is required that . . .* or *it is necessary . . .*) are less comprehensible than expressions with a pronoun (*you must . . .*).[5]

In summary, although there are sometimes valid reasons for the law's reliance on impersonal constructions, use of first- and second-person pronouns is preferable when legal documents address members of the public.

Overuse of Nominalizations and Passives

We saw in chapter 5 that nominalizations are nouns that are derived from verbs and that they often have the purpose or effect of de-emphasizing (or even obscuring) the actor. They also reduce comprehension. Research indicates that nominalizations are usually more difficult to process than their corresponding verb forms.[6]

Unfortunately, legal language tends to use a lot of nominalizations, even when there is no need to de-emphasize or obscure the actor. Consider the language of many credit contracts: *in the event of default on the part of the buyer. . . .* The word *default* can be either a noun or a verb; here, it is a noun. It is far more effective to use the word as a verb, which allows a simpler (and shorter) sentence while communicating exactly the same message: *if the buyer defaults . . .* And because this is a consumer contract, it makes sense to use personal pronouns: *if you default. . . .* Using verbs, instead of their nominalized equivalents, is almost always a more direct and effective way of making a point.

Whether passives cause comprehension problems is a bit less clear. Many plain English proponents urge writers to shy away from the passive voice.[7] But research has shown that this broad generalization needs to be more nuanced. For example, an investigation into the language of jury instructions by Charrow and Charrow found that passives do indeed impede comprehension, but mainly when they occur in subordinate clauses. In main clauses they seem not to cause significant problems.[8]

Furthermore, when the focus is on the object of the action, passives are as easy—and perhaps easier—to understand than active sentences. For example, if a text has been discussing the disability claim of a prison guard (i.e., the guard has already been introduced), it makes more sense to write that *the guard was beaten by a prisoner,* in place of the corresponding active sentence (*a prisoner beat the guard*). Passives are also justified in many court orders, as in *the petition for a writ of certiorari is granted.* The topic here is the petition, so it logically comes first. Note that the actor—the court—is not specifically mentioned, but this has nothing to do with strategic imprecision. There is no need to state who the actor is because it is fully evident from the context.

Passives have less to commend them in jury instructions, where they are also quite common. Consider this gem:

> You must never speculate to be true any insinuation *suggested* by a question *asked* a witness.[9]

Because both of the passives are in subordinate clauses, a sentence of this sort will be quite hard to process. In fact, unless you listen carefully you might think that the witness asked the question.

Overall, it is best to use straightforward, active verbs rather than nominalizations or passives. The basic sentence type, containing a subject, active verb, and object, is easiest for people to process.[10] Occasional use of nominalizations or passive verbs is acceptable, especially in more formal writing, but should be done judiciously.

Modal Verbs

Clear communication generally requires using ordinary modal verbs (*can, could, may, might, must, should, will,* and *would*) where appropriate. In place of *shall*, which has an archaic and legalistic feel to it, language directed at the public should mostly use *must*. Of course, *shall* does have the virtue of signaling that something is an enforceable legal obligation, not just an informal rule or unenforceable agreement. At the same time, because *shall* is little used outside the legal world, we should avoid it when the audience is the lay public.

Similarly, the archaic use of *do* (as in *I do appoint*) is almost always unnecessary in legal language and may falsely suggest emphasis to someone untrained in the law. If the writer needs to unambiguously indicate performativity, *hereby* is quite sufficient.

Finally, personal pronouns followed by an ordinary modal verb, like *you must* or *you can*, are much more clear and intelligible than longer impersonal expressions like *it is necessary (for you)* or *it is your duty* or *it is possible (for you).*[11]

Multiple Negation

The reason that multiple negatives cause processing difficulties should be fairly evident. One negative is not normally a problem, but two in the same sentence cancel each other out in standard English. If the first negation makes it appear that the sentence will be negative, the second forces the reader to reverse course and interpret the sentence as positive. Add a third or fourth negative, and the situation becomes semantically intolerable. Not surprisingly, research indicates that the more negatives a sentence contains, the harder it is to process.[12]

Long and Complex Sentences

Chapter 4 revealed that legal writing tends to consist of very long sentences, sometimes hundreds of words in length. The available research suggests, logically enough, that such long sentences undermine comprehension.[13]

At the same time, sentence length by itself may not be the true culprit, but rather the greater complexity that tends to accompany length. Consider the following sentence:

> Once upon a time there was a young girl and her name was Little Red Riding Hood and her grandmother lived in a small house in the forest and one day Little Red Riding Hood decided to visit her grandmother and she packed a picnic basket and headed off and along the way she met a wolf and. . . .

Plainly, a sentence of this sort can go on *ad nauseam* without causing any processing difficulties. Contrast the following:

> The boy whom the girl whom the gentleman in the white car hit kissed lives next door to me.[14]

Although it is not all that long, this sentence is almost impossible to process, even though linguists claim that it is technically grammatical.

The complexity of sentences is far more of a problem than length. Plain legal language thus strives to avoid unusual, complex, or antiquated syntactic constructions, while promoting clarity through strategies like keeping subject and verb close to each other, reducing the number of clauses in each sentence, and minimizing the depth of embedding.

Poor Organization

The structure of a text or discourse can have a profound impact on how well people understand it. It seems self-evident that a story told in chronological order is easier to follow than one where the events are related randomly. Anyone who has watched a film with a lot of flashbacks realizes how hard it can be to piece the story together. Logical presentation of other types of material is equally essential. For the most part, it makes sense to present the most important things first, the general before the specific, and the overall statement or rule before any conditions or exceptions.[15] Those principles are patently violated in the following statute, where a fairly trivial exception to the general rule begins with the second word:

> Whoever, other than a special Government employee who serves for less than sixty days in a calendar year, having been so employed as specified in subsection (d) of this section, within one year after such employment has ceased, knowingly acts as agent or attorney for, or otherwise represents. . . . [16]

This statute would be far better organized if it began with the general (*whoever knowingly acts . . .*), and subsequently dealt with the specific exception (*a special Government employee*).

Other hallmarks of good organization include dividing complex material into sections and subsections, adding headings when appropriate, and using numbered lists.

Consumer legal documents are notorious not only for poor organization (frequently placing the most important provisions at the end of a long document, where they can readily be overlooked), but also for burying critical contract terms in the smallest type.[17] Typesize roughly corresponds to loudness in speech: we tend to raise our voices to emphasize a point. We reflect this in writing or printing by using larger letters, or all capitals, or a bold or italic typeface. Less crucial matters are placed in smaller letters in out-of-the way locations; footnotes are usually in smaller type and at the bottom of the page or at the end of a document. We thus logically assume that provisions in small type at the end of a contract have little importance. Placing critical consumer information in that position is obviously not the best way to communicate, and if done purposely, can be quite deceptive.

If all went well, this chapter should have produced a sense of *déjà vu* in the reader. More specifically, it may seem to have resembled a recapitulation of many of the points made in part 2 on the nature of legal language. The similarity with part 2 is quite telling. It seems that virtually all the characteristics of legal language reduce comprehension to some extent. Of course, many aspects of the language of the law serve legitimate—or at least, necessary—functions. Their retention may be justified for in-group communication. Yet when the legal profession wishes to communicate effectively with members of the public, it must do so in language that the public understands. Whether the profession decides to adopt the translation approach, or to engage in wholesale simplification of its language, it should address the public in its own language: ordinary English.

CHAPTER THIRTEEN

Plain English

Over the past decades we have learned a great deal about how to improve legal language and increase comprehension. What impact has this research had on the profession? The answer to this question depends to a large degree on the type or genre of legal language at issue, as well as the audience to which it is addressed.

In this chapter we begin by examining what I call **internal legal language.** This is the language used for communications within the profession, and thus addresses an audience mainly of lawyers. We then move on to **consumer documents,** which are intended to be read and understood by the ordinary lay public. Later, in chapter 14, we will turn our attention to **jury instructions,** a specific but very significant type of legal genre that is addressed to jurors, who—like consumers—normally are members of the public and have no legal training.

Internal Legal Language

Lawyers write many documents for an audience of other lawyers. One might argue that here, the use of convoluted legalese should not matter, as long as the targeted audience can decipher it. But of course, lawyers almost invariably work for clients. Surely it is not unreasonable to suggest that even internal legal documents be written in the most intelligible possible way, so that the client who paid to have the document prepared, and whose rights and duties are affected by it, knows what is being proposed on her behalf.

The same applies to statutes, which many lawyers view as a type of "in-group" communication. Yet most statutes confer rights and obligations on the public, or greatly affect the public interest; it is hardly a radical proposal that the public should be able to consult statutes directly, rather than having to engage the services of a professional interpreter.

Actually, there is already an area in American law where courts do— at least in theory—require that ordinary people be able to understand statutes. The United States Supreme Court has held that a criminal statute must put a person of "average intelligence" on notice that something is illegal before that person can be punished for violating it.[1] In the words of Justice Holmes, this constitutional requirement of due process mandates that "a fair warning should be given to the world in language that the common world will understand, of what the law intends to do if a certain line is passed."[2] Yet the courts' assumption that an average person can understand criminal statutes frequently seems quite dubious. In the case of someone convicted of engaging in a *crime against nature*, for example, the Supreme Court held that people generally would understand that this includes cunnilingus.[3] I suspect that to the modern mind, a "crime against nature" consists of cutting down a thousand-year-old redwood or killing a dolphin. Similarly, how many people languishing in prison for engaging in a *pattern of racketeering activity* have any idea what this term means? Even judges have trouble with it.[4] Criminal statutes are simply not written in language that the "common world" is likely to understand very well.

Part of the problem may be that the average person, untrained in the law, will probably never be able to fully understand most statutes, no matter how plain the language. Truly comprehending a statute or similar legal document involves much more than having some familiarity with the words that are written on paper. At a minimum, it demands a great deal of background knowledge, including a basic understanding of the legal system and the general subject matter of the text.

Furthermore, in the Anglo-American system understanding a statute typically requires familiarity with the cases that have interpreted the language of the statute, often in idiosyncratic ways. At the least, it requires legal training to be able to find those precedents. In addition, the subject matter of statutes can be quite complex. It takes intelligent and motivated law students many weeks to understand the general gist of concepts like negligence or proximate cause; it seems overly idealistic to expect a lay person to take the time and effort to learn the meaning of various legal concepts necessary to understand a statute properly.

Perhaps Coke's suggestion that the law was not in English lest the "unlearned" by "bare reading" might "suck out errors . . . and fall into destruction"[5] was not just a cynical attempt by a lawyer to defend the profession's turf. Recently, a rabidly antigovernment group in the United States, called the Montana Freemen, have started to engage in "bare reading" of the Bible, the Constitution, the Magna Carta, and the Uniform Commercial Code. They then prepare verbose legal filings to various state and federal courts, dressed up in "pseudo-scholarly terms and meaningless Latin phrases," typically claiming that for various reasons the courts have no jurisdiction over them. One judge compared this "freemanspeak" to the rantings of someone who is mentally ill. Another was a bit more charitable, commenting that it was "incredibly difficult" to decide what the filings meant. Needless to say, legal papers of this sort are seldom successful.[6] Admittedly, this is an extreme example. But it does illustrate that properly understanding a legal document requires much more than merely knowing what the individual words and sentences mean.

The hope that every man can be his own lawyer, which has existed for centuries,[7] is probably no more realistic than having people be their own doctor. If we receive clearly written instructions and take some time to study them, or receive good oral training, many of us can do some basic medical diagnosis and treatment. But even if we have the required intelligence and aptitude, most of us do not have the time to learn other trades and professions well enough to engage in more complicated procedures. The same is true for the law. With a good, nontechnical explanation, or a well written and relatively straightforward statute, many people can determine what the law is on a particular subject, or even draft a simple will. Yet someone with a more complicated estate plan and lurking tax problems would be foolhardy not to seek professional assistance. Plain legal language will never make lawyers superfluous. In fact, as our society and laws become ever more complex, lawyers will be more essential than ever.

This hardly means that internal legal language should not be reformed. Aiming at full comprehension by every member of the public may be overly optimistic, but there is every reason to make statutes and other legal documents clearer than they have been in the past. This benefits not just the public, but the legal profession itself. Though loathe to admit it, many lawyers struggle to interpret complex laws and other legal documents. Furthermore, there must be thousands of cases each year on the proper construction of such documents, which strongly suggests that clearer writing would benefit both lawyers and their clients.

Statutes and other government documents have actually come a long way toward meeting those goals. Currently, many legislative drafting manuals recommend plain language principles.[8] In fact, Hawaii has embedded in its constitution the precept that governmental writing meant for the public "should be plainly worded, avoiding the use of technical terms."[9] The Renton Commission in the United Kingdom has stated that "[i]deally, statutes should be written in ordinary, straightforward English that can be understood by lawyers and laymen. . . ."[10] Similarly, the Law Reform Commission of Canada has expressed its "dedication to the use of plain language in the drafting of statutes, to the extent possible." The Office of the Legislative Council in Ontario, like other Canadian provinces, has a drafting manual that provides that acts should be primarily written in ordinary language, avoiding redundant or archaic words and phrases.[11] Down Under, several Australian states have endorsed plain language statutory drafting, and at least one has taken the relatively radical step of banning the modal verb *shall* as an indicator of obligation, replacing it with *must*.[12]

Nor has the movement been limited to English-speaking countries. Although one might suppose that legal English is particularly convoluted because of the historical influence of Latin and Law French, it turns out that complex legal language bedevils many countries that do not share the common law tradition. In Sweden, for example, King Charles XII decreed in 1713 that all royal documents be in clear, plain Swedish. Apparently, the decree was not entirely successful, because in the 1960s and 1970s, a government minister became concerned with the lack of comprehensibility of Swedish statutes. A 1982 ordinance requires the Ministry of Justice to ensure that "all statutes and decisions are written in a clear and simple language." To carry these ideas into practice, a team of three language experts working in the Swedish Ministry of Justice reviews and edits most of the material destined for the Riksdag, Sweden's parliament.[13]

In Japan, one of the factors that makes legal language very difficult to read is the use of Chinese characters, which have no phonetic relationship to spoken Japanese. Each character, which roughly speaking represents a word, must be memorized individually. There are about 2000 such characters still in common usage. Concurrently, the Japanese have two phonetically-based (syllabic) writing systems called **katakana** and **hiragana,** each containing 48 symbols. But because Chinese characters continue to be used along with both syllabic systems, Japanese has been described as "the most intricate and complicated writing system ever used by a sizeable population."[14] The consequence is that in the past, ordinary Japanese had great difficulty understanding their laws, which were written predominantly in Chinese characters, many of them very unusual, and with absolutely no punctuation. Furthermore, the writing style was Chinese also and did not represent Japanese syntax very well. The situation improved with the adoption of a new democratic constitution after World War Two, which was written in hiragana, the system used by ordinary Japanese people.[15] Now, several of the codes, such as the Penal Code, have been revised to make them more understandable. They are written in more everyday Japanese, have captions and punctuation, and limit themselves to the use of hiragana and the roughly two thousand Chinese characters in common usage. Although this has greatly improved the situation, the Code apparently remains difficult for many ordinary Japanese to understand, and several popular "translations" into simpler language have been published.[16]

Although statutes will never read as easily as a dime-store novel, these are encouraging signs. Recent statutes virtually never consist of one long sentence that is dozens or hundreds of words long. Almost all jurisdictions these days have headings on their statutes, employ numbers and letters to divide statutes into sections and subsections, and make ample use of lists. Not only has organization dramatically improved, but drafters have tried to use more ordinary vocabulary and better syntax. A recent analysis of the language of Australian statutes concluded that legislation enacted in the 1990s contained dramatically less technical vocabulary than in the past, as well as shorter sentences, positive rather than negative expression, and less use of the passive voice.[17] In the words of Frederick Bowers, "The golden age of statutory flatulence is long gone; when modern critics of legal language trot out their favourite pleonasms they are more often than not exemplifying bureaucratic language and the language of conveyances, wills, and agreements rather than statutory language."[18]

Unfortunately, despite some linguistic improvement, statutes are increasingly complicated in terms of substance. Ironically, it may be that precisely because of better organizational principles, drafters of statutes are now able to make them much longer than before and conceptually far more complex. Furthermore, the overall volume of statutes is growing at a phenomenal rate. No doubt this is necessitated by our ever more technological society, but it is a decidedly mixed blessing.

Other internal legal language presents a more uneven picture. The reform movement has had less impact on pleadings and petitions, which sometimes still recycle formulaic phrases that are decades or even centuries old. Perhaps lawyers fear that—as in the Middle Ages—even a minor slip in pleading can be fatal. While I was still in practice, I drafted what is called a **general denial** to a complaint against a client. Copying language from a form approved by the Judicial Council of California, the text of my proposed answer was simply *Defendant generally denies each and* *every allegation in the complaint.*[19] There is no doubt that it would have been perfectly adequate. The senior partner who reviewed my work was horrified, however. Despite the Judicial Council's seal of approval, this was not the standard denial used by our firm, one which had proven its worth over many decades. I thus revised our answer to conform with tradition:

> Defendant, for himself and himself alone, in answer to the complaint and by virtue of the provisions of Code of Civil Procedure section 431.30, subdivision (d), now files its general denial to the complaint and answering all the allegations of the complaint, denies each and every allegation thereof.

Even though many lawyers espouse plain language in theory,[20] they seem reluctant to change their style in practice. A significant reason for this reluctance is that it is often far easier, and takes much less time, to use old forms as a model. Perhaps this will change as models for plain language pleadings and other court documents become more widely available[21] and as it becomes apparent that courts are receptive to the change.

In fact, there is an interesting way in which the obscurity of pleadings can be strategically turned against their drafters. Consider the case of a comedian who was sued for defamation. His lawyer filed a counterclaim against the plaintiff for ten million dollars, alleging that the plaintiff owed the comedian money. During a deposition, the comedian was asked about his counterclaim. He admitted: "I don't know what it says and I don't understand it." His lawyer wisely decided to drop it.[22]

Although pleadings may still be legalistic sometimes, lawyers writing briefs or memoranda of points and authorities (arguments to a court) are well aware that they need to get to the point as quickly and clearly as possible. Busy judges have no patience for convoluted, redundant, or poorly organized arguments. The object is to persuade the judge, something that convoluted language is unlikely to accomplish. Just as with closing arguments to a jury, most lawyers have learned to lay out their arguments to courts as plainly as possible. They have gauged the sentiment of judges well. Even though the judges are thoroughly familiar with legalese, surveys show that a great majority prefer plain English, and that when presented with samples of writing in plain English versus traditional legalese, they rate the former as more persuasive.[23]

Legal education has been responsive to these trends, and in some cases is stimulating them. In the United States, almost all law schools teach legal writing to their students and require passing such a course for graduation. Although there is much variation in these classes, most stress the importance of avoiding traditional legalese. The textbooks used to teach legal writing in American law schools almost routinely recommend the use of plain English, and illustrate how to do so.[24] One book, Richard Wydick's *Plain English for Lawyers,* originally published as a law review article in 1978, has been especially influential.[25] Similar guidebooks are available in other English-speaking countries.[26] Unfortunately, after students graduate they often go to work for members of the profession who grew up in the old school and are forced to imitate their antiquated style. Still, there is reason to hope that when these recent graduates become their own bosses, they will remember the lessons they learned while students.

Judicial style has likewise improved over the past decades. As an indicator of the change, consider the use of prepositions preceded by *here-, there-* and *where-*. In a sampling of ten United States Supreme Court opinions from 1891, there were numerous such forms, including *hereafter, hereby, herein, hereinbefore, hereof, hereunto, herewith, thereby, therefor, therein, thereof, thereon, thereupon, whereby, wherefrom, whereunto,* and *whereupon.*[27] By 1941, a similar survey of ten Supreme Court cases revealed fewer of these forms, although they were still being used: *herein, thereafter, therefor, therein, thereof, thereto,* and *thereunder*. By 1991, they had become quite rare. In ten Supreme Court opinions decided in that year, only *thereafter, thereby,* and *thereof* occurred.

The same holds for the adjectival use of *said* and *aforesaid*. These legalisms were still quite common in the opinions from 1891. One of the cases begins as follows:

> This is a petition for a writ of prohibition to be directed to the judge of the district court of the United States for the eastern division of the southern district of Georgia, to prohibit *said* judge from taking further cognizance of a certain suit instituted before him in *said* court. The suit sought to be prohibited is a libel filed in *said* court by John Lawton, owner of the steamboat Katie, seeking a decree for limited liability for the loss and damage which accrued by fire on *said* steam-boat in the Savannah river on the 12th of October, 1887.[28]

By 1941 use of *aforesaid* or *said* in this sense was already rare, and by 1991 it seems to have disappeared entirely from the Supreme Court's lexicon. On the other hand, American judicial opinions—like statutes—

have become substantially longer than they were in the past and seem increasingly complex in terms of subject matter.[29]

The language of judgments from the English House of Lords, which functions as the British high court, seems a bit more conservative, based on a survey of 1994 cases. Forms like *thereafter, thereby, thereof, therein, thereon, thereunder,* and *thereupon,* while not terribly common, were not systematically avoided, either. The law lords used *said* only as a verb, however.

Enjoying the literary freedom bestowed by their great job security, some judges have become renowned for their straightforward style. Here is an excerpt from a famous opinion by Judge Cardozo, then on the New York Court of Appeals:

> The defendant is a manufacturer of automobiles. It sold an automobile to a retail dealer. The retail dealer resold to the plaintiff. When the plaintiff was in the car it suddenly collapsed. He was thrown out and injured. One of the wheels was made of defective wood, and its spokes crumbled into fragments.[30]

Across the Atlantic, the British equivalent may be Lord Denning, who wrote in one of his judgments:

> Broadchalke is one of the most pleasing villages in England. Old Herbert Bundy was a farmer there. His farm was at Yew Tree Farm. It went back for 300 years. His family had been there for generations. It was his only asset. But he did a very foolish thing. He mortgaged it to the bank. Up to the very hilt. . . .[31]

Unfortunately, this simple—almost austere—style is much harder to maintain when wading through the morass of legal doctrine, as opposed to merely reciting the facts. But it is surely worth striving for. Many judicial opinions affect not just the parties before the court, but have tremendous implications for the population at large. A court may declare that your children will henceforth be sent by bus to a school miles away from your home to achieve racial balancing, or that you do or do not have a right to an abortion, or that you can be imprisoned for burning the flag. The average person may not understand every detail of a judicial opinion, but a motivated reader should at least be able to grasp the general idea.[32] Justice Earl Warren once wrote a memo to other members of the United States Supreme Court about the famous school desegregation case, *Brown v. Board of Education.* He urged them to write opinions that were "short" and "readable by the lay public."[33] That should be the Court's ideal not just when it is trying to persuade a skeptical public. As a matter of policy, those most affected by a judicial opinion should be able to read and understand it.

Consumer Documents

While court opinions and statutes have discarded the most notorious attributes of legalese, private documents written on behalf of lay clients have lagged behind. This is highly ironic. When a client signs a will or contract, it is the *client*—not the *lawyer*—who is legally "speaking" through that document. Thus, it is the client's intent that is deemed to govern the meaning, even though the client may scarcely understand it!

Some of the most significant documents that the average person signs in a lifetime concern title to his or her house; this is the average person's most valuable asset. An extremely important document in this regard is the **deed of trust** (similar to a mortgage), used in many American states. Here is part of the text of a typical deed of trust:

> Borrower covenants that Borrower is lawfully seised of the estate hereby conveyed and has the right to grant and convey the Property and that the Property is unencumbered, except of the encumbrances of record. Borrower warrants and will defend generally the title to the Property against all claims and demands, subject to any encumbrances of record.[34]

Despite appearances, this is not an ancient English indenture, but a form published in the United States in 1990. Although the borrower may not literally be engaged in the proverbial act of signing her life away, this is a momentous legal obligation that could cost her a large amount of money, or loss of the property, if something goes awry. Still, it is doubtful that most people who sign this form have more than a foggy notion of what it involves.

The available research, though limited in scope, supports this conclusion. A study of ordinary consumers interviewed at a shopping center demonstrated that most of them understood very little of a standard installment purchase agreement and warranty; on the other hand, a plain English version of the same documents was understood much better, especially by low income subjects.[35] The influential *Restatement (Second) of Contracts* notes that consumers "do not in fact ordinarily understand" the terms of a standardized contract.[36] Even highly educated judges may have trouble with consumer documents. During oral argument regarding an insurance policy in 1969, Chief Justice Weintraub of the New Jersey Supreme Court admitted: "I don't know what it means.

I am stumped." Justice Haneman remarked, "I can't understand half of my insurance policies," and Justice Francis suggested that such policies are kept "deliberately obscure."[37]

The Plain English Movement

The notion that people have a right to understand legal documents that affect their rights and obligations ultimately led to the **Plain English Movement**. Because this movement has mainly concentrated on government forms and consumer documents, it is associated with the consumer movement. In fact, Ralph Nader, the American consumer guru, wrote an article entitled *Gobbledygook* for the *Ladies' Home Journal* in 1977. Nader pointed out that even legal experts often could not understand the "mumbo-jumbo" in insurance policies, leases, and loan contracts. He urged consumers to continue exercising "vigilance and pressure" on banks and insurance companies to simplify the language of their forms.[38]

In the United States, some of the earliest efforts to improve legal language directed at consumers were initiated by the federal government, beginning rather modestly in the 1940s.[39] Federal law now requires clear, conspicuous, accurate, or understandable language in many types of consumer transactions, as mandated by the Truth in Lending Act, the Fair Credit Reporting Act, and the Magnuson-Moss Warranty Act.[40] Additionally, in 1978 President Carter signed Executive Order 12044, which aimed to improve federal regulations and required that they be "as simple and clear as possible."[41]

On the state level the movement began with private initiative. In the early 1970s a New York bank, Citibank, decided to experiment with a promissory note in plain English. Virtually every time that people borrow money from a bank, they sign a promissory note, so it is a very common legal document. Despite the misgivings of its legal department, Citibank began to use its innovative form in 1975. It attracted a great deal of favorable media attention. Politicians jumped on the bandwagon, and New York State enacted America's first general plain language law in 1978.[42] (For the original and revised Citibank promissory notes, see appendices E and F.)

Other state legislatures also took note, so that now there are plain English laws governing certain categories of consumer transactions in most of the American states.[43] Especially widespread are regulations requiring plain language in insurance contracts; general plain English legislation that applies to all consumer contracts, as in New York, is unfortunately less common.

Although it is fair to say that the Plain English Movement has recently slowed a bit in the United States, there are hopeful signs, particularly on the federal level. The drafting handbook of the Office of the Federal Register contains much of the standard advice on making proposed rules and regulations more intelligible.[44] More significant for the average consumer is a rule by the Securities and Exchange Commission on disclosure documents relating to securities. The SEC has become concerned that "the technical and dense legalese of current disclosure documents hides the information that is necessary for investors to make informed investment decisions." The rule requires the use of plain English on the cover page, summary, and risk factors sections of prospectuses.[45]

Outside of the United States, Australia has been a leader in the movement. At about the same time that Citibank released its promissory note, the Australian Sentry Life Insurance Company, responding to a survey of its customers, produced a plain language insurance policy. An executive from another insurance company, the National Road Motorists Association of New South Wales, saw the impact of the Citibank form during a visit to New York. Soon thereafter, the Association issued its first plain language automobile insurance policy. Apparently, litigation has declined as a result of such forms, there are fewer invalid claims, and insurance company staff now give more accurate advice to customers. As opposed to the United States, however, the impetus in Australia comes mainly from public pressure and voluntary efforts, rather than being required by legislation.[46]

The United Kingdom has its own movement promoting plain English. An important agitator for reform is the Plain English Campaign, started by a woman in Liverpool who was fed up with unintelligible government forms. She took hundreds of the offending documents, proceeded to Parliament Square, and publicly shredded the lot.[47] The Campaign gives out well-publicized awards for plain English and booby prizes for gobbledygook.[48] The National Consumer Council has likewise been active in plain language issues. Her Majesty's government seems to have been sufficiently embarrassed; it recently began revising large numbers of its forms. It has systematically reviewed thousands of forms, eliminated many as unnecessary, and simplified many others. On the private level, a growing group of English solicitors use plain language drafting in their practices.[49] Many of them are part of a growing international organization called *Clarity*, which publishes a journal by the same name. Yet—as in Australia—efforts to pass a general plain English law have met with resistance.[50]

Plain English likewise has made headway in Canada. The Bank of Nova Scotia redesigned and rewrote its loan forms in the late 1970s, and other banks have followed suit. More recently, there have been efforts at the federal level, as well as in the provinces, to promote more comprehensible legal language, encouraged for a while by a Plain Language Centre in Toronto. There has also been some movement in the provinces. For the most part, however, Canada follows Australia and the United Kingdom in promoting plain English mainly by persuasion and example.[51]

The plain language movement is attracting attention around the world. Such diverse countries as Ghana, India, New Zealand, Papua New Guinea, Singapore, and South Africa have shown interest.[52] Particularly in countries where English is not a native language, but which use English for legal purposes, it makes a great deal of sense.

Plain English Legislation

As the above overview shows, the United States seems more willing to enact legislation requiring private parties to use plain language, while other countries tend to depend more on education and encourage voluntary measures. This brings to the forefront the question of how effective legislation is in achieving reform.

The earliest, and perhaps most general, approach is exemplified by the New York plain language statute.[53] This law applies to leases and consumer agreements for personal, family, or household purposes, and thus has a fairly broad scope. In other words, it covers most consumer legal documents. In terms of language, the law requires that:

> 1. the writing be clear and coherent and the words used have common and everyday meaning; and
> 2. the writing be appropriately divided and captioned by its various sections.

The primary requirement of New York's law—that language be "clear and coherent"—is a very flexible, perhaps even vague, standard. We might call this the **general approach.** It has the virtue of being a plain and straightforward statement of what is required. The problem is that this standard—like all flexible language—is subject to interpretation and discretion. This is a serious potential drawback, because judges and lawyers, who are accustomed to reading legalese, have notoriously bad intuitions about when language is comprehensible to the average person. Those who draft the affected documents are also left to their own devices. How well this approach works depends entirely on the skill and the good will of those who must carry it out.

What might also limit the law's effectiveness is the remedy for violations, which is a mere $50 per occurrence, in addition to actual damages. There is a limit of $10,000 for a class action lawsuit. Because actual damages will be quite hard to prove, few lawyers would take a case of this kind on a contingent fee basis, and injured consumers may not be able to afford a retainer. Most importantly, this law does not provide consumers with an "incomprehensibility" defense. In other words, consumers cannot avoid their obligations by showing that they did not understand a document.[54]

The parsimonious remedy may largely explain why it was possible to enact this law, despite opposition from business. In fact, Citibank itself opposed the law, because it wished to remain free to experiment with the language of its forms without government interference.[55]

A truly effective remedy would provide that people cannot be bound by forms that they do not understand. Like the "unconscionability" defense to contracts, there should be an "incomprehensibility" defense. Naturally, such an approach would call into question the validity of many contracts and other legal documents with consumers, because so many are still written in legalese, and large numbers of consumers who breach or default on obligations would try to avoid them by claiming not to have understood the relevant document. Legislators will no doubt fear that they are opening the doors to a flood of litigation. But I believe that these problems could be solved. We might limit the defense to standardized forms, which are used and drafted by larger corporations that have the resources to hire experts to make the forms more comprehensible. And individual consumers could not avoid their obligations by claiming that they had not read or understood a specific document; we should not reward sloth. Instead, the test should be objective: whether the average consumer would be able to understand the form. In addition, the law would operate only on future documents, to avoid creating uncertainty about existing obligations. Even with these limitations, such a law would quickly produce results.

Despite the compromises made by the New York law, it is reported to have had some success. Many consumer contracts and other documents are simpler than before. And the law has accomplished this with little litigation.[56] On the other hand, it may not be as consumer-friendly as it could be, in large part because of its very general standard of what constitutes plain language and its limited remedy.

Other states have tried to give substance to general provisions requiring "clear" or "plain" language. Not surprisingly, they aim for greater precision and specificity by using a list approach (see chapter 5). A recent Pennsylvania law begins with a broad and general standard: consumer contracts "shall be written, organized and designed so that they are easy to read and understand."[57] The statute then lists specific guidelines to determine whether this general standard has been met:

(1) The contract should use short words, sentences and paragraphs.
(2) The contract should use active verbs.
(3) The contract should not use technical legal terms, other than commonly understood legal terms, such as "mortgage," "warranty" and "security interest."
(4) The contract should not use Latin and foreign words or any other word whenever its use requires reliance upon an obsolete meaning.
(5) If the contract defines words, the words should be defined by using commonly understood meanings.
(6) When the contract refers to the parties to the contract, the reference should use personal pronouns, the actual or shortened names of the parties, the terms "seller" and "buyer" or the terms "lender" and "borrower."
(7) The contract should not use sentences that contain more than one condition.
(8) The contract should not use cross references, except cross references that briefly and clearly describe the substances of the item to which reference is made.
(9) The contract should not use sentences with double negatives or exceptions to exceptions.[58]

It is evident that the drafters of this list were familiar with the research regarding legal language.

The statute also contains "visual guidelines," which state that the type size, line length, column width, margins, and spacing between lines and paragraphs should make a document easy to read. Moreover, a document should have captions in boldface type, and it should use ink that contrasts sharply with the paper.[59]

We might call this method the **guidelines approach.** As opposed to the general approach, it gives drafters some concrete guidance. At the same time, the guidelines are only as good as the people who apply them. If drafters of legal documents do not have some training in applying the guidelines, they will have limited impact. The same is true of judges who have to decide whether a particular form meets the guidelines. Perhaps linguists or other academics could be used as consultants, but that would quickly make the process time-consuming and expensive.

The desire to quickly and cheaply evaluate the language of legal documents has produced an alternative: what can be called the **objective approach.** Connecticut's plain language law, for instance, uses guidelines very similar to those in the Pennsylvania law. It also allows an alternative objective test, however, under which a document is held to be "plain" if it meets the following criteria:

(1) The average number of words per sentence is less than twenty-two; and

(2) No sentence in the contract exceeds fifty words; and

(3) The average number of words per paragraph is less than seventy-five; and

(4) No paragraph in the contract exceeds one hundred fifty words; and

(5) The average number of syllables per word is less than 1.55; and

(6) It uses personal pronouns, the actual or shortened names of the parties to the contract, or both, when referring to those parties; and

(7) It uses no type face of less than eight points in size; and

(8) It allows at least three-sixteenths of an inch of blank space between each paragraph and section; and

(9) It allows at least one-half of an inch of blank space at all borders of each page; and

(10) If the contract is printed, each section is captioned in boldface type at least ten points in size. If the contract is typewritten, each section is captioned and the captions are underlined; and

(11) It uses an average length of line of no more than sixty-five characters.[60]

The great advantage of this objective approach is that it is very easy to apply. In fact, a computer program could make the necessary calculations in no time at all.

Parts of the objective standard used in Connecticut were inspired by what are known as **readability tests.** There are a number of different tests, including the Dale-Chall formula and the Fog Index.[61] Perhaps the most common is the Flesch Reading Ease Test, developed by Rudolf Flesch. It has been incorporated into many state statutes that require insurance contracts to be in plain English. For example, Florida requires that insurance policies receive a minimum score of 45 on the Flesch test.[62] To put this into perspective, a score of 100 is very simple and 0 is extremely difficult; according to Flesch, plain English requires a score of 65 or above.[63] Incidentally, legal documents often receive scores in the negative numbers. In a study conducted in the mid-1980s, the Social Security Act received a score of −130 and the Ethics in Government Act came in at −219![64]

To apply the Flesch test, you begin by calculating the average number of words for every sentence in the text, then multiply this number by 1.015. Next, count the average number of syllables per word and multiply this by 84.6. The sum of these two numbers is subtracted from 206.835, producing the Flesch reading ease score.[65]

Linguists and experts on plain language have subjected the Flesch test to a barrage of criticism.[66] Their basic point is that the test is simplistic. Legal language is hard to understand because of linguistic features such as those described in chapter 12. It cannot be improved by mechanically shortening sentences and using words with fewer syllables. For instance, a recalcitrant insurance company could revise its policies by replacing some commas with periods. The language might be just as obscure as before, but might satisfy the Flesch test because the policies now contain very short sentences.

A problem with the Flesch test is that sentence length is only indirectly tied to comprehensibility. What really matters is complexity: levels of embedding, sentence structure, and so forth. Some very long sentences are perfectly understandable, while quite short ones (*the lis pendens shall be expunged*) may be virtually impossible for the lay public to understand.

Nor is there a direct relationship between the number of syllables in a word and comprehensibility. Some words have three or four syllables but would be understood by virtually any adult speaker of English, including *ambulance, automobile, helicopter, hospital, radio,* or *television.* Other words or phrases are very short, but cause significant comprehension problems, such as *en banc, estop, fee simple, per stirpes,* or *seisin.* What really matters is the likelihood that the average person will know what a word means. Archaic, formal, and technical words are bound to be problematic, regardless of how few syllables they have. Commonly used words will present few comprehension difficulties, even if they have many syllables.

Perhaps a more fundamental problem is that slavishly following guidelines, or applying any objective standard, is not sufficient to guarantee comprehension. Poorly worded plain language does not promote understanding. What guidelines and objective standards cannot measure is how well a complicated concept is being explained. Effective communication, like any other skill, is not just a matter of knowing the rules, but requires experience and perhaps even some intuition.

Ideally, we should require testing of important documents on a representative sample of the population. But although it should be done as often as is feasible, individual testing of the thousands of consumer-oriented documents that are produced each year would be a costly and tedious process.

For this reason, Robert Benson has suggested that readability formulas, with all their shortcomings, perform a valuable function in promoting plain legal language.[67] As an expert on readability has pointed out, word length and sentence length do not *cause* difficulty in reading, but they are reasonable *indices* of difficulty.[68] Thus, as a rough indicator, readability tests work fairly well. Although it is possible to make a list of short legal terms that no lay person would understand, paging through a law dictionary quickly shows that the vast bulk of legal terminology has two syllables and often many more. And although sentence length is not *directly* related to complexity, long sentences *generally* tend to be more complex. Anyone with linguistic sophistication can fool the Flesch test, of course, but we have to assume that its users are not trying to subvert it.

Because it is impossible to legislate writing skills and intuitions about communication, the best practical approach is to rely on both specific guidelines and an objective, easy-to-apply evaluation measure. Those who draft the documents need guidelines and training on how to write legal language in a way that will maximize comprehensibility. Government officials, as well as judges, need a quick and reliable way to determine whether that goal has been met.

Ultimately, computer technology will provide superior evaluation methods. For example, in place of counting syllables, a better way to decide whether words are comprehensible is to use a word frequency dictionary. Such a dictionary records how often a term occurs in a particular corpus, and therefore is a fairly accurate indicator of how common—and presumably, understandable—a word is. Frequency counts could be incorporated into computer programs designed to assess the comprehensibility of texts. Such programs could also review a document for other linguistic features, like sentence complexity, that have been identified as causing comprehension difficulties. In fact, computers can already accomplish many of these goals, but a truly accurate gauge of comprehensibility is probably still in the future.

Some Remaining Challenges

All in all, the movement advocating plain English has made substantial progress in improving the language of consumer contracts. Yet there are many areas in which lack of comprehensibility still creates problems for the public. For instance, a will is an important document for most people, but despite occasional efforts at improvement, the vast majority of wills (and perhaps to a lesser extent, trusts) are still a jumble of legalese.[69]

Another vital document is a medical consent form, where a patient acknowledges the risks of some medical treatment and authorizes a doctor to proceed. They are often drafted by lawyers. Research indicates that patients do not understand these forms very well and that use of plain language principles improves readability.[70] The same issue arises when someone signs a form consenting to allow police to search a building or vehicle. Also drafted by lawyers, these forms likewise tend to be in legalese rather than plain English. Here is an actual example from Washington:

> I, Doug G. Jensen, understanding my Constitutional Right to refuse consent to have a search made of the premises hereafter described and of my right to refuse to consent to a search without a search warrant, hereby authorize the undersigned officers of the Wash. State Patrol to conduct a complete search of the vehicle. . . .[71]

Premises hereafter described is hardly the clearest reference to Mr. Jensen's car. Nonetheless, courts will almost always presume that someone who signs a consent form understands what it means, unless she is clearly incompetent, was compelled by the police, or did not speak English.[72] Such presumptions are obviously helpful in promoting surgeries and searches, but the result would be easier to accept if courts occasionally looked at the language of the forms a bit more critically.

Releases of liability raise similar concerns. Ordinarily, organizers of risky ventures like scuba diving, automobile racing, or skiing require participants to sign such releases before they are allowed to engage in the activity. Somewhat unexpectedly, here judges are less likely to presume that if you signed it, you must have read and understood it. A court in California observed that releases of liability shift the risk of injury from the tortfeasor to the victim, and questioned whether public policy should permit this when the clause was in six point type.[73] Other cases have refused to enforce releases that were expressed in long, convoluted sentences, such as one that consisted of 193 words.[74]

Likewise, there are many occasions on which someone is required to give legal notice to another person or to the public in general. Newspapers often print them by the dozen, ranging from government notices that a particular establishment has applied for a liquor license, to notices that someone has died and that if you have a claim against the estate of the deceased, you must file it promptly. Whether such notices really *notify* the affected persons is frequently subject to grave doubt. For instance, the following is how tenants in Detroit were once informed that their landlord was attempting to evict them:

> PLEASE TAKE NOTICE, That you are hereby required to quit, surrender, and deliver up possession to me of the premises hereinafter described. . . .

Fortunately, these notices were revised to be far more comprehensible:

> Your landlord or landlady wants to evict you. . . .[75]

Large numbers of tenants still receive the proverbial "notice to quit," however.

Products can oftentimes be quite dangerous. Because manufacturers are aware that they may have to pay large damage awards if their product injures a consumer, they seem to have taken an interest in effective warnings. One of the top rungs of my ladder has a conspicuous sticker proclaiming:

> DANGER! Do not stand at or above this level. YOU CAN LOSE YOUR BALANCE.

Obviously, someone who stood on a higher rung, fell off, and then sued the manufacturer for product liability would have a hard time convincing a judge that he did not understand the warning. Far less effective is the language on a bottle of isopropyl rubbing alcohol:

> FOR EXTERNAL USE ONLY
> Will produce serious gastric disturbances if taken internally.

It seems a safe bet that anything labeled *alcohol* will tempt someone to drink it, especially because rubbing alcohol is quite cheap. Unfortunately, some people will not know what *serious gastric disturbances* are. The warning also contains a passive in a subordinate clause (*if taken internally*) and is entirely in the third person, leaving it for the reader to infer that this will happen to *you*. Furthermore, it could be read to suggest that the product is safe, as long as you drink it in the open air, rather than inside a building. The warning would be far more effective if it simply advised users: *Do not drink! You may become very sick.*

Recently, linguists and other language experts have demonstrated some of the problems with existing warnings,[76] and casual observation suggests the situation is improving. In fact, the Food and Drug Administration recently proposed new regulations that would require simpler language on over-the-counter drugs.[77]

There is no doubt that legal language has improved considerably over the past decades, at least in certain areas. Nonetheless, the Plain English Movement still has plenty of work to do.

CHAPTER FOURTEEN

Communicating with the Jury

Jurors are another class of consumers of legal language. As we saw in chapter 11, the instructions that jurors receive at the end of a trial are typically written in very dense legalistic language, and then presented orally. It has been evident for some time that jurors often do not understand their instructions very well. Justice Felix Frankfurter of the United States Supreme Court once suggested that a judge's instructions were "abracadabra."[1] Another renowned jurist, Jerome Frank, observed that the judge's words to the jury "might as well be spoken in a foreign language—that, indeed, for all the jury's understanding of them, they are spoken in a foreign language."[2]

Confusion and its Consequences

Recent research by social scientists has confirmed the observation that instructions often leave many jurors confused and frustrated. Other jurors may be quite confident that they understand the law, but be absolutely wrong.

A seminal study was conducted by Robert and Veda Charrow on the civil pattern instructions normally given in California.[3] The Charrows recorded fourteen instructions on audio tape and played them twice to several subjects. The subjects were then asked to paraphrase the instructions.[4] On average, they correctly paraphrased only about half of the essential parts of each instruction.[5]

The Charrows discovered that a number of linguistic features, such as those discussed in chapter 12, were largely responsible for the low scores.[6] They therefore repeated their experiment, using instructions that had been rewritten to be more intelligible but communicated the same information; in fact, their revisions were quite conservative. This time, the subjects did substantially better.[7]

Laurence Severance and Elizabeth Loftus conducted a similar study with former jurors and people awaiting assignment as jurors in the State of Washington. They showed their subjects a videotaped burglary trial. One group received standard instructions on reasonable doubt and related legal concepts; the other group got the same instructions, but rewritten to be more understandable. Comprehension was measured by a multiple choice questionnaire. Overall, subjects with the revised instructions made fewer errors than those with the pattern instructions.[8] Several other research teams, testing different instructions with varying methodologies, have reached similar conclusions.[9]

The reaction of the profession to research of this sort has varied. Many state court judges continue to drone on in much the same bored way that they always have, continually recycling tired language that has been in service for decades. Trial judges are especially reluctant to deviate from an instruction if at some time an appellate court has given its language a stamp of approval, even if done many decades ago. And as we observed in chapter 11 with the reasonable doubt instruction, courts are hesitant to modify the language of jury instructions that are based on a statute, even though statutes are written in legal language for a professionally-trained audience.

If judges fear to modify existing instructions, or to explain them in ordinary language when jurors return with a question, the only real avenue for reform is the committees that draft the pattern instructions in the first place. Fortunately, here some progress has been made, at least in the realm of good intentions. As early as 1938, California's committee on standard jury instructions informed users: "if you can write [an instruction] that will be clearer to the lay mind . . . we ask that you give to our committee, and to the bar, the benefit of your erudition."[10] More recently, the California committee expressed a desire to draft instructions that are "understandable to the average juror."[11] Other American jurisdictions require that instructions be simple,[12] understandable,[13] conversational,[14] and free of legal jargon.[15] And the federal courts in the Ninth Circuit, expressing an interest in "improv[ing] the quality of communication with jurors," promote writing in short sentences and avoiding negatives. Quite sensibly, they advise against reading statutes to the jury, because the statute was not drafted to be understood by jurors.[16]

Furthermore, lawyers and judges who truly wish to improve communication with jurors now have guidelines at their disposal to help them reach this goal. Among them are a book by the experienced team of Elwork, Sales, and Alfini, as well as suggestions distributed by the Federal Judicial Center.[17]

Unfortunately, despite many expressions of good intentions, actual progress has been quite uneven. Robert Nieland, who conducted a study of jury instructions in 1979, found that meaningful attempts at reform had been made in Pennsylvania, Florida, and Arizona; more limited efforts had been undertaken in Montana, Michigan, Maryland, and Virginia.[18] Since then, there have been reports of advances in other states.[19] Perhaps the most receptive have been the federal courts.[20]

In contrast, jury instructions in many of the remaining American states remain quite antiquated. For example, even though California's committees have voiced an interest in increasing comprehensibility, the state's jury instructions have only been modestly and haphazardly improved, despite the detailed criticisms of the Charrow study.[21] Efforts to draft a more intelligible "reasonable doubt" instruction in California have faltered.[22] There is hope, however. Recently, a commission charged with finding ways to improve the jury system (inspired in part by the failure to obtain a conviction in the O. J. Simpson case) recommended that California jury instructions be revised to make them more comprehensible. A task force has been formed to carry out that mandate.[23]

There will continue to be progress, in my opinion, but sometimes the wheels of justice grind very slowly. Just as their medieval counterparts argued that Law French should be preserved because it was more precise than English, many lawyers and judges today contend that instructions in legalese are far more precise and legally accurate than ordinary language. It took centuries to debunk this myth in England. One hopes that it will not take nearly as long to present modern jurors with more understandable instructions.

Capital Instructions: Comprehension as a Matter of Life or Death

The importance of reform is most starkly evident when comprehension is truly a life-or-death matter. We need not delve into the details of death penalty jurisprudence here. Suffice it to say that in most American jurisdictions with capital punishment, it is the jury that decides the defendant's fate. Yet the jury's power of life and death is limited; the United States Supreme Court has made it clear that its discretion "must be suitably directed and limited so as to minimize the risk of wholly arbitrary and capricious action."[24]

Obviously, the only way to suitably guide the discretion of the jury is by having the judge properly instruct them. If that guidance is to be at all meaningful, the jury will have to understand the judge's instructions. Incomprehensible guidance is an oxymoron.

Yet incomprehensible—or at least, convoluted—guidance is exactly what many death penalty juries receive. Under the typical American death penalty statute, the jury must first decide that the defendant has murdered someone under circumstances that make it a possible capital case; this limits the death penalty to only the most serious crimes. The jury must then consider both the **aggravating** and the **mitigating** circumstances. Typical aggravating factors are that the defendant tortured the victim before killing him or has a long history of committing violent crimes. Mitigating factors could be his unhappy childhood, his remorse, mental problems, or his mother testifying that he was a good boy who fell in with the wrong crowd. If the jurors decide that the aggravation outweighs any mitigation, they should vote for death. Otherwise, they should vote for imprisonment (often without the possibility of parole).[25]

While this scheme does indeed give the jury some guidance on how to decide the defendant's fate, it has a serious flaw: its reliance on the technical terms *aggravation* and *mitigation*. Most courts blithely assume that jurors understand these words in their legal sense. The Supreme Court of Georgia has asserted—with no supporting evidence—that *mitigation* "is a word of common meaning and usage."[26] California's high court apparently agrees, having held that these words do not have to be defined for the jury.[27]

The reality is that even in its ordinary sense, *mitigate* is a formal word that many ordinary jurors will not understand very well.[28] As former Justice Thurgood Marshall observed, in its technical legal usage, *mitigating* is "a term of art, with a constitutional meaning that is unlikely to be apparent to a lay jury."[29] This is confirmed by a study of California's capital jury instructions by Lorelei Sontag, who discovered that even relatively well-educated college students poorly understood the word.[30]

In contrast, *aggravate* is a fairly common word. But familiarity can be deceptive. In fact, it is a legal homonym. As linguist Robin Lakoff has written: "*Mitigation* is an uncommon word, bad enough, but *aggravation* is worse—its meaning here (*worsening*) is far from its normal colloquial sense (*annoying*)."[31] This ordinary meaning of *aggravate,* to which the entire judiciary of the United States seems oblivious, is not exactly a recent innovation. Well over a hundred years ago, John Stuart Mill wrote:

The use of "aggravating" for "provoking," in my boyhood a vulgarism of the nursery, has crept into almost all newspapers and into many books; and when writers on criminal law speak of aggravating and extenuating circumstances, their meaning, it is probable, is already misunderstood.[32]

In fact, Otto Jespersen noted that this meaning can be traced back at least as far as 1611.[33] *Aggravate* therefore ordinarily means "annoy" or "irritate." But surely jurors should not vote to put someone to death merely because the defendant, or his crime, *aggravates* them!

Virtually irrefutable evidence that jurors fail to fully grasp the meaning of these terms comes from several reported cases where capital jurors— after they have been "instructed"—come back to ask the judge to define or clarify what these terms mean, or request a dictionary to look them up. In one California case, the jury sent a note to the judge requesting "a definition of aggravation and mitigation." The judge replied that the words should be given their "commonly accepted and ordinary meaning." The jury responded: "Being unfamiliar with the term of mitigation we would like the dictionary meaning of both mitigation and aggravation, please."[34]

In response to such questions, judges tend to just reread the original instructions. Other judges, trying to be more helpful, read a definition like the following from a legal encyclopedia or dictionary, obviously not written for laymen:

> *Aggravation.* Any circumstance attending the commission of a crime which increases its guilt or enormity or adds to its injurious consequences, but which is above and beyond the essential constituents of the crime itself. I will next define "mitigating." Circumstances such as do not constitute a justification or excuse of the offense in question, but which, in fairness and mercy, may be considered as extenuating or reducing the degree of moral culpability.[35]

Ironically, the judge who read these definitions did so in response to a jury's request for "additional definitions of these words in *layman's* terms."[36]

In the published American opinions alone, there are at least ten capital cases during the past decade or two in which the jury is reported to have requested a definition or clarification of *mitigating* and / or *aggravating*.[37] No doubt these represent merely the tip of the iceberg. Sontag's study of capital juries in California presents further evidence that the problem is endemic.[38] She interviewed jurors who had participated in ten capital cases, half of which reached death verdicts.[39] Of the thirty jurors with whom she spoke, only thirteen showed adequate understanding of *aggravating* and *mitigating*.[40] No less than *half* of the juries asked their trial judges for definitions of these critical terms.[41] One juror reported:

> The first thing we asked for after the instructions was, could the judge define mitigating and aggravating circumstances. . . . I said, "I don't know that I exactly understand what it means." And then everybody else said, "No, neither do I," or "I can't give you a definition." So we decided we should ask the judge. Well, the judge wrote back and said, "You have to glean it from the instructions."[42]

Another member of the jury broke down in tears, confessing "I still don't understand the difference between aggravating and mitigating."[43]

This evidence strongly suggests that there have probably been dozens of people who have been condemned to die by juries who poorly understood the legal principles that were supposed to guide their decision. Ironically, the problem is one of the most basic errors in communicating with the public: throwing technical terminology at a lay audience. Every lawyer realizes, during questioning of witnesses, that technical terms must be explained in ordinary language. Yet once the instruction ritual begins, they seem to have forgotten.

Just as legal language consists of more than technical terminology, the problem with jury instructions transcends vocabulary. The late Professor Hans Zeisel, an expert on the American jury, surveyed potential jurors in Cook County, Illinois, to determine how well they understood the instructions that were typically given in a death penalty case in Illinois. Interestingly, the subjects comprehended several concepts relatively well. For instance, most of them correctly understood that if any individual juror decides that some factor (like the defendant's age) is a mitigating factor, the juror can consider that mitigating circumstance in the weighing process. This point is somewhat counterintuitive, because virtually all other jury determinations must be made unanimously.[44]

Yet other points were more problematic. Consider the following instruction on the nature of mitigating evidence:

> Mitigating factors include but are not limited to the following circumstances.
> One, the Defendant has no significant history of prior criminal activity.
> Two, the murder was committed while the Defendant was un-

der the influence of extreme mental or emotional disturbance, although not such as to constitute a defense to prosecution.

If, from your consideration of the evidence, you find that any of the above mitigating factors are present in this case, or that any other mitigating factors are present in this case then you should consider such factors in light of any existing aggravating factors in determining whether the death sentence shall be imposed.[45]

Observe that jurors are told to consider any *mitigation,* which is a broad or flexible term, and which is then amplified by a list of two specific examples. In other words, jurors are to consider any *X, including but not limited to, a and b.* As noted in detail in chapter 5, there is virtually always some tension between the general and the specific. Here, the law requires maximum flexibility: jurors must be allowed to consider any mitigation whatsoever, no matter how trivial it might seem to others. Yet the existence of a specific list plainly suggests that any mitigation ought to resemble those items on the list. Not surprisingly, Zeisel's survey suggests that this is exactly how many jurors interpreted the instruction. For example, most of Zeisel's subjects concluded that more moderate mental disturbance did not count as mitigation.[46]

As opposed to empirical studies that languish in scholarly journals, the Zeisel survey came to the attention of lawyers who represented James Free, a convicted murderer on the Illinois death row. Free's appeal in state courts had failed.[47] As is quite common in such cases, he then petitioned the federal courts for a writ of habeas corpus, requesting the federal judiciary to overturn his sentence because of an alleged violation of his federal constitutional rights. Specifically, Free asserted that Illinois's death penalty instructions did not properly guide the discretion of the jury that sentenced him to death.

Free's lawyers presented Zeisel's research to a federal district court. After examining the evidence, the judge agreed that in a number of areas, Free's jury most likely did not understand the law correctly. The judge issued a writ of habeas corpus vacating Free's death sentence, but stayed the order pending an appeal.[48] As one of the first cases where a judge seriously examined how well juries actually understand instructions, it was a significant decision.

While vacating Free's death sentence may sound extreme, his conviction would have remained valid. The order would most likely have led to another "penalty phase," in which a properly instructed jury would again balance the aggravating versus mitigating factors to decide whether the penalty should be death or imprisonment. Unfortunately, many—perhaps all—of the prisoners on Illinois' death row had been condemned by juries instructed in very similar language. From the point of view of the legal system, the *Free* decision was not a bold step to reform legal language, but offered a straw to dozens and perhaps hundreds of cold-blooded killers, who could grasp it to avoid—or at least, delay—their executions. And grasp it they did.

One of the first to do so was none other than the infamous John Wayne Gacy, a serial killer who had murdered thirty-three young men and disposed of their bodies under his house. Gacy has been described as the "undisputed champion among American serial killers."[49] Riding on Free's coattails, he made a last desperate attempt to stave off his impending execution. Gacy petitioned the federal courts for a writ of habeas corpus, arguing that his jury instructions were similar to Free's, that Zeisel's survey proved that the jury had not properly understood them, and that his sentence of death should likewise be vacated. A different judge rejected his contentions.[50]

Gacy appealed to the Seventh Circuit Court of Appeals. For various procedural reasons, Gacy's appeal was decided before that of Free. The panel of judges deciding Gacy's appeal admitted that "[p]olysyllabic mystification reduces the quality of justice."[51] Yet it rejected the appeal. The court's primary rationale was that the instructions were complex not just because of language, but because of their complicated content, making them hard to master on first exposure, and perhaps too difficult for jurors to understand at all.[52] This is a common objection to improving jury instructions, and, indeed, to legal use of plain language in general. How can amateurs learn a complicated body of law in a matter of minutes or hours when law students have to study it for three years in law school, followed by extensive training in practice? Of course, if ordinary people cannot understand the law, they should not be forced to decide who should be imprisoned and who should be sentenced to death. Poorly instructed jurors will render poor decisions. In addition, they will leave the process frustrated at being compelled to do something that they are not equipped to handle.

The Gacy panel also raised a more formidable obstacle to his appeal: the presumption that jurors understand their instructions:

> Instead of inquiring what juries actually understood, and how they really reasoned, courts invoke a "presumption" that jurors understand and follow their instructions. . . . [T]his is not a bursting bubble, applicable only in the absence of better evi-

dence. It is a rule of law—a description of the premises underlying the jury system, rather than a proposition about jurors' abilities and states of mind.[53]

This truly converts the jury into the proverbial "black box," with evidence and instructions as input, and an unassailable verdict as output. With such a presumption, what happens inside the box is legally irrelevant.

The presumption that jurors understand the law, and that they follow it, does have the advantage that it lends a finality to verdicts that they would otherwise lack, and it lessens the prospect of the losing party harassing the jurors after their decision has been made. Yet as illustrated above, this presumption flies in the face of all available evidence.

After Gacy's failed appeal, Free's case itself came before the Seventh Circuit Court of Appeals. A different panel of judges reached the same conclusion as had Gacy's, but emphasizing different objections to Zeisel's research. The opinion, authored by well-known Judge Richard Posner, complained that Zeisel had not rewritten the instructions and tried them out on a control group. It was therefore impossible to say that revised instructions would have had any influence on the outcome, according to the court.[54]

Of course, as one judge noted in dissent, the solution to this problem would have been to send the case back to the district court, which could then have allowed Free's academic defenders to conduct another survey with a control group.[55] In fact, a subsequent study did exactly what Judge Posner suggested. It found that rewritten instructions did indeed lead to greater comprehension than the original ones.[56] The study also addressed the issue of deliberation. It is often suggested that lack of comprehension because of poorly worded jury instructions is not really a problem because jurors can deliberate before reaching a verdict. Consistent with earlier studies, the researchers found that deliberation increased comprehension only when a substantial number of subjects already had a correct understanding in the first place.[57] If most jurors did not understand the instruction properly to begin with, deliberation just created further confusion as jurors propounded contrasting interpretations of what the judge meant.

A final point is that we may not be able to attain perfection in our quest to create legal language that the ordinary public can understand. Even revising instructions in the *Free* case led only to around 60 percent comprehension. This is consistent with other studies. The team of Elwork, Sales, and Alfini, who also conducted a study comparing standard instructions with more intelligible equivalents, aimed for a comprehension rate under which two-thirds of all jurors on a panel understood a given point of law, and they hoped to achieve that goal with eight out of ten panels. Of 86 questions testing various points of law, only 16 percent met this level of comprehension using the original (standard) instructions. Using revised instructions led to a great improvement, but even then, just over half of the questions met the desired comprehension level.[58]

Results such as these confirm that the law is indeed quite complex. There are limits to how well even the best instructions in plain language can convey complicated concepts to an untrained lay audience in a short period of time. This should not be unexpected; even after years of rigorous education in law school, a substantial number of students fail the bar examination in New York or California. To expect that we will ever achieve 100 percent comprehension of jury instructions—or other legal documents—may be unrealistic.

Yet there is no excuse for not doing better. Jurors who understand their task will have far more confidence in the system than those who do not. And even though the jury will remain something of a "black box," we will receive a more trustworthy output as we raise the quality of the input.

Unfortunately, the legal profession has many goals and interests that may override efforts to communicate clearly with the jury. Free's lawyers adopted the Zeisel survey not so much because they were proponents of better jury instructions, but because they were desperate for a legally sufficient reason to overturn his sentence. When the law is on their side, lawyers will generally try to convey it as intelligibly as possible to the jury. When the law is against them, they tend to favor obscurity.

Judges have their own agenda. Faced in the *Free* case with the prospect of flinging open the doors of the Illinois death row, and the political fracas that it would evoke, they chose to ignore strong evidence that jurors did not understand their task. The possibility of reversals, especially on a large scale, strikes fear in the hearts of most judges, who will have to spend a great deal of time retrying the cases, or face popular and political pressure because they released convicted criminals. Many prefer to hide behind the presumption that jurors understand their instructions.

We will never know whether Gacy and Free would have received a death sentence if their juries had better understood the law. Gacy's crime was heinous enough that the niceties of the law would have had very little impact. It might have made a difference in Free's case. In any event, it is a moot question: the State of Illinois has executed them both.

CONCLUSION

The language of the legal profession has been criticized as arcane and archaic, complex and convoluted, pompous and ponderous. It has been an object of perplexity, scorn, and derision. Despite significant progress over the centuries, especially by the Plain English Movement during the past decades, legal language has retained many of these undesirable qualities. Members of the public are frequently left with an inadequate understanding of documents that govern their rights and obligations. Even lawyers may have great difficulty understanding the language of their colleagues, as indicated by the tremendous number of cases every year revolving around the meaning of some word or phrase.

In the last analysis, legal language must be judged by how clearly, concisely, and comprehensibly it communicates the rights and obligations conferred by a constitution, the opinions expressed by a court, the regulations embodied in a statute, or the promises exchanged in a contract. In today's world, virtually no one escapes taking out insurance policies, assuming mortgages, signing credit contracts, or making a will. We may not attain perfect comprehension of every aspect of these documents by every member of the public. But consumers should understand the most important provisions of the documents that they sign. They should be made aware of the things that really matter to them, even if they do not grasp every detail.

In light of all this evidence of the need to reform the language of the law, why has change come so slowly? Why do lawyers seem so reluctant to speak and write more clearly?

To some extent, the worst features of legal English may simply be remnants of ages past. The long retention of Law French in England is perhaps the best illustration of the conservative tendencies of the profession. Even today, lawyers are nervous about giving up traditional phrasing that has passed the test of time. Of course, this is not just a matter of inertia, but also because reusing tried and proven phraseology may be the safest course of action. This conservatism should not be exaggerated; the linguistic usage of lawyers can be highly creative and innovative, as illustrated by ready coinage of neologisms and the existence of legal slang. But overall, lawyers hesitate to change long-standing linguistic habits, something that clearly hinders efforts at reform.

Another problem is the large technical vocabulary of the profession. Technical terms can be very handy for facilitating in-group communication, allowing a complex concept to be conveyed in a single word or phrase. Paradoxically, however, fostering communication within the profession by means of an elaborate vocabulary undermines the aim of making legal language more accessible to the public. Probably the only solution is to retain technical terms that perform a useful communicative function and to translate them for the public when necessary.

Strategic concerns can also frustrate the goal of clear communication. Legal counsel for banks and insurance companies may sometimes actually prefer that customers not fully understand the terms of a loan agreement or insurance policy; if they did, they might not sign it.

Similar strategic goals and interests operate in the courtroom. On some occasions, trial lawyers are very much interested in clear communication. Normally, we question someone to determine the truth about some matter. Trial lawyers, on the other hand, use questions not so much to obtain information, but more to convey as clearly as possible to the jury that their client's story is correct. In contrast, the defense may not share this aim, especially if the law or evidence favors the prosecution. In that case, lawyers may deliberately choose to pursue a strategy of obscurity and obfuscation. Thus, how clearly lawyers communicate often depends on the goal that they are pursuing.

Related to strategy is the adversarial nature of the profession. This means that virtually any legal document is liable, at some point in its existence, to be picked apart by an opponent eager to exploit a loophole or ambiguity in order to wiggle out of an agreement or to contest a will. Legislation is no exception; almost any statute will be subjected to intense scrutiny by lawyers trying to poke holes in it on behalf of their clients. Those who draft such documents must anticipate these attacks. Therefore, they obsessively try to cover every base, plug every loophole, and deal with every remotely possible contingency. The result is ever longer, denser, and more convoluted prose.

Economics is yet another factor that helps explain some of the features of the language of the legal system. For one thing, the realities of practice encourage lawyers to make abundant use and reuse of forms. Economic considerations also encourage judges to read "pattern" instructions to the jury, rather than drafting them anew for each trial. Large corporations mass-produce preprinted standardized forms for consumer transactions for the same reason. In each case, legal professionals can save time (and hence, money) by recycling old forms rather than reinventing the wheel for every transaction. The evident result is that antiquated language is kept on life support.

An additional economic factor is how lawyers are paid for their services. Long and redundant legal prose is most likely to be found where lawyers can charge by the page. Charging by the hour is a less direct incentive to be verbose, but it strongly motivates lawyers to produce client documents that are sufficiently long and intricate to justify the lawyer's fee. In contrast, my experience suggests that when lawyers are paid on a contingent or fixed fee basis, their writing gets to the point with remarkable speed.

The linguistic habits of lawyers also serve as a badge of membership in the legal profession. "Talking like a lawyer" enhances an attorney's sense of self-esteem and belonging. Using language to create group cohesion is a natural tendency that other social groups and professions share. Unfortunately, linguistic features that cause certain people to feel included in a group necessarily exclude others. Unlike a fraternity or social club, the legal profession has a duty to serve the public. In this light, exclusionary language is more questionable.

The legal system as a whole likewise has goals that may have an adverse impact on communication. For example, it endeavors to state the law as authoritatively as possible. Formal, archaic, and ritualistic language helps accomplish this goal by conveying an aura of timelessness that makes the law seem almost eternal, and thus more credible and worthy of respect. Courts enhance their sense of legitimacy by depicting themselves as virtually unchanging institutions of ancient lineage. This explains why judges can refer to an opinion written decades or centuries ago as something that *we* decided. Ritualistic language separates legal proceedings from ordinary life, marking a court session as being special and important, or impressing on testators the significance of the will that they are about to sign. Because formal and ritualistic language is not in common usage, however, it almost always comes at the cost of comprehension.

The legal system desires to have the law appear not only authoritative, but maximally objective. Court orders are typically in the passive voice (*the writ of certiorari is granted*), creating the impression that such acts are accomplished without the intervention of a fallible human agent. The objectivity of the law is reinforced by judges' use of the third person, referring to themselves as *the court,* rather than *I.* Broad and impersonal statements of legal rules (*Any person who does X shall be guilty of a misde-meanor*) give the law an aura of supreme impartiality. Whatever its bene-fits, this goal once again reduces clear communication. Broad and sweeping generalizations are far less effective than personal warnings that if *you* do the following, *I* will throw *you* into prison.

Incomprehensible and convoluted phraseology serves yet another goal of the legal system: to make the law appear mysterious and complex. Of course, the conspiratorial view of legal language as merely a ploy to fleece the public is overly cynical. Legal language is complex not only because of its long history, but because the substance of the law itself can be quite complicated. The real issue is that many lawyers routinely draft all documents, even those involving very simple transactions, and regardless of the audience, using complex and convoluted phraseology. There is no doubt that this discourages many people from writing wills and other legal documents for themselves. And it encourages them to seek the advice of an attorney to figure out the meaning of statutes and judicial opinions. Because legal language is so different from ordinary speech, the public is resigned to hiring lawyers as expensive translators. In that sense, a distinctive language helps the profession justify its exis-tence and fees.

Understanding the competing goals and interests of the profession with respect to its language can help us decide which aspects of legal language are worth preserving and which should be cast aside. A few ritualistic phrases are worth keeping as links to the past and markers of the transition from ordinary life to a legal event. Useless and archaic words like *aforesaid* and *to wit,* on the other hand, should be discarded. Careful use of word lists can be quite appropriate. Thoughtless repeti-tion of wordy and redundant phrases is the legal equivalent of overusing banal clichés. If lawyers wish to be truly professional in their use of lan-guage, they need to reconsider old habits and concentrate on how well their speech and writing attains the paramount goal of all language: clear, concise and comprehensible communication.

Visionaries will no doubt continue to hope that the distinctive lan-guage of the law will soon vanish entirely, and with it the need for law-yers, as well as the need for books such as this one. Reality cautions that some type of legal language will always be with us. Rather than reducing the pressure to reform, this reality is perhaps the most compelling reason to separate the wheat from the chaff, keeping those features that en-hance the functioning of the legal system, while discarding those that serve no justifiable purpose.

APPENDIX A

An Anglo-Saxon Legal Document: Grant of Lands by Ulfketel to Bury St. Edmunds

[H]Er switeleþ on þis wríte ihu þat Vlfketel God vthe and sc̄e Eadmunde · þat ís þat lond at Rikínghale and al þat þerto hireð · and þat lond at Rucham · and þat lond at Wlpet · and þat lond at Hildericlea · and þat at Redfaresþorpe · also so ít stonden míd mete and míd manne and míd Sake and Sokne also íc ít aihte. Se þe þís awende · God almíthtín aWende his ansene on domesday from hím buten he ít er her þe rathere bete.

Translation:
Here it is declared in this document that Ulfketel has granted to God and St. Edmund the estate at Rickinghall and all that belongs to it, and the estate at Rougham and the estate at Woolpit and the estate at Hinderclay and that at Redfaresthorpe, as they stand with their produce and their men and with rights of jurisdiction, as he has owned them. If anyone alters this, God Almighty shall avert His countenance from him on the Day of Judgment, unless he has made amends for it here as quickly as possible.

Source: A. J. Robertson, Anglo-Saxon Charters 146–47 (1986).

APPENDIX B

A Case Report in Law French

Anonymous, 1319

Un Richard porta brief de dette vers un abbé et soun commoygne, et dit qe le moygne taunt com il fut seculer avoit apromté de ly x livres, a payer a certeyn jour, a quel jour il ne paya poynt; et de ceo tendist sute saunz especialté.

Migg'. Il demaunde ceste dette par resoun de un aprest fet au moygne taunt com il fut seculer, lequel homme est mort quaunt a la ley de terre en taunt com il est profés en religioun; et demaundoms jugement si a tiel demoustraunce devez estre resceu.

Scrop. Quant l'abbé resceit un moygne il se deit aviser q'il ne seit chargé de dette, quar il ly deit resceyvre ove sa charge auxi com le baroun fra sa femme.

Herle. Ceo n'est pas semblable, quar le moygne est mort quant a la ley, et si n'est pas la femme.

Berr'. Pur ceo qe vous n'avez qe sute, a quei homme ne put alayer, mes l'abbé ne put alayer le fet soun moygne, par quei agarde la court qe vous ne pregnez rien par vostre brief.

Et *Toud'* et *Frisk'* disoyent qe cel jugement ust esté mesq'il ust eu fet: quar autrement ensuereit meschef, qe par fet de un seculer la mesoun purra estre chargé à touz jours. *Set contra posissionem potest fieri opinabilis questio etc.*

Translation:

One Richard brought a writ of debt against an abbot and a monk of his house, and he said that the monk while yet secular had borrowed from him ten pounds, to be paid back on a certain day, and on that day the monk did not pay; and of this he tendered suit without showing specialty.

Miggele. He demands this debt by reason of a loan made to a monk while he was yet secular. Now that man is dead as regards the law of the land, inasmuch as he has professed religious vows, so we ask judgement whether you should be received to make such a demonstrance.

Scrope. When the abbot receives a monk he must consider whether he is not charged with debt, for he must receive him with his charge as a husband shall his wife.

Herle. That is a different matter, for the monk is dead at law and the wife is not.

BEREFORD, C.J. Since you only tender suit which can involve no wager of law, [since] the abbot cannot wage law upon the act of one of his monks, the court awards that you take nothing by your writ.

And *Toudeby* and *Friskeney* said the judgement would have been the same even if the demandant had had a deed. Otherwise mischief would have resulted, for the house [would] be charged for all time by the deed of a secular. But against this position an arguable question could be raised.

Source: Year Books of Edward II.: 12 Edward II., 1319 89 (John P. Collas and Theodore F.P. Plucknett eds., 1953).

APPENDIX C

A Modern Will

KNOW ALL MEN BY THESE PRESENTS, that I, HELEN HOVANE-SIAN, of the Town of New Britain, County of Hartford and State of Connecticut, do hereby make, publish and declare this as and for my Last Will and Testament, hereby revoking all wills and codicils thereto heretofore by me made.

FIRST: I direct my Executor to pay my funeral expenses and all my just debts, except those secured by mortgage or otherwise, out of my estate. . . .

[Article Second deals with payment of taxes]

THIRD: I give and bequeath to my brother, ARCHIE HOVANESIAN, SR. of New Britain, Connecticut, the sum of Five Thousand ($5,000.00) Dollars, to be his absolutely and forever, if he be living ninety (90) days after my death. . . .

[Articles Fourth through Tenth make several similar gifts]

ELEVENTH: I give, devise and bequeath all of said rest, residue and remainder of my property which I may own at the time of my death, real, personal and mixed, of whatsoever kind and nature and wheresoever situate, including all property which I may acquire or to which I may become entitled after the execution of this will, in equal shares, absolutely and forever, to ARCHIE HOVANESIAN, SR., LUCY HO-VANESIAN, his wife, ARCHIBALD HOVANESIAN, JR., JOHN C. HO-VANESIAN, KURKEN S. HOVANESIAN, and ANGELA M. (HOVANE-SIAN) SILLARI, per capita, to any of them living ninety (90) days after my death.

TWELFTH: I hereby nominate and appoint my nephew, ARCHIBALD HOVANESIAN, JR., as Executor of this, my Last Will and Testament. I hereby direct that no bond or other security shall be required of my said Executor (or any successor) for the qualification, discharge and performance of his duties as Executor of this, my Last Will and Testament. . . .

IN WITNESS WHEREOF, I have hereunto set my hand and seal at Hartford, Connecticut, this 2nd day of July, 1986.

/s/ Helen Hovanesian

HELEN HOVANESIAN

Signed, sealed, published and declared by the same HELEN HOVANESIAN as and for her Last Will and Testament, in the presence of us, who, at her request, in her presence and in the presence of each other, have hereunto subscribed our names as witnesses on this 2nd day of July, 1986.

/s/ Kathleen M. Kelleher of West Hartford, CT

KATHLEEN M. KELLEHER

/s/ Peter G. Facey of Hartford, CT

PETER G. FACEY

Source: Hovanesian v. Hovanesian, No. 451371S, 1993 WL 392962 (Conn. Super. Ct., Sept. 14, 1993).

APPENDIX D

Excerpts from Jury Instructions in *People v. Simpson*

Ladies and gentlemen of the jury:

You have heard all the evidence and it is now my duty to instruct you on the law that applies to this case. After I conclude reading these instructions to you, we will commence with the argument of counsel. The law requires that I read these instructions to you here in open court. Please listen carefully. It is also my personal policy that you will have these instructions in their written form in the jury room to refer to during the course of your deliberations.

You must base your decision on the facts and the law.

You have two duties to perform: first, you must determine the fact [*sic*] from the evidence received in the trial and not from any other source. A "fact" is something that is proved directly or circumstantially by the evidence or by stipulation. A stipulation is an agreement between the attorneys regarding the facts. Second, you must apply the law that I state to you to the facts as you determine them and in this way arrive at your verdict and any finding you are instructed to include in your verdict.

You must accept and follow the law as I state it to you, whether or not you agree with the law. . . .

You must not be influenced by pity for a defendant or by prejudice against him. You must not be biased against the defendant because he has been arrested for this offense, charged with a crime or brought to trial. None of these circumstances is evidence of guilt and you must not infer or assume from any or all of them that he is more likely to be guilty than innocent. You must not be influenced by mere sentiment, conjecture, sympathy, passion, prejudice, public opinion or public feeling. Both the prosecution and the defendant have a right to expect that you will conscientiously consider and weigh the evidence, apply the law and reach a just verdict regardless of the consequences. . . .

Statements made by attorneys during the trial are not evidence, although if the attorneys have stipulated to or agreed to a fact, you must regard that fact as conclusively proven.

If an objection was sustained to a question, do not guess what the answer might have been. Do not speculate as to the reason for the objection.

Do not assume to be true any insinuation suggested by a question asked of a witness. A question is not evidence and may be considered only as it enables you to understand the answer. . . .

Evidence consists of the testimony of witnesses, writings, material objects or anything presented to the senses and offered to prove the existence or nonexistence of a fact.

Evidence is either direct or circumstantial.

Direct evidence is evidence that directly proves a fact without the necessity of an inference. It is evidence which by itself, if found to be true, establishes that fact.

Circumstantial evidence is evidence that, if found to be true, proves a fact from which an inference of the existence of another fact may be drawn.

An inference is a deduction of fact that may logically and reasonably be drawn from another fact or group of facts established by the evidence.

It is not necessary that facts be proved by direct evidence. They may be proved also by circumstantial evidence or by a combination of direct evidence and circumstantial evidence. Both direct evidence and circumstantial evidence are acceptable as a means of proof. Neither is entitled to any greater weight than the other.

However, a finding of guilt as to any crime may not be based on circumstantial evidence unless the proved circumstances are not only, one, consistent with the theory that the defendant is guilty of the crime, but two, cannot be reconciled with any other rational conclusion.

Further, each fact which is essential to complete a set of circumstances necessary to establish the defendant's guilt must be proved beyond a reasonable doubt. In other words, before an inference essential to establish guilt may be found to have been proved beyond a reasonable doubt, each fact or circumstance upon which such inference necessarily rests must be proved beyond a reasonable doubt.

Also, if the circumstantial evidence as to any particular count is susceptible of two reasonable interpretations, one of which points to the defendant's guilt and the other to his innocence, you must adopt that interpretation which points to the defendant's innocence and reject that interpretation which points to his guilt.

If, on the other hand, one interpretation of such evidence appears to you to be reasonable and the other interpretation to be unreasonable, you must accept the reasonable interpretation and reject the unreasonable. . . .

Every person who testifies under oath is a witness. You are the sole judges of the believability of a witness and the weight to be given the testimony of each witness.

In determining the believability of a witness, you may consider anything that has a tendency in reason to prove or disprove the truthfulness of the testimony of the witness, including but not limited to any of the following:

> the extent of the opportunity or the ability of the witness to see or hear or otherwise become aware of any matter about which the witness has testified;
> the effects, if any, from the use or consumption of alcohol, drugs or other intoxicant by the witness at the time of the events about which the witness has testified or at the time of his or her testimony;
> the ability of the witness to remember or to communicate any matter about which the witness has testified;
> the character and quality of that testimony;
> the demeanor and manner of the witness while testifying;
> the existence or nonexistence of a bias, interest or other motive;
> evidence of the existence or nonexistence of any fact testified to by the witness;
> the attitude of the witness toward this action or toward the giving of testimony;
> a statement previously made by the witness that is consistent or inconsistent with the testimony of the witness;
> the character of the witness for honesty or truthfulness or their opposites;
> an admission by the witness of untruthfulness.

Discrepancies in a witness' testimony, or between his or her testimony and that of others, if there were any, do not necessarily mean that the witness should be discredited. Failure of recollection is a common experience and innocent misrecollection is not uncommon. It is also a fact that two persons witnessing an incident or transaction often will see or hear it differently. Whether a discrepancy pertains to a fact of importance or only to a trivial detail should be considered in weighing its significance.

A witness who is willfully false in one material part of his or her testimony is to be distrusted in others. You may reject the whole testimony of a witness who willfully has testified falsely as to a material point unless from all the evidence you believe the probability of truth favors his or her testimony in other particulars. . . .

The court has admitted physical evidence such as blood, hair and fiber evidence and experts' opinions concerning the analysis of such physical evidence. You are the sole judges of whether any such evidence has a tendency in reason to prove any fact at issue in this case. You should carefully review and consider all the circumstances surrounding each item of evidence, including but not limited to its discovery, collection, storage and analysis. If you determine any item of evidence does not have a tendency in reason to prove any element of the crimes charged or the identity of the perpetrator of the crimes charged, you must disregard such evidence.

You have heard testimony about frequency estimates calculated for matches between known reference blood samples and some of the bloodstain evidence items in this case. The random match probability statistic used by DNA experts is not the equivalent of a statistic that tells you the likelihood of whether a defendant committed a crime. The random match probability statistic is the likelihood that a random person in the population would match the characteristics that were found in the crime scene evidence and in the reference sample. These frequency estimates are being presented for the limited purpose of assisting you in determining what significance to attach to those bloodstain testing results. . . .

A defendant in a criminal action is presumed to be innocent until the contrary is proved, and in case of a reasonable doubt whether his guilt is satisfactorily shown, he is entitled to a verdict of not guilty. This presumption places upon the prosecution the burden of proving him guilty beyond a reasonable doubt.

Reasonable doubt is defined as follows:

> it is not a mere possible doubt, because everything relating to human affairs is open to some possible or imaginary doubt. It is that state of the case which, after the entire comparison and consideration of all the evidence, leaves the mind of the jurors in that condition that they cannot say they feel an abiding conviction of the truth of the charge.

The prosecution has the burden of proving beyond a reasonable doubt each element of the crimes charged in the information and that the defendant was the perpetrator of any such charged crime. The defendant is not required to prove himself innocent or to prove that any other person committed the crimes charged. . . .

The defendant is accused in counts 1 and 2 of the having committed the crime of murder, a violation of Penal Code section 187.

Every person who unlawfully kills a human being with malice aforethought is guilty of the crime of murder in violation of section 187 of the California Penal Code.

In order to prove such crime, each of the following elements must be proved:

> one, a human being was killed;
> two, the killing was unlawful;
> and three, the killing was done with malice aforethought.

Express malice is defined as when there is manifested an intention unlawfully to kill a human being. The mental state—excuse me.

When it is shown that a killing resulted from the intentional doing of an act with express malice, no other mental state need be shown to establish the mental state of malice aforethought.

The mental state constituting malice aforethought does not necessarily require any ill will or hatred of the person killed.

The word "aforethought" does not imply deliberation or the lapse of considerable time. It only means that the required mental state must precede rather than follow the act.

All killing, which is perpetrated by any kind of willful, deliberate and premeditated killing with express malice aforethought, is murder of the first degree.

The word "willful," as used in this instruction, means intentional. The word "deliberate" means formed or arrived at or determined upon as a result of careful thought and weighing of the considerations for and against the proposed course of action. The word "premeditated" means considered beforehand.

If you find that the killing was preceded and accompanied by a clear, deliberate intent on the part the defendant to kill, which was the result of deliberation and premeditated, so that it must have been formed upon preexisting reflection and not under a sudden heat of passion or other condition precluding the idea of deliberation, it is murder of the first degree. . . .

The purpose of the court's instructions is to provide you with the applicable law so that you may arrive at a just and lawful verdict. Whether some instructions apply will depend upon what you find to be the facts.

Disregard any instruction which applies to facts determined by you not to exist. Do not conclude that because an instruction has been given that the court is expressing any opinion as to the facts of this case.

All right.

Ladies and gentlemen, this concludes the instructions that I am going to give to you prior to the arguments of the attorneys.

Source: People v. Orenthal James Simpson, No. BA097211, Reporter's Transcript of Proceedings, vol. 229 (Sept. 22, 1995).

Original Citibank Promissory Note

FIRST NATIONAL CITY BANK

PERSONAL FINANCE DEPARTMENT · NEW YORK

APPLICATION

NUMBER _____

ANNUAL PER-

CENTAGE RATE _____%

$_____
　　　　TOTAL OF PAYMENTS (4) + (7)

PROCEEDS TO BORROWER	(1)	$_____
PROPERTY INS. PREMIUM	(2)	$_____
FILING FEE	(3)	$_____
AMOUNT FINANCED (1) + (2) + (3)	(4)	$_____
PREPAID FINANCE CHARGE	(5)	$_____
GROUP CREDIT LIFE INS. PREMIUM	(6)	$_____
FINANCE CHARGE (5) + (6)	(7)	$_____

FOR VALUE RECEIVED, the undersigned (jointly and severally) hereby promise(s) to pay to FIRST NATIONAL CITY BANK (the "Bank") at its office at 300 Park Avenue, New York, New York 10022 (i) THE SUM OF

_____ ($ _____) (TOTAL OF PAYMENTS) ( ) IN _____ EQUAL CONSECUTIVE MONTHLY INSTALMENTS OF $ _____ EACH ON THE SAME DAY OF EACH MONTH, COMMENCING _____ DAYS FROM THE DATE THE LOAN IS MADE: OR ( ) IN _____ EQUAL CONSECUTIVE WEEKLY INSTALMENTS OF $_____ EACH ON THE SAME DAY OF EACH WEEK, COMMENCING NOT EARLIER THAN 5 DAYS NOR LATER THAN 45 DAYS FROM THE DATE THE LOAN IS MADE OR ( ) IN _____ EQUAL CONSECUTIVE BI-WEEKLY INSTALMENTS OF $_____ EACH, COMMENCING NOT EARLIER THAN 10 DAYS NOR LATER THAN 45 DAYS FROM THE DATE THE LOAN IS MADE AND ON THE SAME DAY OF EACH SECOND WEEK THEREAFTER: OR ( ) IN _____ EQUAL CONSECUTIVE SEMI-MONTHLY IN-STALMENTS OF $_____ EACH, COMMENCING NOT EARLIER THAN 10 DAYS NOR LATER THAN 45 DAYS FROM THE DATE THE LOAN IS MADE, AND ON THE SAME DAY OF EACH SEMI-MONTHLY PERIOD THEREAFTER. (ii) A FINE COMPUTED AT THE RATE OF 5¢ PER $1 ON ANY INSTALMENT WHICH HAS BECOME DUE AND REMAINED UNPAID FOR A PERIOD IN EXCESS OF 10 DAYS. PRO-VIDED (A) IF THE PROCEEDS TO THE BORROWER ARE $10,000 OR LESS, NO SUCH FINE SHALL EXCEED $5 AND THE AGGREGATE OF ALL SUCH FINES SHALL NOT EXCEED THE LESSER OF 2% OF THE AMOUNT OF THIS NOTE OR $25, OR (B) IF THE ANNUAL PERCENTAGE RATE STATED ABOVE IS 7.50% OR LESS. THE LIMITATIONS PROVIDED IN (A) SHALL NOT APPLY AND NO SUCH FINE SHALL EXCEED $25 AND THE AGGREGATE OF ALL SUCH FINES SHALL NOT EXCEED 2% OF THE AMOUNT OF THIS NOTE, AND SUCH FINE(S) SHALL BE DEEMED LIQUIDATED DAMAGES OCCASIONED BY THE LATE PAYMENT(S): (iii) IN THE EVENT OF THIS NOTE MATURING, SUB-JECT TO AN ALLOWANCE FOR UNEARNED INTEREST ATTRIBUTABLE TO THE MATURED AMOUNT, INTEREST AT A RATE EQUAL TO 1% PER MONTH AND (iv) IF THIS NOTE IS REFERRED TO AN ATTORNEY FOR COLLECTION. A SUM EQUAL TO ALL COSTS AND EXPENSES THEREOF INCLUDING AN ATTORNEY'S FEE EQUAL TO 15% OF THE AMOUNT OWING ON THIS NOTE AT THE TIME OF SUCH REFERENCE. FOR NECESSARY COURT COSTS THE ACCEPTANCE BY THE BANK OF ANY PAYMENT(S) EVEN IF MARKED PAYMENT IN FULL OR SIMILAR WORDING, OR IF MADE AFTER ANY DEFAULT HEREUNDER, SHALL NOT OPERATE TO EXTEND THE TIME OF PAYMENT OF OR TO WAIVE ANY AMOUNT(S) THEN REMAINING UNPAID OR CONSTITUTE A WAIVER OF ANY RIGHTS OF THE BANK HEREUNDER.

IN THE EVENT THIS NOTE IS PREPAID IN FULL OR REFINANCED, THE BORROWER SHALL RECEIVE A REFUND OF THE UNEARNED PORTION OF THE PREPAID FINANCE CHARGE COM-PUTED IN ACCORDANCE WITH THE RULE OF 78 (THE "SUM OF THE DIGITS" METHOD) PRO-

VIDED THAT THE BANK MAY RETAIN A MINIMUM FINANCE CHARGE OF $10, WHETHER OR NOT EARNED, AND, EXCEPT IN THE CASE OF A REFINANCING, NO REFUND SHALL BE MADE IF IT AMOUNTS TO LESS THAN $1. IN ADDITION, UPON ANY SUCH PREPAYMENT OR REFINANCING, THE BORROWER SHALL RECEIVE A REFUND OF THE CHARGE, IF ANY, FOR GROUP CREDIT LIFE INSURANCE INCLUDED IN THE LOAN EQUAL TO THE UNEARNED PORTION OF THE PREMIUM PAID OR PAYABLE BY THE HOLDER OF THE OBLIGATION (COMPUTED IN ACCORDANCE WITH THE RULE OF 78), PROVIDED THAT NO REFUND SHALL BE MADE OF AMOUNTS LESS THAN $1.

AS COLLATERAL SECURITY FOR THE PAYMENT OF THE INDEBTEDNESS OF THE UNDERSIGNED HEREUNDER AND ALL OTHER INDEBTEDNESS OR LIABILITIES OF THE UNDERSIGNED TO THE BANK, WHETHER JOINT, SEVERAL, ABSOLUTE, CONTINGENT, SECURED, UNSECURED, MATURED OR UNMATURED, UNDER ANY PRESENT OR FUTURE NOTE OR CONTRACT OR AGREEMENT WITH THE BANK (ALL SUCH INDEBTEDNESS AND LIABILITIES BEING HEREINAFTER COLLECTIVELY CALLED THE "OBLIGATIONS"), THE BANK SHALL HAVE, AND IS HEREBY GRANTED, A SECURITY INTEREST AND/OR RIGHT OF SET-OFF IN AND TO (a) ALL MONIES, SECURITIES AND OTHER PROPERTY OF THE UNDERSIGNED NOW OR HEREAFTER ON DEPOSIT WITH OR OTHERWISE HELD BY OR COMING TO THE POSSESSION OR UNDER THE CONTROL OF THE BANK, WHETHER HELD FOR SAFEKEEPING, COLLECTION, TRANSMISSION OR OTHERWISE OR AS CUSTODIAN, INCLUDING THE PROCEEDS THEREOF, AND ANY AND ALL CLAIMS OF THE UNDERSIGNED AGAINST THE BANK, WHETHER NOW OR HEREAFTER EXISTING, AND (b) THE FOLLOWING DESCRIBED PERSONAL PROPERTY (ALL SUCH MONIES, SECURITIES, PROPERTY, PROCEEDS, CLAIMS AND PERSONAL PROPERTY BEING HEREINAFTER COLLECTIVELY CALLED THE "COLLATERAL"): ( ) Motor Vehicle ( ) Boat ( ) Stocks ( ) Bonds ( ) Savings and/or _____
SEE CUSTOMER'S COPY OF SECURITY AGREEMENT(S) OR COLLATERAL RECEIPT(S) RELATIVE TO THIS LOAN FOR FULL DESCRIPTION.

IF THIS NOTE IS SECURED BY A MOTOR VEHICLE, BOAT OR AIRCRAFT, PROPERTY INSURANCE ON THE COLLATERAL IS REQUIRED AND THE BORROWER MAY OBTAIN THE SAME THROUGH A PERSON OF HIS OWN CHOICE.

IF THIS NOTE IS NOT FULLY SECURED BY THE COLLATERAL SPECIFIED ABOVE, AS FURTHER SECURITY FOR THE PAYMENT OF THIS NOTE, THE BANK HAS TAKEN AN ASSIGNMENT OF 10% OF THE UNDERSIGNED BORROWER'S WAGES IN ACCORDANCE WITH THE WAGE ASSIGNMENT ATTACHED TO THIS NOTE.

In the event of default in the payment of this or any other Obligation or the performance or observance of any term or covenant contained herein or in any note or other contract or agreement evidencing or relating to any Obligation or any Collateral on the Borrower's part to be performed or observed; or the undersigned Borrower shall die; or any of the undersigned become insolvent or make an assignment for the benefit of creditors; or a petition shall be filed by or against any of the undersigned under any provision of the Bankruptcy Act; or any money, securities or property of the undersigned now or hereafter on deposit with or in the possession or under the control of the Bank shall be attached or become subject to distraint proceedings or any order or process of any court; or the Bank shall deem itself to be insecure, then and in any such event, the Bank shall have the right (at its option), without demand or notice of any kind, to declare all or any part of the Obligations to be immediately due and payable, whereupon such Obligations shall become and be immediately due and payable, and the Bank shall have the right to exercise all the rights and remedies available to a secured party upon default under the Uniform Commercial Code (the "Code") in effect in New York at the time, and such other rights and remedies as may otherwise be provided by law. Each of the undersigned agrees (for purposes of the "Code") that written notice of any proposed sale of, or of the Bank's election to retain, Collateral mailed to the undersigned Borrower (who is hereby appointed agent of each of the undersigned for such purpose) by first class mail, postage prepaid, at the address of the undersigned Borrower indicated below three business days prior to such sale or election shall be deemed reasonable notification thereof. The remedies of the Bank hereunder are cumulative and may be exercised concurrently or separately. If any provision of this paragraph shall conflict with any remedial provision contained in any security agreement or collateral receipt covering any Collateral, the provisions of such security agreement or collateral receipt shall control.

Acceptance by the Bank of payments in arrears shall not constitute a waiver of or otherwise affect any acceleration of payment hereunder or other right or remedy exercisable hereunder. No failure or delay on the part of the Bank in exercising, and no failure to file or otherwise perfect or enforce the Bank's security interest in or with respect to any Collateral, shall operate as a waiver of any right or remedy hereunder or release any of the undersigned, and the Obligations of the undersigned may be extended or waived by the Bank, any contract or other agreement evidencing or relating to any Obligation or any Collateral may be amended and any Collateral exchanged, surrendered or otherwise dealt with in accordance with any agreement relative thereto, all without affecting the liability of any of the undersigned. In any litigation (whether or not arising out of or relating to any Obligation or Collateral or other matter connected herewith) in which the Bank and any of the undersigned may be adverse parties, the Bank and each such undersigned hereby waives their respective right to demand trial by jury and, additionally, each such undersigned waives his right to interpose in any such litigation any counterclaim of any nature or description which he may have against the Bank. In addition, the Bank shall not be deemed to have obtained knowledge of any fact or notice with respect to any matter relating to this note or any Collateral unless contained in a written notice mailed, postage prepaid, or personally delivered to the Personal Finance Department of the Bank at its address set forth above. Each of the undersigned, by his signature hereto, hereby waives presentation for payment, demand, notice of non-payment, protest and notice of protest with respect to the indebtedness evidenced by this note, and each such undersigned hereby agrees that this note shall be deemed to have been made under and shall be construed in accordance with the laws of the State of New York.

Each of the undersigned hereby authorizes the Bank to date this note as of the day the loan evidenced hereby is made, to correct patent errors herein and at its option, to cause the signatures of one or more co-makers to be added without notice to any prior obligor.

Note: This promissory note originally fit onto a single sheet of paper measuring 8½ by 14 inches. The document was procured with the assistance of Ann Moses and Cornell Franklin, both of Citibank. Reprinted by permission.

APPENDIX F

Revised Citibank Promissory Note

First National City Bank

Consumer Loan Note   Date_____, 19____

(In this note, the words **I, me, mine** and **my** mean each and all of those who signed it. The words **you, your** and **yours** mean First National City Bank.)

Terms of Repayment To repay my loan, I promise to pay you_____Dollars ($_____). I'll pay this sum at one of your branches in_____uninterrupted_____ installments of $_____each. Payments will be due_____, starting from the date the loan is made.

Here's the breakdown of my payments:

1. Amount of the Loan $_____
2. Property Insurance Premium $_____
3. Filing Fee for
   Security Interest $_____
4. Amount Financed (1+2+3) $_____
5. **Finance Charge** $_____
6. Total of Payments (4+5) $_____

Annual Percentage Rate_____%

Prepayment of Whole Note Even though I needn't pay more than the fixed installments, I have the right to prepay the whole outstanding amount of this note at any time. If I do, or if this loan is refinanced—that is, replaced by a new note— you will refund the unearned **finance charge,** figured by the rule of 78—a commonly used formula for figuring rebates on installment loans. However, you can charge a minimum **finance charge** of $10.

Late Charge If I fall more than 10 days behind in paying an installment, I promise to pay a late charge of 5% of the overdue installment, but no more than $5. However, the sum total of late charges on all installments can't be more than 2% of the total of payments or $25, whichever is less.

Security To protect you if I default on this or any other debt to you, I give you what is known as a security interest in my ○ Motor Vehicle and/or_____(see the Security Agreement I have given you for a full description of this property), ○ Stocks, ○ Bonds, ○ Savings Account (more fully described in the receipt you gave me today) **and** any account or other property of mine coming into your possession.

Insurance I understand I must maintain property insurance on the property covered by the Security Agreement for its full insurable value, but I can buy this insurance through a person of my own choosing.

Default I'll be in default:
1. If I don't pay an installment on time; or
2. If any other creditor tries by legal process to take any money of mine in your possession.

You can then demand immediate payment of the balance of this note, minus the part of the **finance charge** which hasn't been earned figured by the rule of 78. You will also have other legal rights, for instance, the right to repossess, sell and apply security to the payments under this note and any other debts I may then owe you.

Irregular Payments You can accept late payments or partial payments, even though marked "payment in full", without losing any of your rights under this note.

Delay in Enforcement You can delay enforcing any of your rights under this note without losing them.

261

Collection Costs   If I'm in default under this note and you demand full payment, I agree to pay you interest on the unpaid balance at the rate of 1% per month, after an allowance for the unearned **finance charge.** If you have to sue me, I also agree to pay your attorney's fees equal to 15% of the amount due, and court costs. But if I defend and the court decides I am right, I understand that you will pay my reasonable attorney's fees and the court costs.

Comakers   If I'm signing this note as a comaker, I agree to be equally responsible with the borrower. You don't have to notify me that this note hasn't been paid. You can change the terms of payment and release any security without notifying or releasing me from responsibility on this note.

Copy Received   The borrower acknowledges receipt of a completely filled-in copy of this note.

Signatures   Addresses

Borrower: _____   _____

Comaker: _____   _____

Comaker: _____   _____

Comaker: _____   _____

Hot Line   If something should happen and you can't pay on time, please call us immediately at (212) 559-3061.

Personal Finance Department
First National City Bank

Note: This promissory note originally fit onto a single sheet of paper measuring 8½ by 14 inches. The document was procured with the assistance of Ann Moses and Cornell Franklin, both of Citibank. Reprinted by permission.

NOTES

Part One

Chapter One

1. Thomas Pyles and John Algeo, *The Origins and Development of the English Language* 95–96 (4th ed. 1992).

2. Id. at 292.

3. See Rudolf Thurneysen, "Celtic Law," in *Celtic Law Papers Introductory to Welsh Medieval Law and Government* 49 (1973); D. A. Binchy, *Linguistic and Legal Archaisms in the Celtic Law-Books*, in id. at 109. The reference to poets is in Thurneysen, "Celtic Law," 60.

4. Pyles and Algeo, *English Language*, at 95. See also Otto Jespersen, *Growth and Structure of the English Language* 27–36 (10th ed. 1982).

5. J. H. Baker, *An Introduction to English Legal History* 2 (3d ed. 1990).

6. *The Oxford Illustrated History of England* 52–59 (Kenneth O. Morgan ed., 1984).

7. 2 Sir Frederick Pollock and Frederic William Maitland, *The History of English Law before the Time of Edward I* 11 (2d ed. 1959).

8. Pyles and Algeo, *English Language*, at 97–98.

9. Theodore F. T. Plucknett, *A Concise History of the Common Law* 215 (5th ed. 1956).

10. For a more complete list, see David Mellinkoff, *The Language of the Law* 46–49 (1963).

11. See Florence Elizabeth Harmer, *Anglo-Saxon Writs* (1952).

12. See the will of Wulfgar, in *Anglo-Saxon Charters* 52 (Agnes J. Robertson ed. and trans., 1939).

13. See Jespersen, *Growth and Structure*, at 159.

14. Baker, *English Legal History*, at 4–9.

15. 9 *Oxford English Dictionary* 1062 (2d ed. 1989).

16. Baker, *English Legal History*, at 5.

17. Gottfried von Strassburg, *Tristan and Isolde* 199–207 (Francis G. Gentry trans., 1988).

18. According to Baker, the hot iron was only briefly placed in the party's hand. The hand was then bound and inspected a few days later. If the wound had festered, God had decided against that party. Baker, *English Legal History*, at 5.

19. J. Laurence Laughlin, "The Anglo-Saxon Legal Procedure," in *Essays in Anglo-Saxon Law* 183, 193 (1905).

20. Id. at 195.

21. Id. at 183.

22. The text and translation are taken from *Beowolf: Text and Translation* (John Porter trans., 1991), lines 658–60.

23. Jacob Grimm, *Deutsche Rechtsaltertümer* 8–37 (Andreas Heusler and Rudolf Hübner eds., 4th ed. 1899).

24. "Grant of Lands by Ulfketel to Bury St. Edmunds," in *Anglo-Saxon Charters* at 146.

25. "Record of the Dues Rendered to the Church at Lambourn," in *Anglo-Saxon Charters* at 240. The precise meaning of these terms remains obscure. See 1 William S. Holdsworth, *A History of English Law* 20 (1922–); Florence E. Harmer, *Anglo-Saxon Writs* 74 (1952).

26. See generally Harmer, *Anglo-Saxon Writs* at 85–92.

27. Laughlin, "Anglo-Saxon Legal Procedure," at 195.

28. The example is quoted and discussed in Risto Hiltunen, *Chapters on Legal English: Aspects Past and Present of the Language of the Law* 29 (1990).

29. Id. at 29.

30. Id. at 30.

31. Pyles and Algeo, *English Language*, at 99.

32. Baker, *English Legal History*, at 146–54.

33. 1 Pollock and Maitland, *History of English Law*, at 11. Pollock and Maitland state that these were the first Germanic laws written down in a Germanic language.

34. Pyles and Algeo, *English Language*, at 288–90.

35. Brenda Danet and Bryna Bogoch, "Orality, Literacy and Performativity in Anglo-Saxon Wills," in *Language and the Law* 100, 103 (John Gibbons ed., 1994).

36. For a more extensive discussion, see Mellinkoff, *Language of the Law*, at 51–55.

37. Jespersen, *Growth and Structure*, at 67–68.

Chapter Two

1. Thomas Pyles and John Algeo, *The Origins and Development of the English Language* 134–35 (4th ed. 1992).

2. Otto Jespersen, *Growth and Structure of the English Language* 79 (10th ed. 1982).

3. 3 Blackstone, *Commentaries on the Laws of England* 317–18 (1768).

4. David Mellinkoff, *The Language of the Law* 66 (1963).

5. Sir Walter Scott, *Ivanhoe* 27 (Ian Duncan ed., 1996).

6. George H. McKnight, *The Evolution of the English Language: From Chaucer to the Twentieth Century* 5 (1968).

7. See Robert McCrum et al., *The Story of English* 356 (rev. ed. 1992).

8. George E. Woodbine, *The Language of English Law*, 18 Speculum 395, 404–5 (1943).

9. Mellinkoff, *Language of the Law* at 65–67 (noting that the earliest official document in French dates from 150 years after the Conquest. On the other hand, there were some earlier private legal documents in French. Clanchy reports a French charter from 1140 and an administrative document (apparently quite informal and intended to be replaced by a Latin official version) from 1170. M. T. Clanchy, *From Memory to Written Record: England 1066–1307* 219 (2d ed. 1993).

10. Woodbine, *Language of English Law,* at 405.

11. See Douglas A. Kibbee, *For to Speke Frenche Trewely: The French Language in England, 1000–1600: Its Status, Description and Instruction* 7 (1991).

12. Clanchy, *From Memory to Written Record,* at 27. One possible reason is that while Anglo-Saxon clergy had been quite independent and were inclined to translate scripture and learning into English, the Norman clergy were more closely aligned with Rome and were used to conducting all their affairs in Latin. John H. Fisher, *Chancery and the Emergence of Standard Written English in the Fifteenth Century,* 52 Speculum 870, 877 (1977).

13. These data are derived from the Chronological Table of Statutes in 1 *The Statutes of the Realm* i–x (1810). See also Mellinkoff, *Language of the Law,* at 81, 130; Woodbine, *Language of English Law,* at 401–2 n.4.

14. "Of the Original Language of the Charters and Statutes," in 1 *The Statutes of the Realm* xli; Fisher, *Chancery,* at 879–80.

15. Woodbine, *Language of English Law,* at 417. Woodbine observes that "in the generation before the French speaking lawyers of Edward I's time had perfected an all French law vocabulary . . . an English judge is able to write about English law and use technical English terms and legal expressions." Id. at 418.

16. Kibbee, *For to Speke Frenche Trewely,* at 16.

17. 1 Sir Frederick Pollock and Frederic William Maitland, *The History of English Law before the Time of Edward I* 87 (2d ed. 1959).

18. J. H. Baker, *An Introduction to English Legal History* 211–17 (3d ed. 1990).

19. Mellinkoff, *Language of the Law,* at 67–69. See also Kibbee, *For to Speke Frenche Trewely,* at 6 (noting that according to Orderic Vitalis, English was used in a court case in 1116).

20. J. H. Baker, *Manual of Law French* 1 (2d ed. 1990).

21. Woodbine, *Language of English Law,* at 397–98.

22. Id. at 426.

23. Baker, *English Legal History,* at 204–6. On the year books generally, see Frederic W. Maitland, "Introduction," in *Year Books of Edward II.: 1 & 2 Edward II., A.D. 1307–1309* ix–xx (F. W. Maitland ed., 1903).

24. Woodbine, *Language of English Law,* at 428.

25. See Clanchy, *From Memory to Written Record,* at 209.

26. Id. at 200.

27. Baker, *Manual of Law French,* at 4.

28. Woodbine, *Language of English Law,* at 424.

29. Jespersen, *Growth and Structure,* at 87.

30. Kibbee, *For to Speke Frenche Trewely,* at 39.

31. Id. at 58.

32. Malcolm Richardson, *Henry V, English Chancery, and Chancery English*, 55 Speculum 726 (1980).

33. Kibbee, *For to Speke Frenche Trewely*, at 66.

34. Clanchy suggests that as early as the reign of Henry III, judges probably were native speakers of English. Clanchy, *From Memory to Written Record*, at 209. Even if this is correct, they would most likely also have spoken French.

35. Woodbine, *Language of English Law*, at 419; Kibbee, *For to Speke Frenche Trewely*, at 21 (noting that the courtiers who accompanied Eleanor of Provence helped revitalize French at the upper levels of the aristocracy and in the legal system just when it may well have been falling into disuse).

36. Clanchy, *From Memory to Written Record*, at 214.

37. Kibbee, *For to Speke Frenche Trewely*, at 30–31.

38. See 1 William S. Holdsworth, *A History of English Law* 47–50 (1922–); 1 Pollock and Maitland, *History of English Law*, at 84.

39. 1 Pollock and Maitland, *History of English Law*, at 84–85.

40. See generally Paul Brand, *The Origins of the English Legal Profession* 50–69 (1992); 2 Holdsworth, *A History of English Law*, at 311.

41. 2 Holdsworth, *A History of English Law*, at 313.

42. Woodbine, *Language of English Law*, at 400.

43. Mellinkoff, *Language of the Law*, at 82.

44. *Moberlay v. Morpath*, Docese of York, consistory court, 1509/10, cited in R. H. Helmholz, *Select Cases on Defamation to 1600* 13 (1985).

45. The examples are from various cases in id. at 42–49.

46. Id. at 43.

47. Id. at 62.

48. Id. at 44.

49. Id. at 45. Of course, most Law French words, like these, can ultimately be traced to Latin.

50. Id. at 46.

51. See Baker, *English Legal History*, at 67.

52. See Eduard Graf and Mathias Dietherr, *Deutsche Rechtssprichwörter* (1864).

53. Cited in Woodbine, *Language of English Law*, at 431 n.5. A slightly different version of this saying is quoted in Sir Robert Megarry, *A Second Miscellany-at-Law: A Further Diversion for Lawyers and Others* 229 (1973).

54. Brenda Danet, *Language in the Legal Process*, 14 Law & Soc. Rev. 445, 482–83 (1980).

55. Helmholz, *Select Cases on Defamation*, at xiv & lxvii.

56. This may be related to a statement by Maitland that when reporters who produced the year books tried to explain the motive of a judge or pleader, they used Latin. Maitland, *Year Books of Edward II*, at lxxx.

57. Baker, *Manual of Law French*, at 4.

58. 1 Statutes of the Realm, 36 Edward III, stat. i, ch. 15. See also 2 Holdsworth, *A History of English Law*, at 477–79.

Maitland suggests that while French remained the language of "pleadings," English became the language of "argument," to the extent they could be distinguished. Maitland, *Year Books of Edward II*, at xxxiv–xxxv.

59. Mellinkoff, *Language of the Law*, at 101.

60. 3 Co. Rep. xl (Butterworth 1826).

61. Robert McCrum et al., *The Story of English* 93 (rev. ed. 1992). See also Peter Goodrich, *Languages of the Law: From Logics of Memory to Nomadic Masks* 75 (1990).

62. Maitland, *Year Books of Edward II,* at xxxiv.

63. Id. at xxxvi.

64. Baker, *Manual of Law French,* at 3. See also Sir John Fortescue, *De Laudibus Legum Anglie* 115 (S. B. Chrimes ed., 1942).

65. Baker, *Manual of Law French,* at 5.

66. Id. at 11.

67. Maitland found that in the early 1300s, creating substantives from the past participle was still relatively rare. *Donee* and similar words were still in the future; lawyers at this time said *celui a qi le doun fut fait.* Maitland, *Year Books of Edward II,* at xxxix.

68. For a longer list, see Mellinkoff, *Language of the Law,* at 15; 1 Pollock and Maitland, *History of English Law,* at 81.

69. 1 Pollock and Maitland, *History of English Law,* at 80.

70. Baker, *English Legal History,* at 255–57.

71. Mellinkoff, *Language of the Law,* at 121.

72. Apparently, there is controversy among scholars about whether these repetitive pairs in Middle English function to translate unfamiliar terms. Inna Koskenniemi, *Repetitive Word Pairs in Old and Middle English Prose* 14–15 (1968).

73. Jespersen, *Growth and Structure,* at 90.

74. Baker, *Manual of Law French,* at 35.

75. *Adams' Case,* in Helmholz, *Select Cases on Defamation,* at 79–80.

76. The text is presented, with some explication, in J. H. Baker, *Le Brickbat Que Narrowly Mist,* 100 L.Q. Rev. 544 (1984). Baker notes that the original report has been lost. Id. at 544 n.1.

The passage illustrates the great contempt power of courts of this period. After being condemned, the prisoner threw a stone (not actually a brickbat, according to Baker) at the judge, which narrowly missed. An indictment was immediately drawn up against him, his right hand was cut off, and he was hanged, then and there. It should be mentioned that the hanging must have been for the underlying crime of being a highwayman, not for contempt of court.

77. Id. at 548.

78. M. Dominica Legge, "French and the Law," in *Year Books of Edward II.: 10 Edward II., A.D. 1316–1317* xliv (M. Dominica Legge and William S. Holdsworth eds., 1935).

79. See generally K. M. McCormick, "Code-Switching and Mixing," in 2 *The Encyclopedia of Language and Linguistics* 581 (R. E. Asher ed., 1994).

80. 1 *Reports from the Lost Notebooks of Sir James Dyer* 119 (J. H. Baker ed., 1994).

Chapter Three

1. Frederic W. Maitland, "Introduction," in *Year Books of Edward II.: 1 & 2 Edward II., A.D. 1307–1309* xxxv (F. W. Maitland ed., 1903).

2. David Mellinkoff, *The Language of the Law* 126 (1963).

3. J. H. Baker, *An Introduction to English Legal History* 244 (3d ed. 1990).

4. *An Act for Turning the Books of the Law, and All Proces and Proceedings in Courts of Justice, into English, 1650,* 2 Acts and Ordinances of the Interregnum 1642–60, 455–56 (C. H. Firth and R. S. Rait eds., 1911).

5. 12 Car. II, ch. 3, §4, reprinted in 5 Statutes of the Realm 180 (1819).

6. See generally *Select Cases before the King's Council in the Star Chamber* (I. S. Leadam ed., 1903).

7. J. H. Baker, personal communication with author. See also Baker, *English Legal History,* at 117–18. The equitable jurisdiction was thus called the "English side." In contrast, the court's common law jurisdiction was the "Latin side" and maintained its records in Latin. As to oral proceedings in English, see John H. Fisher, *Chancery and the Emergence of Standard Written English in the Fifteenth Century,* 52 Speculum 870, 888 (1977).

8. Mellinkoff, *Language of the Law,* at 130.

9. 4 Geo. II, ch. 26 (1731); 6 Geo. II, ch. 14 (1733).

10. Baker, *English Legal History,* at 207.

11. The linguist Leonard Bloomfield wrote that "[w]riting is not language, but merely a way of recording language by visible marks." Leonard Bloomfield, *Language* 21 (1933).

12. Brenda Danet and Bryna Bogoch, "Orality, Literacy and Performativity in Anglo-Saxon Wills," in *Language and the Law* 100, 103 (John Gibbons ed., 1994).

13. Id. at 105.

14. Id. at 106.

15. Id. at 108–15.

16. Jesse Dukeminier and Stanley M. Johanson, *Wills, Trusts and Estates* 207–8 (5th ed. 1995).

17. Baker, *English Legal History,* at 212.

18. Mellinkoff, *Language of the Law,* at 267.

19. Baker, *English Legal History,* at 236.

20. Id. at 234–43.

21. T. F. T. Plucknett, *Ellesmere on Statutes,* 60 L.Q. Rev. 242, 248 (1944).

22. Baker, *English Legal History,* at 237.

23. Id. at 200.

24. Id. at 102–4.

25. Matthew Hale, *The History of the Common Law of England* 111–12 (1971 ed.).

26. *Griffith v. Thomas,* 82 Eng. Rep. 755 (Banc Sup. 1652).

27. *Foster v. Browning,* 79 Eng. Rep. 596 (1625). Other illustrations are contained in Benjamin J. Shipman, *Handbook of Common-Law Pleading* 220 (3d ed. 1923).

28. *Dacy v. Clinch,* 82 Eng. Rep. 964, 965 (1673). This is not the holding in the *Dacy* case, but a discussion of the holding of an earlier case in the time of King James.

29. Baker, *English Legal History,* at 203.

30. Hale, *History of the Common Law,* at 112. See also Mellinkoff, *Language of the Law,* at 190; Baker, *English Legal History,* at 129–30.

31. The story is mentioned in Richard Wydick, *Plain English for Lawyers* 1 (3d ed. 1994). See also note 1 to part 4.

32. Matthew Hale, "Considerations Touching the Amendment or Alteration

of Lawes," in 1 *A Collection of Tracts* 286 (Hargrave ed., 1787), cited in Mellinkoff, *Language of the Law,* at 197.

33. Jonathan Swift, *Gulliver's Travels: An Annotated Text with Critical Essays* 215 (Robert A. Greenberg ed., 1961).

34. Id. at 216–17.

35. Edinburgh Review, March 1827, cited in Frederick Bowers, *Linguistic Aspects of Legislative Expression* 330 (1989).

36. Quarterly Review, Jan. 1828, cited in id. at 330.

The situation may have gotten somewhat better during the Victorian period, in the latter half of the nineteenth century. According to Frederick Bowers, the drafting of British legislation "improved tremendously" during this period. He concludes, however, that during the twentieth century, those standards were not maintained, at least in England. Id. at 331.

37. 7 *The Works of Jeremy Bentham* 282 (John Bowring ed., 1843).

38. George Gopen, *The State of Legal Writing: Res Ipsa Loquitur,* 86 Mich. L. Rev. 333, 344–45 (1987).

39. Jonathan Caplan, "Lawyers and Litigants: A Cult Reviewed," in *Disabling Professions* (Ivan Illich et al. eds., 1977).

40. Kermit L. Hall et al., *American Legal History: Cases and Materials* 11 (2d ed. 1996).

41. Lawrence M. Friedman, *A History of American Law* 45–46 (2d ed. 1985).

42. Mellinkoff, *Language of the Law,* at 209.

43. See generally Paul Samuel Reinsch, *English Common Law in the Early American Colonies* (1899).

44. Elizabeth Gaspar Brown, *British Statutes in American Law 1776–1836* 22 (1964); Hall et al., *American Legal History,* at 23–25.

45. Friedman, *History of American Law,* at 102.

46. 1 U.S.C. xlv. (1994).

47. Friedman, *History of American Law,* at 303.

48. Id. at 318–22.

49. Brown, *British Statutes in American Law,* at 24.

50. Id. at 38–9.

51. Id. at 41.

52. Friedman, *History of American Law,* at 326.

53. Thomas Jefferson, "Autobiography," in 1 *The Works of Thomas Jefferson* 67 (Paul Leicester Ford ed., 1904).

54. Id. at 68.

55. Id. at 69–70.

56. Id. at 70.

57. Statement by Oliver Ellsworth. Landholder, V, *Conn. Courant,* Dec. 3, 1787, *Doc. Hist.,* XIV, 335, cited in Jack N. Rakove, *Original Meanings: Politics and Ideas in the Making of the Constitution* 344–45 (1996).

58. Friedman, *History of American Law,* at 44–45.

59. Id. at 19–20.

60. See, e.g., *De Young v. City of San Diego,* 194 Cal. Rptr. 722 (Ct. App. 1983).

61. *Co-operative Central Bank Bhd. v. Belaka Suria Dsn Bhd.,* [1991] 3 M.L.J. 43, 45.

Part Two

Chapter Four

1. 7 *The Works of Jeremy Bentham* 282 (John Bowring ed., 1843).

2. Glanville Williams, *Learning the Law* 63 (11th ed. 1982).

3. It is also possible that the pronunciation derives originally from Law French, where it was sometimes spelled *defendaunt* and presumably had stress on the final syllable.

4. David Mellinkoff, *The Language of the Law* 157 (1963).

5. See *The Chicago Manual of Style* §5.57 at 173 (14th ed. 1993).

6. Lawrence M. Friedman, *Law and Its Language,* 33 Geo. Wash. L. Rev. 563, 567 (1964).

7. Williams, *Learning the Law,* at 62.

8. See Mellinkoff, *Language of the Law,* at 256, noting that "O yes" was the pronunciation in Blackstone's day.

9. 9 *The Oxford English Dictionary* 22 (2d ed. 1989).

10. See "The Pronunciation of Latin," in *Black's Law Dictionary* vii (6th ed. 1990). See also H. A. Kelly, *Lawyer's Latin: Loquenda ut Vulgus?* 38 J. Legal Educ. 197 (1988).

11. Williams, *Learning the Law,* at 63.

12. A. P. Herbert, *Uncommon Law* 360–64 (1935).

13. Id. at 362.

14. 3 *The Works of Jeremy Bentham* 264 (John Bowring ed., 1843).

15. Marita Gustafsson, *Some Syntactic Properties of English Law Language* 9–10 (1975).

16. Risto Hiltunen, *The Type and Structure of Clausal Embedding in Legal English,* 4 Text 107, 108–9 (1984).

17. Arthur D. Austin, *Complex Litigation Confronts the Jury System: A Case Study* 62 (1984).

18. Herbert F. Schwartz, *Patent Law and Practice* 9 (1988). For some examples, see *International Visual Corp. v. Crown Metal Mfg. Co., Inc.,* 991 F.2d 768 (5th Cir. 1993). I thank Margaret Churchill for pointing this out to me.

19. Mitchel de S.-O.-l'E. Lasser, *Judicial (Self-)Portraits: Judicial Discourse in the French Legal System,* 104 Yale L.J. 1325, 1340–42 (1995).

20. 3 *The Works of Jeremy Bentham* 264 (John Bowring ed., 1843).

21. See David Crystal and Derek Davy, *Investigating English Style* 201 (1969).

22. Gustafsson, *Syntactic Properties of English Law Language,* at 13–14; Hiltunen, *Clausal Embedding in Legal English,* at 109 and 119.

23. Cal. Penal Code §324 (West 1988).

24. For an example of a boilerplate and ineffective no contest clause, see *Lipper v. Weslow,* 369 S.W.2d 698 (Tex. Civ. Ct. App. 1963).

25. Reed Dickerson, *The Fundamentals of Legal Drafting* §8.13 at 181–82 (2d ed. 1986)

26. See Lawrence M. Solan, *The Language of Judges* 67–75 (1993); Clark D. Cunningham et al., *Plain Meaning and Hard Cases,* 103 Yale L.J. 1561, 1573–77 (1994).

27. Marita Gustafsson, *The Syntactic Features of Binomial Expressions in Legal English*, 4 Text 123, 132 (1984).

28. William O'Grady, Michael Dobrovolsky, and Mark Aronoff, *Contemporary Linguistics: An Introduction* 134 (1989).

29. Robinson v. Rayner (Diocese of York, consistory court, 1424/25), reprinted in *Select Cases on Defamation to 1600* 7 (R. H. Helmholz ed., 1985) (translated from the Latin).

30. 4 Geo. II, ch. 26 (1731).

31. Arthur Symonds, *Mechanics of Law-Making* 75 (1835).

32. E. Allan Farnsworth and William F. Young, *Selections for Contracts: Statutes, Restatement Second, Forms* 166 (1992).

33. Id. at 164.

34. Id. at 170.

35. Charles Dickens, *David Copperfield* 730 (New York: Dodd, Mead and Co., 1984).

36. See 2A Norman J. Singer, *Sutherland Statutory Construction* §46.06 at 119–20 (5th ed. 1992).

See also *Tabor v. Ulloa*, 323 F.2d 823, 824 (9th Cir. 1963); *Western Washington Cement Masons Health & Sec. Trust Funds v. Hillis Homes, Inc.*, 612 P.2d 436, 441 (Wash. Ct. App. 1980) ("[S]tatutes are to be construed so as to give effect to every word.").

37. See Jesse Dukeminier and Stanley M. Johanson, *Wills, Trusts, and Estates* 39–40 (5th ed. 1995).

38. *In re Florence Land & Public Works Co.*, (1878) 10 Ch. D. 530, 538.

39. Consider the lawyer joke in which a couple walks through a cemetery and sees a tombstone with the inscription *Here lies a lawyer and an honest man.* "My goodness," the woman tells her friend, "they buried two people in one grave!"

40. Crystal and Davy, *Investigating English Style*, at 203.

41. Id. at 204.

42. Id. at 205.

43. Gustafsson, *Syntactic Features of Binomial Expressions in Legal English*, at 19–20.

44. Id. at 22. The same point is made in Vijay Bhatia, "Cognitive Structuring in Legislative Provisions," in *Language and the Law* 136, 147 (John Gibbons ed., 1994).

45. 1 *California Jury Instructions—Civil—Book of Approved Jury Instructions* 2.21 (8th ed. 1994).

46. See *Agricultural Labor Relations Bd. v. Superior Court*, 149 Cal. App. 3d 709, 712 n.2 (1983).

47. Randolph Quirk et al., *A Comprehensive Grammar of the English Language* §6.18 at 350 (1985).

48. Peter Goodrich, *Languages of Law: From Logics of Memory to Nomadic Masks* 191 (1990).

49. *Bennis v. Michigan*, 116 S. Ct. 994, 998 (1996) ("Our earliest opinion to this effect is Justice Story's opinion for the Court in *The Palmyra*, 12 Wheat. 1, 6 L. Ed. 531 (1827).")

Chapter Five

1. See Reed Dickerson, *The Fundamentals of Legal Drafting* §6.1 at 102 (2d ed. 1986). See also Lawrence M. Solan, *The Language of Judges* 121–28 (1993), for an extensive discussion of the legal profession's attempts to avoid pronouns.

2. Reprinted in E. Allan Farnsworth and William F. Young, *Selections for Contracts: Statutes, Restatement Second, Forms* 161 (1992).

3. David Crystal and Derek Davy, *Investigating English Style* 202 (1969). On the other hand, Gustafsson's study concluded that while anaphoric pronominal references between sentences do not exist, pronouns are used for referents within the same sentence, contrary to Crystal and Davy. Marita Gustafsson, *Some Syntactic Properties of Binomial Expressions of English Law Language* 24 (1975).

4. For a drafting guide that actually recommends avoiding pronouns for this reason, see Robert J. Martineau, *Drafting Legislation and Rules in Plain English* 71 (1991).

5. Cal. Civ. Code §14 (West 1998).

6. *Young v. O'Keefe*, 69 N.W.2d 534 (Iowa 1955).

7. Cal. Rules of Court, Standards of Judicial Administration Recommended by the Judicial Council §1.2.

8. *State v. Wanrow*, 559 P.2d 548, 558 (Wash. 1977).

9. See, e.g., Cal. Rules of Court, rule 534(c)(1) (West 1997).

10. Bentham recommended stating that the masculine singular should comprehend both genders and numbers as a remedy for long-windedness. 3 *The Works of Jeremy Bentham* 265 (John Bowring ed., 1843).

11. *Thompson v. Leach*, [1558–1774] All E.R. 39, 40 (K.B. 1697).

12. Edward Finegan, "Form and Function in Testament Language," in *Linguistics and the Professions* 113, 118 (Robert J. Di Pietro ed., 1982) (finding many passives in wills); Risto Hiltunen, *Chapters on Legal English: Aspects Past and Present of the Language of the Law* 76 (1990) (noting that the passive is very common in legal English); Richard C. Wydick, *Plain English for Lawyers* 27–32 (3d ed. 1994) (arguing against overuse of passives).

13. *United States v. Wilson*, 503 U.S. 329, 334–35 (1992).

14. Hiltunen, *Chapters on Legal English*, at 110 (finding that a traditional statute had seventy-six passives for every hundred active constructions).

15. Journal of Proceedings, Sept. 27, 1995, 64 U.S.L.W. 3238 (Oct. 3, 1995).

16. Reprinted in Farnsworth and Young, *Selections for Contracts*, at 164–67.

17. Cal. Penal Code, §602 (West Supp. 1998).

18. Farnsworth and Young, *Selections for Contracts*, at 165–66.

19. See Sanford Schane, *The Corporation Is a Person: The Language of a Legal Fiction*, 61 Tulane L. Rev. 563 (1987).

20. 1 *California Jury Instructions—Civil—Book of Approved Jury Instructions* 2.21 (8th ed. 1994).

21. David Mellinkoff, *The Language of the Law* 20–22 (1963).

22. Reed Dickerson, *The Interpretation and Application of Statutes* 48 (1975).

23. Kathleen Doheny, *Forget Tourniquets for Snakebite—Head to the ER*, L.A. Times, Aug. 8, 1995, at E-1.

24. *Burns v. United States*, 501 U.S. 129, 147 (1991) (citations and internal quotations omitted).

25. *Jacobellis v. Ohio*, 378 U.S. 184, 197 (1964) (Stewart, J., concurring).

26. *Roth v. United States*, 354 U.S. 476, 489 (1957). The test was modified in *Miller v. California*, 413 U.S. 15 (1973).

27. *Martin v. Hunter's Lessee*, 14 U.S. (1 Wheat.) 304, 326 (1816).

28. *McCulloch v. Maryland*, 17 U.S. (4 Wheat.) 316, 415 (1819).

29. See James F. Stratman and Patricia Dahl, *Reader's Comprehension of Temporary Restraining Orders in Domestic Violence Cases: A Missing Link in Abuse Prevention?* 3 Forensic Linguistics 211 (1996).

30. *Dorman v. Satti*, 862 F.2d 432 (2d Cir. 1988).

31. The statute is quoted and discussed in *State v. Ball*, 627 A.2d 892, 894 & n.1 (Conn. 1993).

32. George T. Bogert, *Trusts* §§ 104–6 at 373–90 (6th student ed. 1987).

33. Lawrence M. Solan, *Judicial Decisions and Linguistic Analysis: Is There a Linguist in the Court?* 73 Wash. U. L.Q. 1069, 1076 (1995).

34. See Frederick Bowers, *Linguistic Aspects of Legislative Expression* 119 (1989). For a discussion of the possible linguistic basis of the various maxims of interpretation, see Geoffrey P. Miller, *Pragmatics and the Maxims of Interpretation*, 5 Wis. L. Rev. 1179 (1990).

35. *Pengelley v. Bell Punch Co. Ltd.*, [1964] 2 All E.R. 945.

36. See generally 2A Norman J. Singer, *Sutherland Statutory Construction* § 47.23 at 216 (5th ed. 1992).

37. *The King v. Wallis*, 101 Eng. Rep. 210 (K.B. 1793). On *ejusdem generis* in general, see 2A Norman J. Singer, *Sutherland Statutory Construction* § 47.23 at 188 (5th ed. 1992). There is some debate on whether the canon should also apply when the general class comes before the specific items.

38. A computer search of a database of American state court opinions found the expression over seventeen thousand times. The search was conducted on the "allstates" database of Westlaw in 1996.

39. *Mahoney v. Baldwin*, 543 N.E.2d 435, 436 (Mass. Ct. App. 1989) ("the phrase 'including but not limited to,' which precedes the specification, limits the applicability of [the Consumer Protection Act] to those types of statutes therein particularized."); *Roberts v. General Motors Corp.*, 643 A.2d 956, 960 (N.H. 1994).

40. David Mellinkoff, *The Myth of Precision and the Law Dictionary*, 31 UCLA L. Rev. 423 (1983).

Chapter Six

1. The example is from an insurance policy analyzed in David Crystal and Derek Davy, *Investigating English Style* 203 (1969).

2. See Randolph Quirk et al., *A Comprehensive Grammar of the English Language* § 12.20 at 874 (1985).

3. *Brown v. State*, 13 S.W. 150 (Tex. Ct. App. 1890).

4. See David Mellinkoff, *The Language of the Law* 340 (1963).

5. *Humfrey v. Pyckeryng* (Common Pleas, Easter term 1562), reprinted in *Select Cases on Defamation to 1600* 56 (R. H. Helmholz ed., 1985).

6. *Moberlay v. Morpath* (Diocese of York, consistory court, 1509/10), reprinted in id. at 12.

7. See generally Georgia M. Green, *Pragmatics and Natural Language Understanding* 24–25 (1989).

8. *Hecht v. Superior Court*, 20 Cal. Rptr. 2d 275, 276 (Ct. App. 1993).

9. 159 Eng. Rep. 375, 375 (1864).

10. David Mellinkoff, *Mellinkoff's Dictionary of American Legal Usage* 648 (1992).

11. *Year Books of Edward IV.: 10 Edward IV. and 49 Henry VI., A.D. 1470* 60 (N. Neilson ed., 1931) (*predicti Ricardus [and others on a certain date] vi et armis scilicet gladiis arcubus et sagittis clausum ipsorum archiepiscopi . . . fregerunt*).

12. Westlaw search conducted by the author on January 16, 1997.

13. *People v. Davis*, 49 Cal. Rptr. 2d 890, 894 (Ct. App. 1996).

14. *People v. Aguilar*, 945 P.2d 1204 (Cal. 1997).

15. Quirk et al., *A Comprehensive Grammar*, at 157–58.

16. William Shakespeare, *Romeo and Juliet*, 2.2.33.

17. William T. Betken, *The Other Shakespeare: Romeo and Juliet* 134 (1984) (emphasis in original). Evidence of the common misunderstanding comes from the title of a newspaper article about the movie *Romeo and Juliet*. Judy Brennan, *Where Art Thou? In First Place*, L.A. Times, Nov. 4, 1996, at F-1.

18. See Peter Meijes Tiersma, *Reforming the Language of Jury Instructions*, 22 Hofstra L. Rev. 37, 66 (1993).

19. Mellinkoff, *Language of the Law,* at 312–17.

20. Reprinted in E. Allan Farnsworth and William F. Young, *Selections for Contracts: Statutes, Restatement Second, Forms* 169 (1992).

21. *In re Pearson's Estate*, 33 P. 451, 453 (Cal. 1893). *See also* 19A *Words and Phrases* 24–26 (1970).

22. E. A. Driedger, *Legislative Drafting*, 27 Canadian B. Rev. 291, 306 (1949).

23. See also Mellinkoff, *Language of the Law*, at 12–16.

24. Lawrence M. Friedman, *Law and Its Language,* 33 Geo. Wash. L. Rev. 563, 565 (1964).

25. Otto Jespersen, *Growth and Structure of the English Language* 103 (10th ed. 1982).

26. See Quirk et al., *A Comprehensive Grammar*, § 7.24 at 421.

27. *Cook v. Equitable Life Assurance Society*, 428 N.E.2d 110, 114 (Ind. Ct. App. 1981).

28. Robin Tolmach Lakoff, *Talking Power: The Politics of Language* 94 (1990).

29. Gary Wake, "A Courtly Appearance," *Atlantica*, Summer 1997, at 51.

30. See Arnold van Gennep, *The Rites of Passage* (M. Vizedom and G. Caffee trans., 1960); Peter Meijes Tiersma, *Rites of Passage: Legal Ritual in Roman Law and Anthropological Analogues*, 9 J. Legal Hist. 3 (1988).

31. Taken from *In re Estate of Johnson*, 630 P.2d 1039, 1040 (Ariz. Ct. App. 1981).

32. 7 *The Works of Jeremy Bentham* 282 (John Bowring ed., 1843).

33. Ashbel G. Gulliver and Catherine J. Tilson, *Classification of Gratuitous Transfers*, 51 Yale L.J. 1, 4 (1941).

34. Lon L. Fuller, *Consideration and Form*, 41 Colum. L. Rev. 799, 800 (1941).

35. 16 *West's Legal Forms: Estate Planning with Tax Analysis* §9.6 at 446 (Donald J. Malouf and Henry J. Lischer, Jr., eds., 1996).

36. John L. Austin, *How To Do Things with Words* 57 (2d ed., J. O. Urmson and Marina Sbisà eds., 1962). See also John R. Searle, *Speech Acts: An Essay in the Philosophy of Language* 68 (1969).

37. Mellinkoff, *Language of the Law*, at 92.

38. *In re Pavlinko's Estate*, 148 A.2d 528, 529 (Pa. 1959).

39. Cal. Pen. Code, §290(a) (West 1988).

40. Cal. Pen. Code, §1 (West 1988) (emphasis added).

41. Reprinted in Farnsworth and Young, *Selections for Contracts*, at 164.

42. Frederick Bowers, *Linguistic Aspects of Legislative Expression* 80 (1989).

43. Mellinkoff, *Language of the Law*, at 18.

44. William O'Grady, Michael Dobrovolsky, and Mark Aronoff, *Contemporary Linguistics: An Introduction* 341–43 (1989).

45. See Victoria Fromkin and Robert Rodman, *An Introduction to Language* 301–2 (5d ed. 1993).

46. See *Allen v. United States*, 164 U.S. 492 (1896); *Booth v. Mary Carter Paint Co.*, 202 So. 2d 8 (Fla. Dist. Ct. App. 1967); *Miranda v. Arizona*, 384 U.S. 436 (1966); *Terry v. Ohio*, 392 U.S. 1 (1968); *In re Totten*, 71 N.E. 748 (N.Y. 1904).

47. Mellinkoff, *Language of the Law*, at 293, and also 388. Nonetheless, Mellinkoff bemoaned the fact that this gave rise to the unjustified assumption that the law is precise in other areas as well.

For another discussion of technical terms, see Mary Jane Morrison, *Excursions into the Nature of Legal Language*, 37 Clev. St. L. Rev. 271 (1989).

48. See Brian A. Garner, *The Elements of Legal Style* 7–15 (1991) (estimating there are fewer than fifty true legal terms of art); Robert W. Benson, *Plain English Comes to Court*, Litigation, Fall 1986, at 21, 24 (stating that there are no more than a hundred legal terms of art).

49. *Black's Law Dictionary* 787 (Henry Campbell Black ed., 4th rev. ed., 1968).

50. See Lawrence M. Solan, *The Language of Judges* 45–55 (1993).

51. For a large number of cases going both ways, see 22A *Words and Phrases* 554 et seq. (1958).

52. For other examples, see Mellinkoff, *Language of the Law*, at 12.

53. Quoted in Roger J. Miner, *Confronting the Communication Crisis in the Legal Profession*, 34 N.Y.L. Sch. L. Rev. 1, 6 (1989).

54. See, e.g., *Estate of McKenzie*, 246 Cal. App. 2d 740, 744 (1966) (if it "satisfactorily appears that the will was drawn solely by the testator, and that he was unacquainted with [the] technical sense" a court may deviate from the technical sense to give effect to the testator's intent); *Ocasio v. Bureau of Crimes Compensation Division of Workers' Compensation*, 408 So. 2d 751, 753 (Fla. Dist. Ct. App. 1982) ("Technical words and phrases that have acquired a peculiar and appropriate meaning in law cannot be presumed to have been used by the legislature in a loose popular sense."); *Wells Fargo Bank v. Huse*, 129 Cal. Rptr. 522, 524 (Ct. App. 1976) (when an instrument is drafted by a legal practitioner, use of technical terms is evidence that the term has been used as a term of art).

55. See William P. Statsky, *Legislative Analysis and Drafting* 177 (2d ed. 1984).

56. Mellinkoff, *Language of the Law*, at 349.

57. See Peter Meijes Tiersma, *Nonverbal Communication and the Freedom of "Speech,"* 1993 Wis. L. Rev. 1525.

Chapter Seven

1. See Shirley Brice Heath, *A National Language Academy?: Debate in the New Nation,* 189 Linguistics 33 (1977).

2. Dennis E. Baron, *Grammar and Good Taste: Reforming the American Language* 95 (1982).

3. Cal. Civ. Code § 1761(c) (West Supp. 1998).

4. *Henrich v. Lorenz,* 448 N.W.2d 327, 332 (Iowa 1989).

5. Essentially the same point is made in Frederick Bowers, *Linguistic Aspects of Legislative Expression* 161 (1989).

6. *Young v. O'Keefe,* 69 N.W.2d 534, 537 (Iowa 1955) (comma added).

7. *Gilbane Building Co. v. Nemours Foundation,* 666 F. Supp. 649, 654 (D. Del. 1985).

8. Cal. Civ. Code § 1798.3(g) (West 1998).

9. See generally 1A Norman J. Singer, *Sutherland Statutory Construction* § 21.16, at 138 (5th ed. 1992).

10. J. Smith, *Using 328 Words When, in the End, Just One Would Do,* L.A. Times, May 18, 1992, at E1.

11. Cited in Michèle M. Asprey, *Plain Language for Lawyers* 115 (2d ed. 1996). For other examples of odd statutory definitions, see Reed Dickerson, *The Fundamentals of Legal Drafting* § 7.3 at 141 (2d ed. 1986).

12. 42 U.S.C. § 2000e(b) (1995).

13. 29 U.S.C. § 1002(10) (1995).

14. When the act in question was re-enacted, it omitted the term, so it apparently no longer exists. R. A. R. Bennion, *Statutory Interpretation* § 369 at 812 (1984).

15. See, e.g., *Lawson v. Suwannee Fruit & SS Co.,* 336 U.S. 198 (1949) (holding that statutory definitions usually control, but not where an obvious incongruity in language would be created); *Central Television Serv., Inc. v. Isaacs,* 189 N.E.2d 333, 337 (Ill. 1963) (stating that it is unconstitutional to define a term in a statute contrary to its ordinary meaning or contrary to the spirit and purpose of the statute); *People v. Kukkanen,* 56 Cal. Rptr. 620 (App. Dept., Super. Ct. 1967) (holding that where a word has clear meaning, the legislature cannot change it).

16. 3 *The Works of Jeremy Bentham* 265 (John Bowring ed., 1843).

17. E. A. Driedger, *Legislative Drafting,* 27 Canadian B. Rev. 291, 307–8 (1949).

18. A suggestion of this kind is also made in Bernard S. Jackson, *Making Sense in Law: Linguistic, Psychological and Semiotic Perspectives* 136 (1995).

19. Gottlob Frege, "On Sense and Reference," in *Translations from the Philosophical Writings of Gottlob Frege* 56 (P. T. Geach and M. Black eds., 1952).

20. *National Soc'y for the Prevention of Cruelty to Children v. Scottish Nat'l Soc'y for the Prevention of Cruelty to Children,* [1915] A.C. 207.

21. *In re Herlichka,* [1969] 3 D.L.R.3d 700, [1969] 1 O.R. 724.

22. The scene is reproduced in print in *Why a Duck?* 200–207 (Richard J. Anobile ed., 1971). The quotation is on page 201.

23. See *Metropolitan Exhibition Co. v. Ewing*, 42 F. 198, 200 (C.C.S.D.N.Y. 1890).

24. Lawrence M. Solan, *The Language of Judges* 126 (1993).

25. Georgia M. Green, *Pragmatics and Natural Language Understanding* 39 (1989).

26. See generally William M. McGovern, Jr., et al., *Wills, Trusts and Estates, Including Taxation and Future Interests* 397 (Hornbook Series 1988).

27. Of course, laws referring to a specific person are quite possible. An example is *bills of attainder*, which are legislative acts against a particular person, pronouncing him guilty of a crime without a trial. These bills were considered so abusive by the American colonists that they are prohibited by the United States Constitution in article I, section 9, clause 3.

Furthermore, most legislatures pass *private laws*. An American federal example is private law 89-431, which declared that for purposes of the Immigration and Nationality Act, Renato Camacho Castro would be held to have been lawfully admitted to the United States as of February 20, 1958. 80 Stat. 1699 (1966).

28. An allegation of this kind was made by Ellen Hawkes, *Family Secrets Today*, L.A. Times Magazine, Feb. 28, 1993, at 16.

29. See generally Paul Grice, "Utterer's Meaning, Sentence-Meaning and Word-Meaning," in *Studies in the Way of Words* 117 (1989); Diane Blakemore, *Understanding Utterances: An Introduction to Pragmatics* 5 (1992).

30. See generally 2A Singer, *Sutherland Statutory Construction* § 46.01 at 81. For a recent case stating the rule, see *Omnitrus Merging Corp. v. Illinois Tool Works, Inc.*, 628 N.E.2d 1165, 1167–68 (Ill. Ct. App. 1993).

31. Oliver Wendell Holmes, *The Theory of Legal Interpretation*, 12 Harv. L. Rev. 417, 419 (1899).

32. See William N. Eskridge, Jr., *The New Textualism*, 37 UCLA L. Rev. 621 (1990).

33. See Lawrence Solan, *When Judges Use the Dictionary*, 68 Am. Speech 50 (1993); Note, *Looking It Up: Dictionaries and Statutory Interpretation*, 107 Harv. L. Rev. 1437 (1994).

34. See generally Solan, *When Judges Use the Dictionary*.

35. Wallace L. Chafe, "Integration and Involvement in Speaking, Writing, and Oral Literature," in *Spoken and Written Language: Exploring Orality and Literacy* 35, 45 (Deborah Tannen ed., 1982).

36. Paul Kay, "Language Evolution and Speech Style," in *Sociocultural Dimensions of Language Change* 21 (Ben G. Blount and Mary Sanches eds., 1977).

37. John Chipman Gray, *The Nature and Sources of the Law* 173 (2d ed. 1909).

38. See William N. Eskridge, Jr., and Philip P. Frickey, *Foreword: Law as Equilibrium*, 108 Harv. L. Rev. 27, 97 (1994), for a list of canons of construction recently applied by the United States Supreme Court. While some are textual, and thus deal with interpretation, most are based on public policy, constitutional principles, and similar considerations. See also Cass Sunstein, *After the Rights Revolution* (1990).

39. The terms *interpretation* and *construction* are not always distinguished in legal usage, nor, if so, are they distinguished consistently. The distinction I draw is elaborated in Peter M. Tiersma, *The Ambiguity of Interpretation: Distinguishing Interpretation from Construction*, 73 Wash. U. L.Q. 1095 (1995).

A similar distinction is made in Reed Dickerson, *The Interpretation and Application of Statutes* 15 (1975). Dickerson distinguishes between the cognitive function of interpretation (the ascertainment of meaning) and the creative function (the assignment of meaning).

40. Benjamin N. Cardozo, *The Nature of the Judicial Process* 124 (1921).

41. See also Solan, *When Judges Use the Dictionary*, at 127.

42. See, e.g., *Ocasio v. Bureau of Crimes Compensation Division of Workers' Compensation*, 408 So. 2d 751, 753 (Fla. Dist. Ct. App. 1982) (Legislature's deliberate use of different terms in different portions of the same statute is strong evidence that it intended different meanings); *State v. Roth*, 479 P.2d 55, 58 (Wash. 1971) ("Where different language is used in the same connection in different parts of a statute, it is presumed that a different meaning was intended.").

43. Karl N. Llewellyn, *Remarks on the Theory of Appellate Decision and the Rules or Canons about How Statutes Are to Be Construed*, 3 Vand. L. Rev. 395, 401–6 (1950).

Chapter Eight

1. *Singh v. State of Rajasthan*, I.L.R. (1986) 36 Raj. 551, 552.

2. Id. at 553.

3. Shiv Chandra Manchandra and Gyanendra Kumar, *Law of Wills in India and Pakistan* 127 (4th ed. 1988).

4. See generally Eileen Fitzpatrick, Joan Bachenko and Don Hindle, "The Status of Telegraphic Sublanguages," in *Analyzing Language in Restricted Domains: Sublanguage Description and Processing* 39 (Ralph Grishman and Richard Kettridge eds., 1986).

5. See *Lafayette Morehouse Inc. v. Chronicle Publishing Co.*, 44 Cal. Rptr. 2d 46 (Ct. App. 1995).

6. Louis A. Arena, "The Language of Corporate Attorneys," in *Linguistics and the Professions* 143, 153 (R. J. Di Pietro ed., 1982).

7. See generally Lawrence M. Solan, *The Language of Judges* (1993).

8. *Fisher v. Lowe*, 333 N.W.2d 67 (Mich. Ct. App. 1983).

9. *Texas Pig Stands, Inc. v. Hard Rock Cafe Int'l Inc.*, 951 F.2d 684, 688, 698 (5th Cir. 1992). For further examples, see Adalberto Jordon, *Imagery, Humor, and the Judicial Opinion*, 41 U. Miami L. Rev. 693 (1987).

10. William L. Prosser, *The Judicial Humorist: A Collection of Judicial Opinions and Other Frivolities* vii (1952). See also Richard Delgado and Jean Stefancic, *Scorn*, 35 Wm. & Mary L. Rev. 1061 (1994); Marshall Rudolph, *Note, Judicial Humor: A Laughing Matter?* 41 Hastings L.J. 175 (1989). My thanks to Loyola student Marc Tocker for these references.

11. See Haig Bosmajian, *Metaphor and Reason in Judicial Opinions* (1992).

12. *Texas v. Johnson*, 491 U.S. 397, 423 (1989) (Rehnquist, C.J., dissenting).

13. *Commonwealth v. Robin*, 218 A.2d 546, 556, 561 (Pa. 1966) (Musmanno, J., dissenting).

14. See J. Gillis Wetter, *The Styles of Judicial Opinions: A Case Study in Comparative Law* (1960).

15. For another discussion of this topic, see Dennis R. Klinck, *The Word of the Law: Approaches to Legal Discourse* 139–42 (1992).

16. One person who has argued that lawyers speak a separate language is Fred Rodell, *Woe Unto You, Lawyers!* 7 (1939) (stating that "The Law is carried on in a foreign language.").

17. Arnold M. Zwicky and Ann D. Zwicky, "Register as a Dimension of Linguistic Variation," in *Sublanguage: Studies of Language in Restricted Semantic Domains* 213, 213–15 (Richard Kettridge and John Lehrberger eds., 1982) (hereinafter *Sublanguage*) (noting the difficulty of defining and applying terms like *dialect*, *register*, and *style*, but arguing that they are nonetheless useful concepts).

18. David Crystal and Derek Davy, *Investigating English Style* 9–10 (1969).

19. Lynette Hirschman and Naomi Sager, "Automatic Information Formatting of a Medical Sublanguage," in *Sublanguage* 27.

20. The examples are from Richard Kettridge, "Variation and Homogeneity of Sublanguages," in *Sublanguage* 107, 127.

21. Richard Kettridge and John Lehrberger, introduction to *Sublanguage*, 1.

22. Naomi Sager, "Syntactic Formatting of Science Information," in *Sublanguage* 9, 9 ("We use the term sublanguage for that part of the whole language that can be described by such a specialized grammar.").

23. John Lehrberger, "Automatic Translation and the Concept of Sublanguage," in *Sublanguage* 81, 102.

24. Veda R. Charrow, Jo Ann Crandall, and Robert P. Charrow, "Characteristics and Functions of Legal Language," in *Sublanguage* 175.

Part Three

Chapter Nine

1. For a description of some of the theories, see Dennis R. Klinck, *The Word of the Law: Approaches to Legal Discourse* 291–334 (1992).

2. Jacob and Wilhelm Grimm, *The Complete Grimm's Fairy Tales* 139–43 (1944).

3. J. H. Baker, *An Introduction to English Legal History* 179 (3d ed. 1990).

4. J. H. Baker, *Manual of Law French* 79–80 (2d ed. 1990).

5. Taken from Baker, *English Legal History,* at 629.

6. Peter N. Simon, *The Anatomy of a Lawsuit* 13–14. The names of the parties and some other details were altered by Simon.

Chapter Ten

1. Douglas W. Maynard, *Inside Plea Bargaining: The Language of Negotiation* 85 (1984) (punctuation added).

2. Id. at 80, 81, 133, 144, 192, 224.

3. This possibility was suggested to me by Laurie Levenson, a former federal prosecutor and presently associate dean of Loyola Law School in Los Angeles.

4. *The Supreme Court of the United States* 14 (pamphlet published by the United States Supreme Court, n.d.).

5. J. H. Baker, *Manual of Law French* 215 (2d ed. 1990).

6. Philip B. Heyman and William H. Kenety, *The Murder Trial of Wilbur Jackson: A Homicide in the Family* (2d ed. 1985).

7. *People v. Orenthal James Simpson*, No. BA097211, Reporter's Transcript of Proceedings (hereinafter *Simpson Transcript*). A copy of the transcripts is housed at the library of Loyola Law School, Los Angeles.

8. William O'Barr, *Linguistic Evidence: Language, Power, and Strategy in the Courtroom* 25 (1982).

9. For an overview of some of the studies, see Susan Berk-Seligson, *The Bilingual Courtroom: Court Interpreters in the Judicial Process* 146 (1990).

10. Frederick A. Philbrick, *Language and the Law: The Semantics of Forensic English* 20 (1949).

11. Thomas A. Mauet, *Trial Techniques* 45 (4th ed. 1996).

12. *Trial of Ford Lord Grey*, 9 Howell's State Trials 127, 176 (1682).

13. Examination of Ronald Shipp, *Simpson Transcript*, vol. 79, at 12700 (Feb. 1, 1995).

14. Heyman and Kenety, *Murder Trial of Wilbur Jackson*, at 138.

15. Id. at 140.

16. On questioning in general, see Randolph Quirk et al., *A Comprehensive Grammar of the English Language* § 11.4 et seq. (1985). For a discussion of questioning in the legal context, see Brenda Danet et al., "An Ethnography of Questioning in the Courtroom," in *Language Use and Uses of Language* 225–26 (Roger W. Shuy and Anna Shnukal eds., 1980); Hanni Woodbury, *The Strategic Use of Questions in Court*, 48 Semiotica 197 (1984).

17. Heyman and Kenety, *Murder Trial of Wilbur Jackson*, at 138.

18. Id. at 141.

19. John M. Conley and William M. O'Barr, *Rules versus Relationships: The Ethnography of Legal Discourse* 48 (1990).

20. See generally Diana Eades, "A Case of Communicative Clash: Aboriginal English and the Legal System," in *Language and the Law* 234 (John Gibbons ed., 1994); Michael Cooke, *A Different Story: Narrative versus "Question and Answer" in Aboriginal Evidence*, 3 Forensic Linguistics 273 (1996).

21. Heyman and Kenety, *Murder Trial of Wilbur Jackson*, at 135.

22. Id. at 122.

23. Id. at 106.

24. *Simpson Transcript*, vol. 79, at 12708 (Feb. 1, 1995).

25. John Henry Wigmore, *Evidence at Common Law* § 773 at 165 (James H. Chadbourn ed., 1970). Leading questions are permissible on direct examination when dealing with preliminary matters that are not controversial. Id., § 775 at 168. And they can be used when a witness turns out to be "hostile." Id., § 774 at 167.

26. See id. § 769 at 155.

27. Edward W. Cleary, *McCormick on Evidence* § 6 at 11 (3d ed. 1984).

28. Quirk, *A Comprehensive Grammar*, § 11.7 at 808–10.

29. Mauet, *Trial Techniques*, at 225.

30. Danet et al., "An Ethnography of Questioning," at 227 (an analysis of two trials found that declarative questions comprised 53 percent of all questions during cross-examination, as opposed to nine percent of questions on direct examination). See also Hanni Woodbury, *The Strategic Use of Questions in Court*, 48 Semiotica 197, 210–12 (1984).

31. *Simpson Transcript*, vol. 106, at 18702–703 (Mar. 14, 1995).

32. Id., vol. 107, at 18899 (Mar. 15, 1995).

33. Id., vol. 231, at 47788 (Sept. 27, 1995).

34. Heyman and Kenety, *Murder Trial of Wilbur Jackson,* at 103.

35. Danet et al., "An Ethnography of Questioning," at 228.

36. Mark Brennan, "Cross-Examining Children in Criminal Courts: Child Welfare under Attack," in *Language and the Law* 199 (John Gibbons ed., 1994). It has been suggested that this is also the case with Australian Aboriginals, for instance. Cooke, *Aboriginal Evidence,* at 273, 276.

37. Saul M. Kassim and Lawrence S. Wrightsman, *The American Jury on Trial* 130 (1988).

38. See Atkinson and Drew, *Order in the Court,* at 61–62.

39. Heyman and Kenety, *Murder Trial of Wilbur Jackson,* at 103, 115, 117, 120.

40. Conley and O'Barr, *Rules versus Relationships,* at 26.

41. See, e.g., *Simpson Transcript,* vol. 79, at 12737 (Feb. 1, 1995).

42. Id., vol. 79, at 12710 (Feb. 1, 1995).

43. Id., vol. 84, at 13847 (Feb. 8, 1995). Clark herself suggests that Judge Ito was generally condescending to her, addressing her by her first name, while speaking respectfully to the defense, using "Mr. Cochran" or "Mr. Shapiro." Marcia Clark, *Without a Doubt* 147 (1997).

44. Elizabeth F. Loftus, *Eyewitness Testimony* 90–94 (1979); A. Daniel Yarmey, *The Psychology of Eyewitness Testimony* 194 (1979).

45. Elizabeth F. Loftus and John C. Palmer, *Reconstruction of Automobile Destruction: An Example of the Interaction between Language and Memory,* 13 J. Verbal Learning & Verbal Behavior 585 (1974).

46. Elizabeth F. Loftus, *Leading Questions and the Eyewitness Report,* 7 Cognitive Psychology 560, 561 (1975).

47. Elizabeth F. Loftus, "Language and Memories in the Judicial System," in *Language Use and the Uses of Language* 257, 260–62 (Roger W. Shuy and Anna Shnukal eds., 1976).

48. Mauet, *Trial Techniques,* at 85.

49. Wigmore, *Evidence at Common Law,* §767 at 149–50.

50. Richard C. Wydick, *The Ethics of Witness Coaching,* 17 Cardozo L. Rev. 1 (1995).

51. Id. at 11–12, using an example provided by Michael Sherrard, Q.C., of Middle Temple.

52. See, e.g., Conley and O'Barr, *Rules versus Relationships;* John M. Conley, William M. O'Barr, and E. Allan Lind, *The Power of Language: Presentational Style in the Courtroom,* 78 Duke L.J. 1375 (1978).

53. Id. at 1380.

54. Id. at 1380–81. For use of the powerless style during police interrogation and its consequences for invoking the right to counsel, see Janet Ainsworth, *In a Different Register: The Pragmatics of Powerlessness in Police Interrogation,* 103 Yale L.J. 259 (1993).

55. Conley et al., *The Power of Language,* at 1385.

56. Id. at 1390.

57. See studies cited in Susan Berk-Seligson, *The Bilingual Courtroom: Court Interpreters in the Judicial Process* 146–49 (1990).

58. Theodore I. Koskoff, "The Language of Persuasion," in ABA Section of Litigation, *The Litigation Manual: A Primer for Trial Lawyers* 110, 111 (1983).

59. Clark D. Cunningham, *The Lawyer as Translator, Representation as Text: Towards an Ethnography of Legal Discourse,* 77 Cornell L. Rev. 1298, 1317 (1992).

60. Anne Graffam Walker, "Language at Work in the Law: The Customs, Conventions, and Appellate Consequences of Court Reporting," in *Language in the Judicial Process* 203, 231 (Judith N. Levi and Anne Graffam Walker eds., 1990).

61. 500 U.S. 352 (1991).

62. 409 U.S. 352 (1973).

63. Id. at 354.

64. H. P. Grice, "Logic and Conversation" in *Syntax and Semantics: Speech Acts* (P. Cole and J. Morgan eds., 1975).

65. See Peter M. Tiersma, *The Language of Perjury: "Literal Truth," Ambiguity, and the False Statement Requirement,* 63 S. Cal. L. Rev. 373 (1990).

Chapter Eleven

1. See, e.g., Gail Stygall, *Trial Language: Differential Discourse Processing and Discursive Formation* 123 (1994) (discussing how the plaintiff's narrative was broken up into various nonsequential pieces during the questioning process).

2. Brenda Danet, *"Baby" or "Fetus"? Language and the Construction of Reality in a Manslaughter Trial,* 32 Semiotica 187, 193 (1980). For other examples, see Frederick A. Philbrick, *Language and the Law: The Semantics of Forensic English* 84 (1949).

3. Danet, *Language and Reality,* at 197, 209.

4. Philip B. Heyman and William H. Kenety, *The Murder Trial of Wilbur Jackson: A Homicide in the Family* 246 (2d ed. 1985).

5. Id. at 251.

6. Id.

7. Id. at 250.

8. Summarized in Janet Ainsworth, *Book Review,* 2 Forensic Linguistics 194, 197 (1995).

9. Danet, *Language and Reality,* at 214.

10. Stygall, *Trial Language,* at 161.

11. Kenneth Reich, *Judges' Role in Cruise Sponsored by Lawyers' Group Raises Questions,* L.A. Times, Oct. 6, 1997, at B3.

12. *People v. Orenthal James Simpson,* No. BA097211, Reporter's Transcript of Proceedings, vol. 230, at 47220–21 (Sept. 26, 1995) (hereinafter *Simpson Transcript*) (available in the Rains Library of Loyola Law School, Los Angeles). On Clark's negative image, see Jeffrey Toobin, *The Run of His Life: The People v. O.J. Simpson* 193 (1996).

13. Roberto Aron et al., *Trial Communication Skills* § 40.02 at 40–42 (1996).

14. On the relative importance of feelings and relationships for women, see Carol Gilligan, *In a Different Voice: Psychological Theory and Women's Development* (1982).

15. See also Bettyruth Walter, *The Jury Summation as Speech Genre: An Ethno-*

graphic Study of What It Means to Those Who Use It 104 (1988). On rhetorical questions, see Randolph Quirk, Sidney Greenbaum, Geoffrey Leech and Jan Svartvik, *A Comprehensive Grammar of the English Language* §11.23 at 826–27 (1985).

16. *Simpson Transcript*, vol. 230, at 47226–27 (Sept. 26, 1995).

17. Id., vol. 231, at 47509 (Sept. 27, 1995).

18. Id., vol. 230A, at 47494–95 (Sept. 26, 1995).

19. Id., vol. 233, at 48264–65 (Sept. 29, 1995).

20. Id., vol. 231, at 47525 (Sept. 27, 1995).

21. This was a very conscious strategy. See Marcia Clark, *Without a Doubt* 50 (1997).

22. *Simpson Transcript*, vol. 230A, at 47498 (Sept. 26, 1995).

23. I conducted an analysis of a substantial part of Clark's closing argument using the computer program Grammatik (version 6.0). A grade level of 6.99 was reported using the Flesch-Kincaid test, although it strikes me that she was actually speaking on at least a high school level. And the program calculated that 5 percent of her finite verbs were passives. The reliability of such tests is discussed in part 4.

24. *Simpson Transcript*, vol. 231, at 47601 (Sept. 27, 1995).

25. Id., vol. 231, at 47607 (Sept. 27, 1995).

26. Id., vol. 232, at 47833 (Sept. 28, 1995).

27. Id., vol. 231, at 47756 (Sept. 27, 1995). See also Henry Weinstein, *Trial's Crucial Phase to Link High Drama, Logic,* L.A. Times, Sept. 25, 1995, at A1, A11 (noting that federal prosecutor Barry Kowalski had characterized Los Angeles police who beat Rodney King as *bullies with badges,* and Gerry Spence used a rhyme in the Karen Silkwood case: *If the lion got away, Kerr-McGee has to pay.*)

28. *Simpson Transcript*, vol. 232, at 47982 (Sept. 28, 1995).

29. Id., vol. 231, at 47650 (Sept. 27, 1995).

30. Id. at 47777.

31. Apparently, some African American lawyers do use Black English Vernacular during trial. See Walter, *Jury Summation*, at 168.

32. *Simpson Transcript*, vol. 231, at 47696–697 (Sept. 27, 1995). The spelling *pitard* is the court reporter's. See *Hamlet*, 3.4.206.

33. *Simpson Transcript*, vol. 231, at 47603 (Sept. 27, 1995).

34. See also William M. O'Barr, Linguistic Evidence: Language, Power, and Strategy in the Courtroom 37 (1982).

35. *Simpson Transcript*, vol. 231, at 47765 (Sept. 27, 1995).

36. Id. at 47791.

37. Id., vol. 232, at 47834 (Sept. 28, 1995).

38. Aron et al., *Trial Communication Skills,* §40.4 at 40–48.

39. *Blacks More Religious Than Whites, Study Says,* L.A. Times, Apr. 19, 1997, at B4.

40. Walter, *Jury Summation*, at 18.

41. *Simpson Transcript*, vol. 232, at 48033–34 (Sept. 28, 1995).

42. In actuality, jury instructions can either precede closing argument (as in the *Simpson* case), or follow (as in *Jackson*). In addition, many judges give preliminary instructions before the presentation of evidence begins.

43. Robert G. Nieland, *Pattern Jury Instructions: A Critical Look at a Modern Movement to Improve the Jury System* (1979); see also William W. Schwarzer, *Communicating with Juries: Problems and Remedies,* 69 Calif. L. Rev. 731, 732–40 (1981).

44. *Simpson Transcript,* vol. 229, at 47136–37 (Sept. 22, 1995).

45. Id. at 47150.

46. Bernard S. Jackson, *Some Semiotic Features of a Judicial Summing Up in an English Criminal Trial: R. v. Biezanek,* 7 Int'l J. Semiotics L. 201, 202 (1994).

47. 59 Mass. 295, 320 (1850).

48. *People v. Brigham,* 25 Cal. 3d 283, 295 (1979) (Mosk, J., concurring).

49. 114 S. Ct. 1239 (1994).

50. 35 Cal. Rptr. 2d 830 (Ct. App. 1994).

51. Id. at 834.

52. Id. at 836.

53. Geoffrey P. Kramer and Dorean M. Koenig, *Do Jurors Understand Criminal Jury Instructions? Analyzing the Results of the Michigan Juror Comprehension Project,* 23 J. L. Reform 401, 403 n.14 (1990).

54. Laurence J. Severance and Elizabeth F. Loftus, *Improving the Ability of Jurors to Comprehend and Apply Criminal Jury Instructions,* 17 Law & Soc'y Rev. 153, 162–73 (1982).

55. Phoebe C. Ellsworth, *Are Twelve Heads Better Than One?* 52 Law & Contemp. Probs. 205, 223–24 (Autumn 1989).

56. *People v. Klee Green Matthews,* 30 Cal. Rptr. 2d 330, 336 (Ct. App. 1994).

57. See Nancy Pennington and Reid Hastie, "The Story Model of Juror Decision Making," in *Inside the Juror: The Psychology of Juror Decision Making* 192 (Reid Hastie ed., 1993).

58. *The Abbot of Tewkesbury v. Calewe, Year Books of Edward II.,* 7 *Edward II.* 161 (William Craddock Bolland ed., 1922).

59. Mrs. Ben T. Head, *Confessions of a Juror,* 44 F.R.D. 330, 336 (1967).

60. Aron et al., *Trial Communication Skills,* §40.08 at 40-16.

61. *Simpson Transcript,* vol. 234, at 48304 (Oct. 3, 1995).

Part Four

1. Cecil Monro, *Acta Cancellariae; or Selections from the Records of the Court of Chancery* 692–93 (1847). See also 1 George Spence, *The Equitable Jurisdiction of the Court of Chancery* 376 (1846). The information reprinted by Spence suggests that the son "used no advice of counsel therein." This may have been part of the reason that the judge was annoyed.

Another source seems less reliable and mentions the case only in passing. It lists the date as 1566 and spells the names of the parties as "Milward" and "Welden." See 21 Eng. Rep. 136 (Ch. 1566).

2. 7 *The Works of Francis Bacon* 362 (James Spedding et al. eds., 1864).

3. 3 *The Works of Jeremy Bentham* 260 (John Bowring ed., 1843).

4. Id. at 207–8.

5. Id. at 271.

6. Joseph Story, "Report of the Commissioners to the Governor of the Commonwealth of Massachusetts (1837)," quoted in Kermit L. Hall et al., *American Legal History: Cases and Materials* 319–20 (2d ed. 1996).

7. See, e.g., in chronological order: Dagobert D. Runes, *Our Obsolete Legal English*, 99 N.Y.L.J. 1964 (1938); Fred Rodell, *Woe Unto You, Lawyers!* (1939); Charles A. Beardsley, *Beware of, Eschew and Avoid Pompous Prolixity and Platitudinous Epistles!* 16 Cal. St. B.J. 65 (1941); Robert A. Morton, *Challenge Made to Beardsley's Plea for Plain and Simple Legal Syntax*, 16 Cal. St. B.J. 103 (1941); Charles A. Beardsley, *Wherein and Whereby Beardsley Makes Reply to Challenge*, 16 Cal. St. B.J. 106 (1941); John W. Hager, *Let's Simplify Legal Language*, 32 Rocky Mountain L. Rev. 74 (1959); Ray J. Aiken, *Let's Not Oversimplify Legal Language*, 32 Rocky Mountain L. Rev. 358 (1960).

8. See, e.g., Robert W. Benson, *The End of Legalese: The Game Is Over*, 13 N.Y.U. Rev. L. & Soc. Change 519 (1985); Robert C. Dick, *Plain English in Legal Drafting*, 18 Alberta L. Rev. 509 (1980); F. Reed Dickerson, *Should Plain English Be Legislated?* 24 Res Gestae 332 (1980); John R. Forshey, *Comment, Plain English Contracts: The Demise of Legalese?* 30 Baylor L. Rev. 765 (1978); George D. Gopen, *The State of Legal Writing: Res Ipsa Loquitur*, 86 Mich. L. Rev. 333 (1987); Harold A. Lloyd, *Plain English Statutes: Plain Good Sense or Plain Nonsense*, 78 Law Libr. J. 683 (1986); Stephen M. Ross, *On Legalities and Linguistics: Plain Language Legislation*, 30 Buffalo L. Rev. 317 (1981).

Chapter Twelve

1. The ensuing discussion is based largely on Robert W. Benson, *The End of Legalese: The Game Is Over*, 13 N.Y.U. Rev. L. & Soc. Change 519 (1985); Robert P. Charrow and Veda R. Charrow, *Making Legal Language Understandable: A Psycholinguistic Study of Jury Instructions*, 79 Colum. L. Rev. 1306 (1979); and Richard C. Wydick, *Plain English for Lawyers* (3d ed. 1994).

2. Peter Meijes Tiersma, *Dictionaries and Death: Do Capital Jurors Understand Mitigation?* 1995 Utah L. Rev. 1, 20–21.

3. See Daniel B. Felker et al., *Guidelines for Document Designers* 31–33 (1981).

4. See Todd T. Rakoff, *Contracts of Adhesion: An Essay in Reconstruction*, 96 Harv. L. Rev. 1173 (1983).

5. Charrow and Charrow, *Making Legal Language Understandable*, at 1324.

6. Felker et al., *Guidelines for Document Designers*, at 38.

7. See, e.g., Wydick, *Plain English for Lawyers*, at 27.

8. Charrow and Charrow, *Making Legal Language Understandable*, at 1325–26.

9. *California Jury Instructions, Criminal*, No. 1.02 (3d rev. ed., 1970). It has recently been modified.

10. Frederick Bowers, *Linguistic Aspects of Legislative Expression* 339 (1989).

11. Charrow and Charrow, *Making Legal Language Understandable*, at 1324.

12. Felker et al., *Guidelines for Document Designers*, at 69–70.

13. Id. at 43.

14. Charrow and Charrow, *Making Legal Language Understandable*, at 1319.

15. See generally Felker et al., *Guidelines for Document Designers*, at 9–12.

16. 18 U.S.C. §207(c) (1982), cited in Benson, *The End of Legalese*, at 525 (1985).

17. For some great examples, see David Mellinkoff, *How to Make Contracts Illegible*, 5 Stan. L. Rev. 418 (1953).

Chapter Thirteen

1. *United States v. Mazurie,* 419 U.S. 544, 553 (1975). See also *Kolender v. Lawson,* 461 U.S. 352, 357 (1983) (requiring that a penal statute define a criminal offense so that "ordinary people" can understand what conduct is prohibited).

2. *McBoyle v. United States,* 283 U.S. 25, 27 (1931). See also Mary Jane Morrison, *Excursions into the Nature of Legal Language,* 37 Clev. St. L. Rev. 271, 276–87 (1989).

3. *Rose v. Locke,* 423 U.S. 48 (1975).

4. For a discussion of this language, see Lawrence M. Solan, *The Language of Judges* 104–6 (1993).

5. 3 Co. Rep. xl (Butterworth 1826).

6. Tom Laceky, *Inmates Use Jailed Freemen as Role Models,* Santa Barbara News-Press, Oct. 26, 1997, at A6.

7. A book entitled *Every Man His Own Lawyer* was first published in 1736. David Mellinkoff, *The Language of the Law* 198 (1963).

8. See Robert J. Martineau, *Drafting Legislation and Rules in Plain English* (1991); Reed Dickerson, *The Fundamentals of Legal Drafting* (2d ed. 1986).

9. Haw. Const. art. XVI, § 13.

10. D. Renton, *The Preparation of Legislation: Report of a Committee Appointed by Lord President of the Council* 36 (1975), cited in Frederick Bowers, *Linguistic Aspects of Legislative Expression* 329 (1989).

11. Joseph Kimble, *Plain English: A Charter for Clear Writing,* 9 Cooley L. Rev. 1, 49 (1992).

12. Michèle M. Asprey, *Plain Language for Lawyers* 177 (2d ed. 1996).

13. Barbro Ehrenberg-Sundin, *Plain Language in Sweden,* 33 Clarity 16 (1995).

14. Florian Coulmas, *The Writing Systems of the World* 122 (1989).

15. Kyoko Inoue, *MacArthur's Japanese Constitution: A Linguistic and Cultural Study of Its Making* 30–31 (1991).

16. Mami Hiraike Okawara, *The Comprehensibility of Japanese Legal Language,* presented at the annual meeting of the Law and Society Association, Glasgow, Scotland, July 11, 1996, and personal communication.

17. Duncan Berry, *A Content Analysis of Legal Jargon in Australian Statutes,* 33 Clarity 26 (1995).

18. Bowers, *Linguistic Aspects,* at 196.

19. Cal. Rules of Court, rule 982(a)(13).

20. Michèle M. Asprey, *It's Official: New South Wales Solicitors Favour Plain Language,* 32 Clarity 3 (1995); Joseph Kimble and Joseph A. Prokop, *Strike Three for Legalese,* 69 Mich. B.J. 418 (1990).

21. See, e.g., Irwin Alterman, *Plain and Accurate Style in Court Papers* (1987); Carol Ann Wilson, *Plain Language Pleadings* (1996).

22. Roger J. Miner, *Confronting the Communication Crisis in the Legal Profession,* 34 N.Y.L. Sch. L. Rev. 1, 4 (1989).

23. Robert W. Benson and Joan B. Kessler, *Legalese v. Plain English: An Empirical Study of Persuasion and Credibility in Appellate Brief Writing,* 20 Loy. L.A. L. Rev. 301 (1987); Joseph Kimble and Joseph A. Prokop, *Strike Three for Legalese,* 69 Mich. B.J. 418 (1990).

24. See, e.g., Gertrude Block, *Effective Legal Writing* 113 (4th ed. 1992); Charles R. Calleros, *Legal Method and Writing* 198, 403 (1990); Veda Charrow and Myra K. Erhardt, *Clear and Effective Legal Writing* (1986); Helene S. Shapo et al., *Writing and Analysis in the Law* 172 (3d ed. 1995); Larry L. Teply, *Legal Writing, Analysis, and Oral Argument* 48 (1990).

25. Richard C. Wydick, *Plain English for Lawyers*, 66 Calif. L. Rev. 727 (1978). It is now published as a book. Richard C. Wydick, *Plain English for Lawyers* (3d ed. 1994).

26. See, e.g., Mark Adler, *Clarity for Lawyers* (1990) (United Kingdom); Asprey, *Plain Language* (Australia).

27. These lists exclude *therefore, hereinafter,* and *thereafter,* which have become lexicalized adverbs. It also excludes any examples that are quoted from other sources.

28. *Ex Parte Garnett,* 141 U.S. 1 (1891).

29. See Sharon Wagner-Wells, *Legal Language in the 90's: Comparing Supreme Court Language of 1796, 1896, & 1996* (unpublished manuscript).

30. *McPherson v. Buick Motor Co.,* 111 N.E. 1050 (N.Y. 1916).

31. *Lloyds Bank v. Bundy* [1975] Q.B. 326, [1974] 3 All E.R. 757, 761 (C.A.).

32. See Joseph Goldstein, *The Intelligible Constitution* 6 (1992).

33. Id. at 58.

34. The original is in possession of the author.

35. Jeffrey Davis, *Protecting Consumers from Overdisclosure and Gobbledygook: An Empirical Look at the Simplification of Consumer-Credit Contracts,* 63 Va. L. Rev. 841, 872 (1977).

36. Restatement (Second) of Contracts, §211 comment b (1979).

37. Melvin Aron Eisenberg, *The Limits of Cognition and the Limits of Contract,* 47 Stan. L. Rev. 211, 242 (1995).

38. Ralph Nader, *Gobbledygook,* Ladies' Home Journal, Sept. 1977, at 68.

39. Reed Dickerson, *The Fundamentals of Legal Drafting* §8.2 at 156–57 (2d ed. 1986).

40. 15 U.S.C. §§1601–1665b (1988); id. §§1681–1681t (1988); id. §§2301–2312 (1988). See also Kimble, *Plain English,* at 31–32.

41. The order is reprinted in Carl Felsenfeld and Alan Siegel, *Writing Contracts in Plain English* 263 (1981). Apparently, Carter first publicized the idea during a "fireside chat." Reed Dickerson, *The Fundamentals of Legal Drafting* §8.11 at 179 (2d ed. 1986).

42. See Carl Felsenfeld, "The Plain English Experience in New York," in *Plain English: Principles and Practice* 13 (Erwin R. Steinberg ed., 1991).

43. For an overview, see the appendix in Kimble, *Plain English.*

44. Federal Register Document Drafting Handbook, published on the World Wide Web at http://www.nara.gov/nara/fedreg/ddh/ddhout.html.

45. News release: *SEC to Consider Plain English Proposal, Handbook Draft,* published on the World Wide Web at http://www.sec.gov/news/plaineng.htm.

46. Robert D. Eagleson, "The Plain English Movement in Australia and the United Kingdom," in *Plain English: Principles and Practice* 30 (Erwin R. Steinberg ed., 1991).

47. See Kimble, *Plain English,* at 51–54.

48. See generally Plain English Campaign, *Born to Crusade: One Woman's Battle to Wipe Out Gobbledygook and Legalese* (n.d.).

49. Presentation of Mark Adler at the annual meeting of the Law and Society Association, Glasgow, Scotland, July 11, 1996.

50. Eagleson, "The Plain English Movement," at 39.

51. See generally Asprey, *Plain Language,* at 37–39; Gail Dykstra, "A Plain Language Centre for Canada," in *Plain English: Principles and Practice* 43 (Erwin R. Steinberg 1991); Kimble, *Plain English,* at 45–51.

52. See, e.g., *Cutt Visits India,* 36 Clarity 3 (1996); Robert D. Eagleson, *Singapore Embraces Plain English,* 36 Clarity 3 (1996); Stephen Hunt, *Drafting: Plain English versus Legalese,* 3 Waikato L. Rev. 163 (1995) (New Zealand); Joe Kimble and Chris Balmford, *Plain Language Takes Off in South Africa,* 33 Clarity 8 (1995); Phillippa Wearne and Chris Tricker, *Papua New Guinea Welcomes Plain Language,* 38 Clarity 29 (1997); *Crusade for Plain English Reaches Ghana,* Campaign International, Sept. 1996, at 1.

53. N.Y. Gen. Oblig. §5-702 (West 1997–98).

54. Id. at §5-702(a)–(b).

55. Felsenfeld, "The Plain English Experience," at 14–15.

56. Id. at 15.

57. Pa. Stat. Ann. tit. 73, §2205(a) (1997).

58. Id. §2205(b).

59. Id. §2205(c).

60. Conn. Gen. Stat. §42-152(c) (1997).

61. The various readability formulas are discussed in Robert W. Benson, *The End of Legalese: The Game Is Over,* 13 N.Y.U. Rev. L. & Soc. Change 519, 547–50 (1985), and Daniel B. Felker et al., *Document Design: A Review of the Relevant Research* 69–93 (1980).

62. Fla. Stats. Ann. §627.4145 (1998).

63. Rudolf Flesch, *How to Write Plain English: A Book for Lawyers and Consumers* 25–26 (1979).

64. Benson, *The End of Legalese,* at 555.

65. Flesch, *How to Write Plain English,* at 24–25. For another description of the test, along with some criticism, see Carl Felsenfeld and Alan Siegel, *Writing Contracts in Plain English* 221–29 (1981).

66. See, e.g., L. Campbell and V. M. Holland, "Understanding the Language of Documents Because Readability Formulas Don't," in *Linguistics and the Professions* 157 (R. J. DiPietro ed., 1982); Janice C. Redish and Susan Rosen, "Can Guidelines Help Writers?" in *Plain English: Principles and Practice* 83, 84 (Erwin R. Steinberg ed., 1991); Reed Dickerson, *The Fundamentals of Legal Drafting* §8.9 at 173–74 (2d ed. 1986) ("A document can meet the Flesch (or Gunning) test 100 percent without rising above gibberish.").

67. Benson, *The End of Legalese,* at 551–58.

68. George R. Klare, *Assessing Readability,* 10 Reading Research Q. 62, 97–98 (1974–1975).

69. See Thomas S. Word, Jr., *A Brief for Plain English Wills and Trusts,* 14 U. Rich. L. Rev. 471 (1980).

70. Benson, *The End of Legalese,* at 544; T. M. Grundner, *On Readability of Surgi-*

cal Consent Forms, 302 New Eng. J. Med. 900 (1980); David S. Kaufer, Erwin R. Steinberg and Sarah D. Toney, *Revising Medical Consent Forms: An Empirical Model and Test,* 11 Law, Medicine & Health Care 155 (1983).

71. *State v. Jensen,* 723 P.2d 443, 444 (Wash. Ct. App. 1986).

72. See, e.g., *People v. Devine,* 424 N.E.2d 823, 830 (Ill. Ct. App. 1981); *People v. Jakubowski,* 472 N.Y.S.2d 853 (App. Div. 1984); *State v. Jensen,* 723 P.2d 443, 444–45 (Wash. Ct. App. 1986).

73. *Celli v. Sports Car Club,* 29 Cal. App. 3d 511, 521 (1972).

74. *Conservatorship of Link,* 158 Cal. App. 3d 138 (1984). See also *Ferrell v. Southern Nevada Off-Road Enthusiasts,* 147 Cal. App. 3d 309, 319 (1983).

75. Jonathan I. Rose and Martin A. Scott, *"Street Talk" Summonses in Detroit's Landlord-Tenant Court: A Small Step Forward for Urban Tenants,* 52 J. Urban L. 967, 1017, 1021 (1975).

76. See, e.g., Bethany K. Dumas, *Adequacy of Cigarette Package Warnings: An Analysis of the Adequacy of Federally Mandated Cigarette Package Warnings,* 59 Tenn. L. Rev. 261 (1992); Mark R. Lehto and James M. Miller, "The Effectiveness of Warning Labels," in *Product Liability 1989: Warnings, Instructions and Recalls* 167, 180 (Kenneth Ross and Barbara Wrubel eds., 1989); Roger W. Shuy, *Warning Labels: Language, Law, and Comprehensibility,* 65 Am. Speech 291 (1990).

77. Marlene Cimons, *New Labeling Proposed for Patent Drugs,* L.A. Times, Feb. 27, 1997, at A14.

Chapter Fourteen

1. *Andres v. United States,* 333 U.S. 740, 765–66 (1948) (Frankfurter, J., concurring).

2. Jerome Frank, *Law and the Modern Mind* 181 (1935).

Frank's point was not that instructions should be made comprehensible, but rather that ordinary jurors cannot reasonably be expected to understand the law in such a short period of time. He claimed that the "realistic theory" was that the jury simply determines the law itself. Id. at 303–4.

3. Robert P. Charrow and Veda R. Charrow, *Making Legal Language Understandable: A Psycholinguistic Study of Jury Instructions,* 79 Colum. L. Rev. 1306 (1979).

4. Id. at 1311–14.

5. To determine the level of comprehension, the Charrows broke each instruction into segments, often a clause or a phrase. They then determined how many of these segments the subjects correctly paraphrased; the result was the "full performance" score. Subjects did not do very well on full performance; the mean score was 0.386; this means that only about one-third of the segments were correctly paraphrased. An alternative scoring method, the "approximation measure," isolated the critical information in each instruction. Yet even here the subjects did not do well, with a mean score of 0.540. Id. at 1314–16.

6. Id. at 1317–28.

7. Id. at 1331–34. The full performance score for the fourteen revised instructions rose from 0.310 for the original BAJI version to 0.427 for the revised version. The approximation measure rose from 0.447 to 0.592.

8. Laurence J. Severance and Elizabeth F. Loftus, *Improving the Ability of Jurors to Comprehend and Apply Criminal Jury Instructions,* 17 Law & Soc'y Rev. 153 (1982); Laurence J. Severance, Edith Greene and Elizabeth F. Loftus, *Toward Criminal Jury Instructions That Jurors Can Understand,* 75 J. of Crim. L. & Criminology 198 (1984).

9. See, e.g., Phoebe C. Ellsworth, *Are Twelve Heads Better Than One?* 52 Law & Contemp. Probs. 205 (Autumn 1989); Robert F. Forston, *Sense and Nonsense: Jury Trial Communication,* 1975 B.Y.U. L. Rev. 601 (1975); Reid Hastie, Steven Penrod, and Nancy Pennington, *Inside the Jury* (1983); Geoffrey P. Kramer and Dorean M. Koenig, *Do Jurors Understand Criminal Jury Instructions? Analyzing the Results of the Michigan Juror Comprehension Project,* 23 J. L. Reform 401 (1990); O'Reilly, *Why Some Juries Fail,* 41 D.C. B.J. 69 (1974); Walter W. Steele and Elizabeth G. Thornburg, *Jury Instructions: A Persistent Failure to Communicate,* 67 N.C. L. Rev. 77, 92 (1988); Charles L. Weltner, *Why the Jury Doesn't Understand the Judge's Instructions,* Judges' J. 19 (Spring, 1979).

10. *California Jury Instructions—Civil* xxvii–xxviii (3d rev. ed. 1943).

11. *California Jury Instructions—Civil* vi (7th ed. 1986).

12. Idaho R. Civ. P. 51(a)(2) (1997).

13. U.S. Dist. Ct. Rules (D. Haw.), Civil Rule 235-11. Also, the North Dakota Pattern Jury Instruction Commission has as one of its goals to improve "juror comprehension of instructions." North Dakota Supreme Court Administrative Rules and Administrative Orders, administrative rule 23.

14. Mich. Ct. R. 2.516(D)(4) (West 1992).

15. U.S. Dist. Ct. Rules (E.D. Cal.), Civil Rule 51.163 (1997).

16. *Manual of Model Criminal Jury Instructions for the District Courts of the Ninth Circuit* iv (1992).

17. Amiram Elwork, Bruce D. Sales, and James J. Alfini, *Making Jury Instructions Understandable* (1982); Federal Judicial Center, *Pattern Criminal Jury Instructions* (1988) (Appendix A, entitled *Suggestions for Improving Juror Understanding of Instructions,* by Allan Lind and Anthony Partridge, makes suggestions for drafting comprehensible instructions based on the work of the Charrows and the Elwork, Sales and Alfini team).

18. Robert G. Nieland, *Pattern Jury Instructions: A Critical Look at a Modern Movement to Improve the Jury System* 24–25 (1979).

19. See generally John H. Neiman, *Letter: Iowa Jury Instructions,* 74 Judicature 336 (1991); Bernard S. Meyer and Maurice Rosenberg, *Questions Juries Ask: Untapped Springs of Insight,* 55 Judicature 105, 106 (1971) (Montana and Oregon); Harvey S. Perlman, *Pattern Jury Instructions: The Application of Social Science Research,* 65 Neb. L. Rev. 520, 531–41 (1986) (Alaska). Of course, without careful analysis it is impossible to determine how successful these efforts have been.

20. See Federal Judicial Center, Pattern Criminal Jury Instructions (1988). See also *Manual of Model Criminal Jury Instructions for the District Courts of the Ninth Circuit* (1995).

21. Peter Meijes Tiersma, *Reforming the Language of Jury Instructions,* 22 Hofstra L. Rev. 37 (1993).

22. Committee on Standard Jury Instructions-Criminal, *Alternative Definitions of Reasonable Doubt,* L.A. Daily Journal Special Report 87-10 (May 22, 1987).

23. J. Clark Kelso, *Final Report of the Blue Ribbon Commission on Jury System Improvement*, 47 Hastings L.J. 1433, 1517 (1996).

24. *Gregg v. Georgia*, 428 U.S. 153, 189 (1976).

25. For further details on the legal standards, see Peter Meijes Tiersma, *Dictionaries and Death: Do Capital Jurors Understand Mitigation?* 1995 Utah L. Rev. 1.

26. *Cape v. State*, 272 S.E.2d 487, 493 (Ga. 1980).

27. *People v. Lang*, 782 P.2d 627 (Cal. 1989).

28. See Tiersma, *Dictionaries and Death*, at 14.

29. *Watkins v. Murray*, 493 U.S. 907, 910 (1989) (Marshall, J., dissenting from denial of certiorari).

30. Lorelei Sontag, *Deciding Death: A Legal and Empirical Analysis of Penalty Phase Jury Instructions and Capital Decision-making* 76 (1990) (available from University Microfilms International in Ann Arbor, Michigan; order number 9033148).

31. Robin Lakoff, *Life-or-Death Confusion in the Law: State Supreme Court Realized Issue Wasn't Only Semantics*, L.A. Times, Jan. 3, 1986, at 5.

32. Stuart Mill, *A System of Logic* 451 (People's ed., 1886), *cited in* Otto Jespersen, *Growth and Structure of the English Language* 111 (10th ed. 1982).

33. Jespersen, *Growth and Stucture*, at 111–12.

34. *People v. McLain*, 757 P.2d 569, 580 (Cal. 1988).

35. *People v. Hamilton*, 756 P.2d 1348, 1362 (Cal. 1988).

36. Emphasis added. The definitions came from *Black's Law Dictionary*. Id. at 1362.

37. Tiersma, *Dictionaries and Death*, at 15–18.

38. See generally Sontag, *Deciding Death*.

39. Id. at 89–90.

40. Id. at 115. See also Craig Haney and Mona Lynch, *Comprehending Life and Death Matters: A Preliminary Study of California Death Penalty Instructions*, 18 Law & Hum. Behavior 411, 420–21 (1994) (fewer than half of the subjects could provide even a partially correct definition of mitigation).

41. Two judges told the jurors to derive the meaning from the instructions as a whole. One gave them definitions out of *Black's Law Dictionary*. Another jury got definitions, but the source was unclear. And as to the fifth, the juror who was interviewed recalled only that the judge's response was very obscure. Sontag, *Deciding Death*, at 121.

42. Id. at 111.

43. Another juror also reported that her jury did not understand "aggravating" and "mitigating" on the verdict forms. Id. at 124–25.

44. Tiersma, *Dictionaries and Death*, at 20–21.

45. Id. at 27.

46. Id. at 26–28.

47. *People v. Free*, 447 N.E.2d 218 (Ill. 1983); 492 N.E.2d 1269 (Ill. 1986) (denying postconviction relief); 522 N.E.2d 1184 (Ill. 1988) (affirming dismissal of second postconviction petition).

48. *United States ex rel. Free v. Peters*, 806 F. Supp. 705 (N.D. Ill. 1992).

49. *The Tortuous Tale of a Serial Killer*, Newsweek, April 25, 1994, at 30.

50. *United States ex rel. Gacy v. Welborn*, 1992 WL 211018 (N.D. Ill.), *motion to suspend judgment denied*, 1992 WL 358851.

51. *Gacy v. Welborn,* 994 F.2d 305, 314 (7th Cir. 1993).

52. Id. at 311.

53. Id. at 313 (citations omitted).

54. *Free v. Peters,* 12 F.3d 700 (7th Cir. 1993).

55. Id. at 709.

56. Shari Seidman Diamond and Judith N. Levi, *Improving Decisions on Death by Revising and Testing Jury Instructions,* 79 Judicature 224, 230 (1996).

57. Id.

58. Elwork, Sales, and Alfini, *Making Jury Instructions Understandable,* at 54–55.

SELECT BIBLIOGRAPHY

The list below contains some of the more important resources for those interested in legal language. For a detailed bibliography emphasizing social science sources, see Judith N. Levi, *Language and the Law: A Bibliographic Guide to Social Science Research in the U.S.A.* (American Bar Association, Teaching Resource Bulletin No. 4, 1994). At the end of the list are some sites on the World Wide Web that deal with language and the law.

Part One: Origins

Baker, J. H. *An Introduction to English Legal History*. 3d ed. London: Butterworths, 1990.

———. *Manual of Law French*. 2d ed. Aldershot, Eng.: Scolar Press, 1990.

Blake, N. F. *A History of the English Language*. New York: New York University Press, 1996.

Clanchy, M. T. *From Memory to Written Record: England 1066–1307*. 2d ed. Oxford: Blackwell Publishers, 1993.

Danet, Brenda, and Bryna Bogoch. "Orality, Literacy and Performativity in Anglo-Saxon Wills." In *Language and the Law*, edited by John Gibbons, 100. London and New York: Longman, 1994.

Fisher, John H. "Chancery and the Emergence of Standard Written English in the Fifteenth Century." 52 *Speculum* 870 (1977).

Friedman, Lawrence M. *A History of American Law*. 2d ed. New York: Simon and Schuster, 1985.

Holdsworth, William Searle. *A History of English Law*. Boston: Little, Brown and Co., 1922–.

Jespersen, Otto. *Growth and Structure of the English Language*. 10th ed. Chicago: University of Chicago Press, 1982.

Kibbee, Douglas A. *For to Speke Frenche Trewely: The French Language in England, 1000–1600: Its Status, Description and Instruction*. Amsterdam: John Benjamins Publishing Co., 1991.

Laughlin, J. Laurence. "The Anglo-Saxon Legal Procedure." 1905. In *Essays in Anglo-Saxon Law*. South Hackensack, N.J.: Rothman Reprints, 1972.

Legge, M. Dominica. "French and the Law." In *Year Books of Edward II.: 10 Edward II., A.D. 1316–1317*, edited by M. Dominica Legge and William S. Holdsworth, xliv. London: Bernard Quaritch, 1935.

Maitland, Frederic William. "Of the Anglo-French Language in the Early Year

Books." In *Year Books of Edward II.: 1 & 2 Edward II.*, A.D. *1307–1309,* edited by Frederic W. Maitland, xxxiii. London: Bernard Quaritch, 1903.

McKnight, George H. *The Evolution of the English Language: From Chaucer to the Twentieth Century.* New York: Dover Publications, 1968.

Mellinkoff, David. *The Language of the Law.* Boston: Little, Brown and Co., 1963.

Plucknett, Theodore F. T. *A Concise History of the Common Law.* 5th ed. Boston: Little, Brown and Co., 1956.

Pollock, Sir Frederick, and Frederic William Maitland. *The History of English Law before the Time of Edward I.* 2d ed. Washington, D.C.: Lawyers Literary Club, 1959.

Richardson, Malcolm. "Henry V, English Chancery, and Chancery English." 55 *Speculum* 726 (1980).

Woodbine, George E. "The Language of English Law." 18 *Speculum* 395 (1943).

Part Two: The Nature of Legal Language

Bentham, Jeremy. *The Works of Jeremy Bentham.* Edited by John Bowring. Edinburgh: W. Tait, 1843.

Bhatia, Vijay. "Cognitive Structuring in Legislative Provisions." In *Language and the Law,* edited by John Gibbons, 136. London and New York: Longman, 1994.

Bosmajian, Haig. *Metaphor and Reason in Judicial Opinions.* Carbondale: Southern Illinois University Press, 1992.

Bowers, Frederick. *Linguistic Aspects of Legislative Expression.* Vancouver: University of British Columbia Press, 1989.

Crystal, David, and Derek Davy. *Investigating English Style.* Bloomington: Indiana University Press, 1969.

Cunningham, Clark D., et al. "Plain Meaning and Hard Cases." 103 *Yale L.J.* 1561 (1994).

Dickerson, Reed. *The Interpretation and Application of Statutes.* Boston: Little, Brown and Co., 1975.

Eskridge, William N. "The New Textualism." 37 *UCLA L. Rev.* 621 (1990).

Finegan, Edward. "Form and Function in Testament Language." In *Linguistics and the Professions,* edited by Robert J. Di Pietro, 113. Norwood, N.J.: Ablex Publishing Co., 1982.

Friedman, Lawrence M. "Law and Its Language." 33 *Geo. Wash. L. Rev.* 563 (1964).

Garner, Bryan A. *A Dictionary of Modern Legal Usage.* 2d ed. Oxford: Oxford University Press, 1995.

Gibbons, John. *Language and the Law.* London and New York: Longman, 1994.

Goodrich, Peter. *Languages of Law: From Logics of Memory to Nomadic Masks.* London: Weidenfeld, 1990.

———. *Legal Discourse: Studies in Linguistics, Rhetoric and Legal Analysis.* New York: St. Martin's Press, 1987.

Gustafsson, Marita. *Some Syntactic Properties of English Law Language.* University of Turku, Publications of the Department of English, 1975.

Hiltunen, Risto. *Chapters on Legal English: Aspects Past and Present of the Language of the Law.* Helsinki: Suomalainen Tiedeakatemia, 1990.

Jackson, Bernard S. *Making Sense in Law: Linguistic, Psychological and Semiotic Perspectives.* Liverpool: Deborah Charles Publications, 1995.

Kaplan, Jeffrey P. "Syntax in the Interpretation of Legal Language: The Vested versus Contingent Distinction in Property Law." 68 *Am. Speech* 58 (1993).

Kettridge, Richard, and John Lehrberger. *Sublanguage: Studies of Language in Restricted Semantic Domains.* Berlin: W. de Gruyter, 1982.

Klinck, Dennis R. *The Word of the Law: Approaches to Legal Discourse.* Ottawa: Carlton University Press, 1992.

Kurzon, Dennis. *It Is Hereby Performed: Legal Speech Acts.* Amsterdam: John Benjamins Publishing Co., 1986.

Maley, Yon. "The Language of the Law." In *Language and the Law,* edited by John Gibbons, 11. London and New York: Longman, 1994.

Mellinkoff, David. "The Language of the Uniform Commercial Code." 77 *Yale L.J.* 185 (1967).

———. *Mellinkoff's Dictionary of American Legal Usage.* St. Paul: West Publishing Co., 1992.

———. "The Myth of Precision and the Law Dictionary." 31 *UCLA L. Rev.* 423 (1983).

Miller, Geoffrey. "Pragmatics and the Maxims of Interpretation." 5 *Wis. L. Rev.* 1179 (1990).

Morrison, Mary Jane. "Excursions into the Nature of Legal Language." 37 *Clev. St. L. Rev.* 271 (1989).

Quirk, Randolph, et al. *A Comprehensive Grammar of the English Language.* London: Longman, 1985.

Schane, Sanford. "The Corporation Is a Person: The Language of a Legal Fiction." 61 *Tul. L. Rev.* 563 (1987).

Singer, Norman J. *Sutherland Statutory Construction.* 5th ed. Deerfield, Ill.: Clark Boardman Callaghan, 1992.

Solan, Lawrence M. *The Language of Judges.* Chicago: University of Chicago Press, 1993.

———. "When Judges Use the Dictionary." 68 *American Speech* 50 (1993).

Tiersma, Peter M. "The Ambiguity of Interpretation: Distinguishing Interpretation from Construction." 73 *Wash. U. L.Q.* 1095 (1995).

Winter, Stephen L. "Transcendental Nonsense, Metaphoric Reasoning, and the Cognitive Stakes for Law." 137 *U. Pa. L. Rev.* 1105 (1989).

Part Three: In the Courtroom

Ainsworth, Janet. "In a Different Register: The Pragmatics of Powerlessness in Police Interrogation." 103 *Yale L.J.* 259 (1993).

Aron, Roberto, et al. *Trial Communication Skills.* Colorado Springs: Shepard's/McGraw-Hill, 1996.

Atkinson, J. Maxwell, and Paul Drew. *Order in the Court: The Organization of Verbal Behavior in Judicial Settings.* Atlantic Highlands, N.J.: Humanities Press, 1979.

Conley, John M., and William M. O'Barr. *Rules versus Relationships: The Ethnography of Legal Discourse.* Chicago: University of Chicago Press, 1990.

Conley, John M., et al. "The Power of Language: Presentational Style in the Courtroom." 78 *Duke L.J.* 1375 (1978).

Danet, Brenda. " 'Baby' or 'Fetus'? Language and the Construction of Reality in a Manslaughter Trial." 32 *Semiotica* 187 (1980).

———. "Language in the Legal Process." 14 *Law & Society Rev.* 445 (1980).

Danet, Brenda, et al. "An Ethnography of Questioning in the Courtroom." In *Language Use and Uses of Language*, edited by Roger W. Shuy and Anna Shnukal, 225. Washington, D.C.: University of Georgetown Press, 1980.

Eades, Diana. "A Case of Communicative Clash: Aboriginal English and the Legal System." In *Language and the Law*, edited by John Gibbons, 234. London and New York: Longman, 1994.

Jackson, Bernard S. "Some Semiotic Features of a Judicial Summing Up in an English Criminal Trial: *R. v. Biezanek.*" 7 *Intl. J. Semiotics of Law* 201 (1994).

Levi, Judith N., and Anne Graffam Walker. *Language in the Judicial Process.* New York and London: Plenum Press, 1990.

Loftus, Elizabeth F. *Eyewitness Testimony.* Cambridge: Harvard University Press, 1979.

Loftus, Elizabeth F., and John C. Palmer. "Reconstruction of Automobile Destruction: An Example of the Interaction between Language and Memory." 13 *J. Verbal Learning & Verbal Behavior* 585 (1974).

Mauet, Thomas A. *Trial Techniques.* 4th ed. Boston: Little, Brown and Co., 1996.

Maynard, Douglas W. *Inside Plea Bargaining: The Language of Negotiation.* New York: Plenum Press, 1984.

O'Barr, William M. *Linguistic Evidence: Language, Power, and Strategy in the Courtroom.* San Diego: Academic Press, 1982.

Philbrick, Frederick A. *Language and the Law: The Semantics of Forensic English.* New York: Macmillan, 1949.

Shuy, Roger W. *Language Crimes: The Use and Abuse of Language Evidence in the Courtroom.* Cambridge, Mass.: Blackwell Publishers, 1993.

Stygall, Gail. *Trial Language: Differential Discourse Processing and Discursive Formation.* Amsterdam: John Benjamins Publishing Co., 1994.

Tiersma, Peter M. "The Language of Perjury: 'Literal Truth,' Ambiguity, and the False Statement Requirement." 63 *S. Cal. L. Rev.* 373 (1990).

Walker, Anne Graffam. "Language at Work in the Law: The Customs, Conventions, and Appellate Consequences of Court Reporting." In *Language in the Judicial Process*, edited by Judith N. Levi and Anne Graffam Walker, 203. New York and London: Plenum Press, 1990.

Walter, Bettyruth. *The Jury Summation as Speech Genre: An Ethnographic Study of What It Means to Those Who Use It.* Amsterdam: John Benjamins Publishing Co., 1988.

Woodbury, Hanni. "The Strategic Use of Questions in Court." 48 *Semiotica* 197 (1984).

Part Four: Reforming the Language of the Law

Asprey, Michèle M. *Plain Language for Lawyers.* 2d ed. Leichhardt, N.S.W.: The Federation Press, 1996.

Benson, Robert W. "The End of Legalese: The Game Is Over." 13 *N.Y.U. Rev. L. & Soc. Change* 519 (1985).

Charrow, Robert P., and Veda R. Charrow. "Making Legal Language Understandable: A Psycholinguistic Study of Jury Instructions." 79 *Colum. L. Rev.* 1306 (1979).

Davis, Jeffrey. "Protecting Consumers from Overdisclosure and Gobbledygook: An Empirical Look at the Simplification of Consumer-Credit Contracts." 63 *Va. L. Rev.* 841 (1977).

Dickerson, Reed. *The Fundamentals of Legal Drafting.* 2d ed. Boston: Little, Brown and Co., 1986.

Dumas, Bethany K. "Adequacy of Cigarette Package Warnings: An Analysis of the Adequacy of Federally Mandated Cigarette Package Warnings." 59 *Tenn. L. Rev.* 261 (1992).

Eagleson, Robert D. "The Plain English Movement in Australia and the United Kingdom." In *Plain English: Principles and Practice,* edited by Erwin R. Steinberg, 30. Detroit: Wayne State University Press, 1991.

Elwork, Amiram, Bruce D. Sales, and James J. Alfini. *Making Jury Instructions Understandable.* Charlottesville, Va.: The Michie Co., 1982.

Felker, Daniel B., et al., *Guidelines for Document Designers.* Washington, D.C.: American Institutes for Research, 1981.

Felsenfeld, Carl. "The Plain English Experience in New York." In *Plain English: Principles and Practice,* edited by Erwin R. Steinberg, 13. Detroit: Wayne State University Press, 1991.

Felsenfeld, Carl, and Alan Siegel. *Writing Contracts in Plain English.* St. Paul: West Publishing Co., 1981.

Flesch, Rudolf. *How to Write Plain English: A Book for Lawyers and Consumers.* New York: Harper and Row, 1979.

Gopen, George D. "Let the Buyer in the Ordinary Course of Business Beware: Suggestions for Revising the Prose of the Uniform Commercial Code." 54 *U. Chi. L. Rev.* 1178 (1987).

———. "The State of Legal Writing: Res Ipsa Loquitur." 86 *Mich. L. Rev.* 333 (1987).

Kimble, Joseph. "Plain English: A Charter for Clear Writing." 9 *Cooley L. Rev.* 1 (1992).

Kramer, Geoffrey P., and Dorean M. Koenig. "Do Jurors Understand Criminal Jury Instructions? Analyzing the Results of the Michigan Juror Comprehension Project." 23 *J. L. Reform* 401 (1990).

Kurzon, Dennis. "Clarity and Word Order in Legislation." 5 *Oxford J. Legal Stud.* 269 (1985).

Martineau, Robert J. *Drafting Legislation and Rules in Plain English.* St. Paul, Minn.: West Publishing Co., 1991.

Mellinkoff, David. "How to Make Contracts Illegible." 5 *Stan. L. Rev.* 418 (1953).

Nieland, Robert G. *Pattern Jury Instructions: A Critical Look at a Modern Movement to Improve the Jury System.* Chicago: American Judicature Society, 1979.

Schwarzer, William W. "Communicating with Juries: Problems and Remedies." 69 *Cal. L. Rev.* 731 (1981).

Severance, Laurence J., and Elizabeth F. Loftus. "Improving the Ability of Jurors to Comprehend and Apply Criminal Jury Instructions." 17 *Law & Society Rev.* 153 (1982).

Shuy, Roger W. "Warning Labels: Language, Law, and Comprehensibility." 65 *American Speech* 291 (1990).

Sontag, Lorelei. *Deciding Death: A Legal and Empirical Analysis of Penalty Phase Jury Instructions and Capital Decision-making.* Ann Arbor: University Microfilms International, 1990.

Steinberg, Edwin R. *Plain English: Principles and Practice.* Detroit: Wayne State University Press, 1991.

Tiersma, Peter M. "Dictionaries and Death: Do Capital Jurors Understand Mitigation?" 1995 *Utah L. Rev.* 1 (1995).

———. "Reforming the Language of Jury Instructions." 22 *Hofstra L. Rev.* 37 (1993).

Wilson, Carol Ann. *Plain Language Pleadings.* Upper Saddle River, N.J.: Prentice Hall, 1996.

Wydick, Richard C. *Plain English for Lawyers.* 3d ed. Durham, N.C.: Carolina Academic Press, 1994.

Internet Resources

http://ljp.la.utk.edu (Language in the Judicial Process; has information of interest to forensic linguists, including citations to recent literature and reviews of books and articles).

http://www.adler.demon.co.uk/clarity.htm (site for Clarity, an international organization devoted to promoting plain legal language).

http://www.legaltheory.demon.co.uk (information on legal semiotics).

http://www.sec.gov/consumer/plaine.htm (contains draft of Plain English Handbook proposed by Securities and Exchange Commission).

http://www.web.net/raporter/English/LegalLanguage/index.html (Canadian site on plain legal language).

WORD AND PHRASE INDEX

GENERAL INDEX

abbreviations. *See* acronyms; clipping
Aboriginals, Australian, 161, 281n. 36
abortion trial, 182–84
abridgments, 37
accents, 51
acronyms, 137–38
actor: formations with *-or* to indicate, 99;
  obscuring of, 75, 77, 187–88
ademption, 123
adjectives: following noun in Law French,
  30; made into nouns, 138; *such,* 91
adverbs and adverbials: phrasal, 59–60;
  preceding participles, 65; scope of, 60–
  61
Aethelbert (king of Kent), 10, 16
Africa, 46
African Americans: 157–58, 175, 176; in
  Simpson case, 166–67, 185, 188, 190–
  92
aggravating circumstances, 234–38
Alfini, James, 232, 239
allegation, 148
alliteration, 13–15, 26–27, 60, 188–89
ambiguity: of *(afore)said,* 89–90; of *aggrava-*
  tion and *mitigation,* 234–37; of pronouns, 68, 72; of reference, 121; of
  same, 88; of *such,* 91; of word lists, 64–
  65
anaphoric usage, 91
Anglo-Saxon language, 10–17; conjoined
  phrases in, 31; continuing influence on
  the law, 21; example of document in,
  245; oral ceremonies in, 36–37; as written language before Conquest, 25
Anglo-Saxons, 10–16
answer: effect of question on, 170–75; to
  complaint, 150–51. *See also* questioning
  of witnesses
antonyms, 114, 182
archaic language, 87–97, 192–93, 204–5

argot, 106–7, 142, 163
argument. *See* closing argument; opening
  statement; persuasive language
Arizona, 233
articles, 89–91
Articles of Confederation, 44
assertion, 148
attributive descriptions, 123
Austin, J. L., 104
Australia, 46, 134, 161, 214–15, 221
Australian Sentry Life Insurance Co.,
  221
authoritative written texts. *See* autonomous language; writing
autonomous language, 127–28, 177–79

Bacon, Sir Francis, 199
Bailey, F. Lee, 166
Baker, J. H., 21, 22, 32
Bank of Nova Scotia, 222
Benson, Robert, 227
Bentham, Jeremy: and bonding, 51; and
  conspiracy theory, 42, 102; as critic of
  legal language, 199; and definitions,
  120; and long-windedness, 55, 56; and
  redefinitions, 272n. 10
Beowulf, 13
Berkeley, Lady Henrietta, 159
Bible, 29, 96
bilingualism, 23, 32, 177, 201
bill of attainder, 277n. 27
binomial expressions. *See* conjoined
  phrases
Birmingham, England, 84–85
black people. *See* African Americans
Black English Vernacular, 157, 175, 190–
  92
Blackstone, William, 44
Bogoch, Bryna, 36
boilerplate, 59